RESEARCHING BRITISH MILITARY ═ MEDALS ═

A PRACTICAL GUIDE

RESEARCHING BRITISH MILITARY ═ MEDALS ═

A PRACTICAL GUIDE

STEVE DYMOND

The Crowood Press

DEDICATION

This book is dedicated to
22888 Private David Boyce
9th Battalion, Royal Irish Fusiliers
Wounded 16 August 1917, Langemarck (Third Ypres)

First published in 1999 by
The Crowood Press Ltd
Ramsbury, Marlborough,
Wiltshire SN8 2HR

British Library Cataloguing-in-Publication Data
A catalogue record for this book is available from
The British Library

ISBN 1 86126 282 5

Edited by Martin Windrow
Designed by Frank Ainscough / Compendium
Printed and bound by in Great Britain

CONTENTS

INTRODUCTION

The places and dates on British campaign medals tell the story of the nation's illustrious military past, from before Waterloo in 1815 to the present day. Few other collectors' items represent such a tangible investment in our history.

Many medals are officially named - engraved with the name and unit of the recipient - thus creating a direct link between the medal you hold in your hand and the man who once fought on the battlefield and who wore it pinned on his chest. This feature enables collectors to research the lives of individuals caught up in the military campaigns of yesteryear, through numerous archives and other sources which this book sets out to explain.

Researching medals is a huge subject and no single volume could hope to cover every aspect. This book explains how to research British campaign medals and decorations up to and including the Second World War. Medals awarded to servicemen from the Commonwealth and Dominions are not covered, although often the sources for research are very similar. Likewise, medals awarded to women are not dealt with specifically here, although, again, many of the sources quoted are equally applicable. Indian Army medals are mentioned in passing, as are Polar and life-saving awards, but these too are each major topics in their own right and outside the scope of these pages.

This book is not intended as a guide to collecting medals, only to researching their recipients. Therefore it does not cover numismatic details such as styles of naming, renaming, dimensions, or the periods or other requirements for qualification; these and other matters of importance to collectors are already adequately covered in numerous books, of which many will be found in the Bibliography.

Masculine pronouns are used throughout. No offensive discrimination is intended; many women have been decorated with gallantry awards and have earned campaign medals during this century, but the overwhelming majority have been presented to men and the use of the male form simplified matters. It may also be noticed that the detailed spelling and abbreviation of ranks sometimes differ between my text and actual period quotations - these forms have varied over the years.

Anyone with a sense of history and a little imagination can quickly become hooked on researching the past - ask anybody who has started looking at their family tree! Medals are a particularly exciting avenue of research, since the student is propelled back to defining moments in our national history. Each great battle carved on the nation's memory was won through the efforts of individuals - ordinary men of their time, who happened to be there. Such men rarely gave a thought to the historical importance future generations would place on the events in which they were caught up; they just wanted to survive, and not to let their comrades down. However, it was their courage and resolution which ensured that history was made. From Nelson's Royal Navy through to "the Few" of the Battle of Britain, their lives were recorded - and we can find out about them. Each medal explored seems to develop a personality of its own as a tiny fragment of history is brought back to life.

This book describes the sources available to medal researchers and explains, by the progressive tracing of actual examples, how they can be employed to gradually build a picture of the person who was awarded the medal. Sources quoted range from major national archives like the Public Record Office to local telephone directories. Medal collectors and genealogists are the two groups most associated with researching medals. This book covers sources familiar to both, and it is to be hoped that each will learn something from it. Readers new to the subject should learn from these pages how to find their way through the maze of surviving documentation, and should be able to commence research into any medals that come their way.

Researching medals is addictive; it turns the researcher into a detective, and the hunt often leads to fascinating human stories. It can be frustrating, is often time-consuming, but most of all it is absorbing and thoroughly enjoyable.

ACKNOWLEDGMENTS

I would like to acknowledge the following, who supplied information, photographs and advice during the preparation of this book. Without them it would have been a much harder struggle:

The late George Rice
Bob Scarlett for the photographs
Amanda Moreno, Royal Irish Fusiliers Museum
Rachel Watson, Northamptonshire Record Office
Margaret Oliver, East Yorkshire FHS
Matthew Sheldon, Royal Naval Museum
Mary Eddie, Priaulx Library
Mr K.H.Tough, HM Greffier, Guernsey
Mrs P.Pleasance, The Greffe, Guernsey
Nathan Coyde, Guernsey Archive Service
Brian Owen, Guernsey Militia Museum
Mrs M.G.Vidamour, La Societié Guernaise
J.S.E.Brookbank, IX Squadron Association
Matthew Little, Royal Marines Museum
Miss Eunice Wilson
Diana Gregg, Portsmouth Museums and Record Service

My thanks also to Jean Nordon, Stephen Escreet, Pam Spenceley, F.W.Richardson and Bessie Hodgson for information and photos of Thomas Davis; to David Kreckeler, Bob Brown, Rosemary Booth and Mr & Mrs Colin Grant for assistance regarding Henry Harvey; to Constance Ponsford and Maxine Bonner for information about Charles Hoggett. Thanks also to all staff at the Public Record Office, Commonwealth War Graves Commission, Royal Air Force Museum, British Newspaper Library, India Office Library, Family Records Centre, Somerset House, National Army Museum, National Maritime Museum, Imperial War Museum, and King's Own Scottish Borderers Museum. Also to the *Holderness Gazette, Western Morning News, Guernsey Evening Press* and *Portsmouth Journal.*

CHAPTER 1: MEDALS IN GENERAL

It would be difficult to think of anything more interesting to collect than British military medals, their titles recalling famous battles and campaigns from the annals of our nation's history. However, there is more to medal collecting than mere accumulation. The thrill derived from obtaining attractive items associated with dramatic historical events is heightened by another exciting aspect of the hobby, a single feature which separates medals from other collectables and adds an absorbing and intimate dimension to the pursuit.

Most British medals are named to the individual soldier, sailor or airman to whom they were awarded, thus forging a uniquely personal link between the small token of a nation's gratitude and respect and the person who earned it. Diligent research through plentiful and accessible archives may unearth the story of the man behind the medal and bring his memory to life. While many collect medals for their own sake, others find this potential for research the principal attraction.

Today, few men and women in the street could name many examples from the great variety of medals awarded to British servicemen. Yet strangely, they continue to inspire respect and curiosity whenever they are worn. Onlookers may possess family medals, gathering dust in a drawer, without realising that they can discover the story behind them. The personal details inscribed on many medals entice growing numbers of family historians into the hobby, eager to explore their military ancestry

and track down medals earned by their forebears. Medals represent the most personal heirloom it is possible to imagine, almost sacred to a family historian. Discovering family names in a parish register cannot compare with the thrill of holding an ancestor's medal in the palm of your hand when your research has enabled you to imagine not only the surroundings and events of the campaign for which it was presented, but sometimes even the physical appearance of the man who wore it.

Apart from dedicated collectors and genealogists, anyone who happens to own one or two British medals can find out something about the person who earned them. The wide assortment of surviving military documentation makes it unusual to find a soldier or sailor about whom absolutely nothing can be discovered. Not everyone wants to research individuals for their own sake; some concentrate on medals and information linked to a specific regiment, squadron or ship. Others seek medals and material related to a particular campaign, battle or incident. Another might collect and research items awarded to people from his home town; the permutations are endless.

The type of research undertaken varies in other ways. One person may look at the man's role in a single event, like the Charge of the Light Brigade. Another might want to find out everything about the person's military career. Others, particularly genealogists, may view the medal recipient's military career as but a small part of his researchable life.

The 1914-18 British War Medal, Victory Medal, and Imperial Service Medal to 22888 Pte.David Boyce, Royal Irish Fusiliers.

This book covers some subjects well known to the experienced medal researcher, and others familiar to family historians. Hopefully, somewhere along the way there may be some cross-fertilization, and everyone may learn something they did not know before.

Some may ask, why bother with research? Why not just collect? The simple answer is - because you can! Few collectables lend themselves to any form of research into individual bygone lives. So why not make use of the resources available to broaden ones knowledge and enliven the pursuit? Finding out about the recipient and his war breathes life into the medal, recapturing the segment of history lost when they passed out of his hands; thus a tiny forgotten chapter of our national past is brought back to the surface . Medals are hard won and proudly cherished by those who earn them. The present owner can repay the compliment by keeping the story alive.

Research often leads to unusual discoveries. The medal may be rarer than first thought, or the recipient might be entitled to other awards. He may have gone on to great things later in life, adding interest to the dullest medal. If you don't look, you can't find out. After all, to be purely mercenary, no collector will need reminding that a spectacular anecdote can hugely enhance the price of a medal. No doubt for some this is the main reason to undertake research - it would be foolish to pretend otherwise. For most, however, such discoveries are simply a bonus.

Considerations of money value rarely interest genealogists. Most are prepared to follow up any leads to add details to their family story, and medals are just another avenue to investigate. Unfortunately, being confined to ancestral awards, they cannot choose which medals to study; family history cannot be rewritten. No amount of wishful thinking can place a great-great-grand-father on the deck of the *Victory* or charging the guns at Balaclava; but the fascination of history is not limited to those few moments which Hollywood has heard of - a little reading can reveal the inherent drama and pathos of any military campaign.

Occasionally a conflict of interest occurs between collectors, museums and family researchers. Many find it sad that medals are sold to collectors. They inspire strong feelings, and some passionately believe that they should remain with the family to whom they are linked. Collectors often feel sympathy with this viewpoint and can be persuaded to part with medals to descendants. That said, some people feel no attachment to medals earned by their ancestors and see a financial bonus as ample justification to sell. Their feelings sometimes change years later, and they may come to regret impulsive sales when they discover that the cost of buying back family medals has risen spectacularly.

Sadly, not all old soldiers had a choice. Poverty often led treasured medals to the pawnbroker's window, and hard-won awards went over the counter never to be seen again. Sentiment does not put food in hungry bellies.

It is certain that many collectors cherish medals as much as the original recipients. Once sold, it is pleasing to see them in the hands of someone who treats them with the respect they are due. Of course, medals retained in private collections are rarely seen by the public, but most come back into circulation sooner or later. Many feel that the best place for historic medals is in the safekeeping of a museum and argue the benefits of placing

The issue box which survives with David Boyce's "pair", stamped B WAR and VICTORY. The mishapen lump of metal at the right is the remains of the German machine gun bullet removed from his leg after he was wounded, and kept as a souvenir.

notable awards, such as the Victoria Cross, on display for all to see. Such exhibits help keep Britain's military tradition alive and stimulate public interest. On the other hand, regimental museums often possess literally hundreds of examples of common campaign medals, some of which never see the light of day. In one instance known to the author a regimental museum was totally unaware of medals which had been left in a storeroom; this neglect resulted in some being damaged and others lost altogether. Such a fate would not have befallen them in the hands of a collector. This is an extreme example, and the vast majority of museums lavish care upon all regimental memorabilia; indeed, some make impressive displays specifically by massing together many examples of the same campaign medal. However, it does show that there is more than one side to the argument, and provides a strong case for museums owning prestigious awards to relinquish some more humble and commonly available types.

Before embarking upon research it is obviously useful to know something about the history of medals. That said, this book is not the place for detailed numismatic information about the range of medals which have been awarded, nor for quoting the elaborate regulations and qualifying periods pertaining to each - a number of other books already cover these subjects, and readers are directed to the Bibliography.

Medals are traditionally awarded to recognize achievement in all walks of life. The simple metal disk or star is usually intrinsically worthless; its significance and value arise from the endeavours it represents. Each campaign medal symbolises operations undertaken by the British forces. The recipient may have suffered hardship, privations, wounds or even death to earn the right to wear it upon his chest.

Monarchs and generals have always sought to reward the efforts of their soldiers; the bestowal of gifts on particularly valiant men was not only a tangible demonstration of the value put on their service, but also earned the soldier respect from the world at large. Today medals are universally accepted as the currency by which military exploits are measured. They display

George Reeve, 1st Royal Irish Fusiliers, is presented with a sports prize at Shorncliffe, Kent, in 1913. (RIF Museum)

the services rendered in a recognizable form.

In the forces of the United Kingdom all medals are awarded sparingly. Campaigns are only deemed suitable to be recognized by a medal or clasp after strict criteria have been set. Gallantry awards are graded, the more prestigious medals being presented for the most impressive deeds of valour. Committees are established to adjudicate which category of award is suitable in each case. Some medals are rarely awarded; the Victoria Cross provides the best example of a significant number of years - even decades - elapsing between one award and another, since no act has been performed in the meantime which is considered worthy of this ultimate accolade.

Medals are also awarded to acknowledge outstanding service in civil life, graded in a similar way to military decorations. However, this book is primarily concerned with researching campaign and gallantry medals awarded to British military personnel.

There are several distinct types of award, each offering differing scope for research.

Orders

Orders of knighthood are bestowed by the reigning monarch in published Honours Lists. The oldest orders originate from the Middle Ages and are traditionally associated with personal service to the monarch. The most prestigious award is the Most

Noble Order of the Garter, instituted in 1348. The Orders of the Thistle, St Patrick and the Bath all date from the 18th century or earlier.

Orders maybe ranked into as many as five distinct classes; Grand Cross is highest, followed by Knight Commander, Commander, Officer and finally Member. Each class of award brings entitlement to different badges of office. Holders of the Grand Cross wear a large breast star and a sash bearing a badge. Knight Commanders are awarded a smaller breast star and badge on a neck ribbon. Commanders wear a neck badge, and the two lesser classes wear the medal or badge suspended from a ribbon.

Although most orders were originally purely military awards, the majority have been divided into military and civil divisions over the years. For example, the Most Honourable Order of the Bath, instituted as a military decoration in 1725, has military and civil divisions each further divided into Knight Grand Cross, Knight Commander and Companion, making six categories in all. The badges of chivalric orders are usually issued unnamed and do not command wide attention from medal collectors (although they may have a higher intrinsic value due to the precious metals and stones sometimes employed in their manufacture). Like other unnamed medals, orders lack the personal connection to a particular individual. Having said that, many can be attributed to individuals through supporting documentation or by virtue of accompanying named medals.

Decorations

Decorations are the category of medal with which most people are familiar - those awarded to recognize gallantry or distinguished service. They are extremely desirable to collectors and probably offer more research opportunities than any other type of medal. Acts of bravery become woven into the framework of regimental history and attract wide attention from newspapers and authors.

Strangely, there was no formalised system for recognizing acts of bravery until the Crimean War of 1854-56. Prior to that the Meritorious Service Medal was occasionally awarded to "other ranks" (the traditional British Army term for men of ranks below commissioned officer) who had performed acts of gallantry, although this was not the purpose for which it was intended. Before the Crimea distinguished conduct was rewarded in a variety of ways, ranging from monetary awards to specially struck medals awarded and paid for at regimental level. The only exception was the Indian Order of Merit, created by the Honourable East India Company in 1837 to acknowledge brave deeds. The bravery of officers could be recognized in several ways, but no clearcut system existed. They were sometimes awarded specially struck gold or silver medals. Senior officers could be made Commanders of the Bath (CB), while junior officers might be brevetted - promoted to a higher rank - for bravery in the field. The only other way in which bravery could be publicly endorsed was by a Mention in Despatches (MID), but other ranks did not qualify for this until 1843. Servicemen are still "Mentioned" today for gallant behaviour which is considered short of that for which an actual gallantry medal would be awarded.

The institution of the Distinguished Conduct Medal in 1854 marked the arrival of the first true gallantry decoration. The medal provided a yardstick by which the bravery of ordinary soldiers and NCOs could be recognized, and was universally respected throughout the Army (as it still is, being considered second only to the Victoria Cross). The Conspicuous Gallantry Medal followed in 1855 for naval ratings; and the Victoria Cross was instituted shortly afterwards as the supreme gallantry award for all ranks and services, which it remains to this day.

Thereafter a scale of awards was introduced over a number of years, intended to match an act of bravery to an appropriate level of decoration, befitting the rank and service of the recipient. Some decorations were often awarded for exceptional service rather than a specific display of individual bravery.

From 1886 officers of the British Army, the Royal Navy and eventually the Royal Air Force were eligible for admission to the Distinguished Service Order. The Military Cross was instituted for junior and warrant officers of the Army at the end of 1914. The Royal Navy and Royal Marines already had the Conspicuous Service Cross, dating from 1901, and late in 1914 this was retitled the Distinguished Service Cross and its conditions of award broadened to include junior officers. Royal Air Force officers were eligible for the Distinguished Flying Cross and Air Force Cross, depending upon the nature of their service, from mid-1918.   Other ranks might be awarded the Distinguished Conduct Medal or Military Medal, naval ratings the Conspicuous Gallantry Medal or Distinguished Service Medal, NCOs and men of the RAF the Distinguished Flying Medal or Air Force Medal.

Such a system became unacceptable to the so-called "classless society" of today. In 1993 decorations based upon those formerly applicable to officers only were introduced for all ranks, and a sergeant was soon awarded a Military Cross for gallantry while serving with the multi-national peace-keeping forces in Bosnia. The decision to alter the structure of British gallantry decorations met with a mixed reaction from the military establishment, and not only from officers - the other ranks hold their own specific decorations in considerable regard. However, the reception seems to be generally favourable, and the new system is certainly easier to understand.

Surprisingly, gallantry decorations do not always bear the name of the recipient. As a general rule officers' awards were issued unnamed, while those presented to other ranks were impressed with the details of the man concerned. There are exceptions, and a great many officers arranged engraving at their own expense.

A souvenir postcard incorporating a portrait photograph of a soldier from the Norfolk Regiment during the Great War.

Campaign Medals

These represent the largest group of medals awarded to British military personnel. They indicate simply that the man was "there". He may not have performed heroic feats, but he was in the named region or present within the environs of a battle during the specified qualification period. Campaign medals cover the whole range of British military service, and a single clasp can signify months or years of exhausting, dangerous service under the most arduous conditions.

The practice of presenting campaign medals to British troops began with the defeat of the Spanish Armada in 1588 and continued sporadically over the next 150 years. Early issues were unnamed, although certain individuals paid to have them engraved. The criteria of qualification for these early medals is generally uncertain. It seems probable the first medals were not issued to all persons present, but only to selected individuals for bravery. As the 18th century progressed it gradually became customary to reward everyone involved. However, these medals were still struck on an *ad hoc* basis, often financed by commanding generals from their own pocket. There was no mechanism to establish which campaigns merited a medal or the criteria for allocating an award.

The Battle of Waterloo in 1815 was an important milestone in the history of campaign medals. It was the first action for which the British government saw fit to reward *all* participants with a medal, regardless of rank, and including the next-of-kin of those killed in action. It was also the first named medal, machine-impressed around the rim with the recipient's name, unit, and sometimes rank; this founded a tradition which continues to this day. Thus began the unique bond between medal and man - even after death - from which researchers still benefit.

By issuing a medal to all participants the government conferred greater status on medals, making them an official symbol of services rendered. Thenceforth, with several notable exceptions, it became customary to commemorate wars, campaigns and battles by issuing a medal, or a clasp - a metal bar specifying particular details, to be attached to the suspension ribbon of an existing medal.

Although the Waterloo medal was the first issued to all men present, three medals were instigated later to commemorate actions fought prior to Waterloo. The Naval General Service Medal, Military General Service Medal and Army of India Medal were all issued years - in the latter two cases, many years - after the events they commemorated, to surviving participants from actions which took place at sea or on land between 1793 and 1840. A list of actions was published in each case, and applications invited from men who considered themselves entitled to the medal in question, which could not be issued without one or more specific clasps. Large numbers of participants had died in these campaigns or in the intervening years. Given the standards of literacy at the time, it is likely that many surviving veterans did not apply for the medal to which they were entitled; the numbers awarded represent only a fraction of the men involved in the campaigns.

General Service Medals continue to be awarded to the present day. They are open-ended awards, approved for periods of intermittent hostilities on land and sea, to which clasps are added when actions take place. Soldiers or sailors are presented with the medal for involvement in any operation commemorated by a clasp, and can earn further clasps - but not a second medal - if present at subsequent actions. Therefore a soldier could serve in several significant campaigns, yet only wear one medal.

(**NB:** Collectors usually refer to the clasps added to campaign medal ribbons as **bars** - e.g., "MGS with bars Badajoz, Ciudad Rodrigo", etc. In this text I have used the term **clasp** throughout, to avoid any possible confusion with the other meaning of "bar", that of a second or subsequent award of a gallantry decoration, e.g. "MC and bar", etc.)

After Waterloo, medals were issued to commemorate campaigns great and small fought by the British services in all corners of the globe. Sometimes a medal was struck to recognize an apparently insignificant battle, while another seemingly more important campaign was only recognized by a clasp, or even passed unmarked. Controversy continues to the present day about some almost forgotten campaigns overlooked by the authorities.

British soldiers and seamen were kept busy throughout the 19th century, and medals were issued for expeditions which now fail to strike a chord with any but the specialist. They were particularly active around the borders of the Indian sub-continent, quelling localised uprisings, mounting punitive expeditions and policing hostile tribes. Some medals were issued unnamed, others were impressed or engraved; styles varied from medal to medal, and even differed for the same award.

The Boer War of 1899-1902 involved troops from across the length and breadth of the British Empire. For the first time the war reached beyond the ranks of professional soldiers, drawing recruits from all walks of life to the adventure in South Africa. Families with no previous military connection suddenly found they had a personal stake in happenings far away from home.

The First World War took this process a huge step further. Virtually every family in the land was affected by a conflict in which a high proportion of Britain's prewar professional soldiers became casualties during the first year, to be replaced at first by volunteers, and later by conscripts, in their millions. Many of us have known participants in the Great War, perhaps our own fathers or grandfathers, which brings this period of our history within touching distance. In many cases medals awarded for the Great War remain within family hands. A variety of related artefacts and documents survive to this day, making research into the period 1914-18 especially meaningful, particularly where it involves members of our own families. Some of the stories discovered are deeply poignant.

The Second World War saw the birth of another generation of medals. Unfortunately, most were issued unnamed. This is more of a drawback to medal collectors than family researchers, where the provenance of medals is rarely in doubt. In this day and age collectors have to be wary of misrepresented medals and remain suspicious of those which appear on the market without strong supporting credentials.

Long Service and Good Conduct Medals

Long Service and Good Conduct Medals (LSGCs) regularly surface on their own or in company with other types of medal. They have been awarded in varying styles to all three of the regular services. LSGCs are also presented to reservists, territorials, police officers and various other groups affiliated to the forces and emergency services. Long Service medals nearly always bear the name of the recipient and are therefore particularly important when accompanying unnamed medals.

The Naval Long Service and Good Conduct Medal was introduced in 1830, followed by the Army LSGC in 1831. Qualification for each requires a high level of conduct as well as prolonged service. A long service medal as part of a group often indicates good research potential. It stands to reason that the longer a man spent in service the more chance there is of discovering documentation concerning his career. This does not always follow; but as a collector, knowing nothing else about two men except that one spent more time in the forces than another, I would go for the long service group every time.

Coronation and Jubilee Medals

Coronation and Jubilee medals are issued to celebrate royal events. Historically, medals were often struck to commemorate milestone events in the reign of a monarch; but the first intended for wear was the Empress of India Medal 1887, created to celebrate the proclamation of Queen Victoria as Empress of India. Thereafter medals were generally issued to soldiers and police officers involved in royal coronation and jubilee parades, until 1911 when the Edward VII Coronation Medal was made eligible for issue to personnel not actually present. Latterly, medals of this type have been issued on a fairly arbitrary basis to those considered deserving at the time of the event. Included in this category are medals commemorating royal visits to Ireland and Scotland, as well as the Delhi Durbar Medals of 1903 and 1911.

Few examples issued to military personnel were named, limiting their research potential unless found with other named medals. However, medals awarded to police officers and ancillary services were invariably named, and offer opportunities to delve into police archives.

Outside the five main categories of military medal there are many other miscellaneous categories. Some provide excellent opportunities for research - often better than the mainstream medals outlined above.

Life-saving medals are a prime example; on their own or accompanying other awards, these offer outstanding opportunities for research. The type of feats for which they are awarded generally attract the attention of the media, and the bodies which present them maintain their own records. There are numerous types, including Royal National Lifeboat Institution Medals, Liverpool Shipwreck and Humane Society Medals, Royal Humane Society Medals, and many others. They are a fascinating subject in their own right and attract many specialist collectors.

There are also Polar Medals, Arctic Medals, Shooting Medals, sporting medals and commemorative regimental medals. They all offer potential for research and the chance to examine diverse types of information. Each medal must be examined on its merits as regards the scope available, but some are very well documented.

*   *   *

To demonstrate the diversity of material waiting to be uncovered, several medal groups have been selected to illustrate points made in the text of this book. At the end of each chapter the research source covered will be examined for information about the chosen groups, gradually building up a picture of each of these characters. Medals were selected to cover different periods, ranks and services, rather than because of their research potential, although from the outset some provided more hope than others (however, that is always the way of it, and it would have been of little value to the reader to pick a series of "open goals"). **The groups chosen for research are as follows:**

(1) Naval General Service Medal 1793-1840, clasp Syria, awarded to Charles Hoggett.

(2) Sutlej Campaign Medal, Aliwal reverse, clasp Sobraon, awarded to Edward Heymer, 16th Lancers.

(3) Afghanistan Medal 1878 awarded to Captain H.J.Harvey, 1st Battalion, 25th Regiment.

(4) Egypt Medal 1882-89, no clasps; Khedive's Star; Long Service and Good Conduct Medal, all awarded to Private Joseph Full, Royal Marines; HMS *Tamar* impressed on Egypt Medal and HMS *Fox* on LSGC.

(5) First World War British War Medal and Victory Medal awarded to 22888 Private David Boyce, Royal Irish Fusiliers (the author's grandfather).

(6) First World War Military Cross and Military Medal awarded to Lieutenant (ex-Sgt 7574) George Reeve, Royal Irish Fusiliers.

(7) Second World War aircrew group to Flight Sergeant T.R.Davis, RAF.

CHAPTER 2: FIRST STEPS

Before embarking upon research, it makes sense to accumulate as much information as possible. Examining document archives takes time. Prior knowledge pinpoints where worthwhile results may be achieved and effort well spent. It cuts corners - and saves money. Some "digging" prior to visiting research establishments can also prevent mistakes. Where *known* facts contradict those on documents found in an archive, then papers may refer to a different individual - soldiers with the same names are not uncommon. Foreknowledge guards against being led off onto hopeless tangents.

Researching medals can be rewarding and enjoyable. It can also be laborious and very frustrating. The pleasure of handling ancient documents withers to bitter disappointment after a long day spent in a dusty archive without discovering anything significant. Every researcher will experience bad days - the important thing is to adopt methods which minimise the chance of negative results. Otherwise enthusiasm wanes, and the man behind the medals remains buried in the archives.

It is important to decide what the objects of your research are; until goals are established, it is difficult to work out a plan of action. Objectives may change during the course of research - an interesting lead may present itself at any stage - but there should be some end in view at the outset. By thoroughly organizing the information to hand and giving priority to realistic research targets you can ensure that you use your time effectively, and hopefully one step should lead to another. The important word here is "realistic". It is patently obvious that certain medals offer greater research potential than others. Some just do not lend themselves to productive detective work, and no amount of time spent in record offices will change this.

Not surprisingly, medals to high ranking officers are likely to be the most productive. Even where they played no identifiable leading role in any campaign, their very rank made their actions noteworthy. Their name will appear in many different archives, and normally a full picture of their life can be assembled.

Other Ranks are less well recorded than officers, but this certainly does not preclude them from research. This is where being realistic comes in. Within the limitations imposed by their lowly station in life, there is a surprising amount of information about ordinary soldiers, sailors and airmen waiting to be uncovered. There is a lot of satisfaction to be obtained from building up a rounded picture of an insignificant private soldier's life 100 years after his time.

There is another factor to consider. A lot of officers' medals

have already been well researched. This deprives the purchaser of the chance to explore fresh territory - he is likely to be treading over old ground. Other ranks' medals tend to be unresearched and offer genuine opportunities to delve into the forgotten past.

Gallantry groups present mixed potential. With certain exceptions, the deed which earned the decoration is normally fully documented. However, while this single fragment of the recipient's life is highlighted the rest may be shrouded in mystery. First World War awards at the lower end of the scale can be particularly disappointing. Citations were not always published, and the only proof that an act of gallantry took place is a single-line entry in the London Gazette.

The exciting thing about medal research is that while it is usually possible to predict fairly accurately the potential offered, there are always exceptions. So although it is preferable for a collector/researcher to select medals which offer immediate results, never write off those which apparently promise little; just be prepared for failure. The unpredictability is the thrill. Until the faded pages of history have been turned, there is no knowing what lies in wait.

As outlined in the previous chapter, collectors are in a more favourable position than those researching family medals. They can select suitable groups and, if one medal proves frustrating, set it aside and look elsewhere. Family researchers are stuck with their ancestor's medals and cannot make a silk purse out of a sow's ear; and, if the family name is relatively common, they are doubly handicapped. They can recoup some of this disadvantage through greater enthusiasm and a genuine personal interest. Pursuing a lost cause can occasionally pay dividends, but don't bank on it. Years could be spent searching for material which simply does not exist. Once primary sources of information have been exhausted without result, there is usually little to be gained from ploughing on along more obscure pathways without anything concrete to go on.

Although it may be impossible to uncover facts about the individual concerned, there are often opportunities to find out about the campaign fought by his battalion or the role played by his ship. Given the dates between which he served, it is possible to discover at least the sort of life he lived in uniform. This may not be as satisfying as a personal record, but in some cases it is the best one can hope for.

The medals themselves are the best source of information, providing a definite factual starting point. Each medal and clasp indicates a campaign, battle or expedition in which the

Postcard of Edmonton Military Hospital sent by David Boyce during his convalescence to a Miss.M.Griffin of Portadown, asking to be remembered to all at home.

recipient took part. However, personal details inscribed or impressed on the rim or reverse of the medal really provide the starting points. The amount of detail varies from medal to medal, but many bear the name, initials, rank, number, regiment, ship, trade and sometimes the battalion of the recipient. All of these help to guide research in the right direction. Gallantry awards may be engraved with the date of the deed recognized by the decoration.

The service number is particularly important, differentiating between men of the same surname who may have campaigned together in the same regiment or ship. The number can also reveal other details. Some medal researchers have analysed numbers for regiments in which they have an interest. Regimental numbers allocated in blocks during the First World War can pinpoint the date and place of enlistment.

Family medal researchers are in a strong position to accumulate information before visiting archives, drawing upon sources not open to medal collectors. Nearly every family has some knowledge of its own ancestry, and the researcher has a good chance of gaining some pointers about military forebears, even if only hearsay and speculation.

Elderly relatives possess the greatest family knowledge and should know the most about military service. They will almost certainly remember members of the family killed or wounded in the two World Wars. However, their recollections can be disappointing. Whilst young they may have paid no attention to talk of military life. They may have forgotten everything they heard; they will often be unable to remember dates, regiments or any specific facts. However, they will normally retain the most interesting anecdotes, albeit confused as to time, place or even the person concerned. By careful questioning it is often possible to sift through information and work out the details by a process of elimination. The facts deduced may then be verifiable. It is important to remember that some family legends are based upon the shallowest of pretexts and may bear no resemblance to the truth. Remember, too, that military men can often tell a good tale. It is not unusual to find that an old soldier has embellished the less than heroic truth about his military endeavours with a few additions from his own imagination. Few like to highlight their deficiencies, so be prepared to see long-cherished family stories disintegrate under the spotlight of research.

Each time an elderly relation dies their knowledge dies with them. Even if there are no immediate plans to undertake research, try to note down any information they possess - tomorrow may be too late. Better still, record their memories on tape, so nothing is missed. My own experiences with an elderly relative, detailed in a later chapter, provide a salutary lesson.

Documentary evidence is more reliable than memory and some original paperwork might survive to provide a sound base for research. Family researchers may benefit from well preserved documents in family hands, although it is not unusual to find some papers with medals purchased from a dealer.

Collectors who specialise in one regiment, campaign or type of medal are also in a strong position. They accumulate a strong base of knowledge and often possess relevant reference books and material dedicated to their subject.

Everyday sources can be extremely informative. Photograph albums are a good example. Some families are fortunate enough to have retained extremely old photographic coverage. Military men have always been proud to appear in photographs, and it was fashionable during the late 19th and early 20th century to pose in uniform for postcard photographs. Thousands survive from the time of the First World War. A picture is worth a thousand words, and besides the immediate value of identifiable uniform details a photo of the man behind the medal is a very pleasing thing to have, bringing your research to life. No amount of description can equal a single, simple photograph which enables you to look into the eyes of the man whose story you are searching out.

Photographs are especially helpful if you are researching family medals and military achievements but are not in possession of the actual medals. It may be possible to identify the regiment an ancestor served with - the British Army is particularly rich in distinctive cap badges - and his uniform and equipment might pin down the period. Over the last twenty years many reference books have been published which illustrate these details in sufficient depth for you to at least date a photograph

The Under-Secretary of State for Air presents his compliments and by Command of the Air Council has the honour to transmit the enclosed Awards granted for service in the war of 1939-45. The Council share your sorrow that FLIGHT SERGEANT T.R. DAVIS. in respect of whose service these Awards are granted did not live to receive them.

to "not before" a particular date on the basis of a cap, tunic or belt equipment. Naval cap tallies, badges of rank and shoulder titles provide other clues. More importantly, some soldiers were even pictured wearing medals, and with the help of a magnifying glass it might be possible to identify them. Distinctive styles of clasp and ribbon patterns stand out, and fairly accurate conclusions can usually be drawn.

These comments apply equally to postcards, with the occasional added bonus of a few lines scrawled upon the reverse. Unfortunately many were despatched without being written on, and those with writing tend to offer little. Sometimes the address to which the card was sent may prove noteworthy, but often there is only the satisfaction of knowing that the card was despatched by "our man".

Photographs or postcards rarely bear the name of the subject pictured. Although a photograph accompanying a group of medals makes their acquisition a little more attractive, medals and photograph may have been married together by some unscrupulous person and may actually have no connection. The purchaser must decide whether he takes the two together on trust or looks for some form of provenance.

Occasionally postcards may indicate where the man was stationed. Field Post Office numbers can establish an exact location where the item was posted. Even the censor's unique identity code can reveal details of the sector where a man was deployed during the Great War.

Letters and diaries seldom accompany medals appearing on the open market - they are usually snapped up long before. However, such attractive and informative articles may remain with medals in family hands. They are a Godsend to the researcher, providing tremendous first hand accounts of life as the medal recipient knew it. Few other sources can ever provide such colourful, personal information about any individual. They represent a goldmine to the researcher, but alas, few of us are so lucky.

A wide variety of other paperwork can sometimes be found with a group of medals. Some items provide fascinating insights into a military career, others personal detail, and some merely nondescript background material. The man himself obviously kept the items for a reason, but often purely as keepsakes. Each must be considered on its merits for research potential.

Discharge documents and original pay books frequently outline a serviceman's career. These fall into the same category as letters and diaries - gold dust! They are likely to mention medal entitlements, movement orders, wounds and other information. Some men transferred between units during major conflicts, making it hard to keep track of their service, and any original documents help to piece the career together.

The paperwork most commonly found with medals relates to the death of the man in service. Condolence slips, memorial scrolls and letters from commanding officers were usually retained by the grieving family. Unfortunately the most

The official condolence slip accompanying medals sent to the family of Flight Sergeant T.R.Davis, RAF, after the war.

The medal issue box posted to
F/Sgt. Davis' father at an address in
Streatham, south London.

memorable feature of many a military career was the manner of death; frequently the last moments of the medal recipient's life become the starting point of research and, sadly, all too often form the only noteworthy part of it.

Genealogists are usually interested in all aspects of an ancestor's life, not just medal campaigns. Other researchers can benefit by taking a step away from military records to obtain a more rounded picture of the man under the microscope. By doing so, an exciting episode could be discovered, to make him a more compelling figure than the fairly mundane soldier they have so far encountered. Genealogists are better placed than medal collectors to make this sort of discovery; their unique access to family knowledge should stand them in good stead, while medal researchers have less to go on. However, there are sources of family history open to anyone, which will be covered in more detail in a later chapter.

It is possible for "non-family" medal researchers to level the playing field somewhat by making local enquiries where the medal recipient lived. Advertisements appealing for information placed in local papers can prove fruitful and cost little. A simple telephone directory can be employed to contact descendants. Even in the "global village" of today many families still reside close to their ancestors, especially in areas outside the major cities. Such an approach might disclose information which could never be found by conventional means.

Once every stone has been overturned and the researcher is in possession of as much backround information as possible, it is time to organize the material and decide on the next course of action. Some researchers might have already discovered everything they wished to know, or established the single fact they sought. For most, however, the background material discovered is only the starting point. Now is the time to plan the next step along the road. Normally this will be a visit to the Public Record Office at Kew, but not necessarily. Those who have discovered that their man was involved in a particularly noteworthy event may feel drawn towards the newspaper library at Colindale, or regimental magazines at the National Army Museum.

There is one pitfall to beware of. Researching several medals at once is economical and saves time, but can lead to confusion. It makes sense to combine interests when visiting an archive, but do make clear notes about the work carried out, otherwise it is easy to lose track of results. Accurate records form an important part of research - without them the whole exercise is a waste of time.

Every researcher will have a preferred method of recording

what they have found. For some it will be meticulous notes in carefully annotated notebooks. Others maintain card indexes with individual cards relating to each medal recipient. Nowadays many medal researchers use personal computers, taking advantage of the storage and retrieval abilities at their disposal. There is no doubt that computers offer greater flexibility than paper systems, although the financial outlay if buying a system for this purpose alone is considerable. Genealogists will be aware of the vast range of software available to assist with their hobby. There are few packages on the market designed for military research; however, it is a simple matter to tailor a programme for individual requirements.

Once the groundwork is complete it is time to start looking through public archives. In the following chapters we will look at the various establishments where documentation is held and what type of information they offer. But before we do, let us look at the material it has been possible to glean about our selected subjects before visiting any research establishments, and to set out our goals.

Research Notes

Charles Hoggett
Naval General Service Medal 1793-1840, bar Syria. No documentation accompanied the medal, and Hoggett appeared totally unresearched to date.

My intentions were to discover as much as possible about Hoggett's naval career. Was this the only campaign in which he

Typical of the ephemera which may be found with medals in family collections, and which may sometimes be of great help to researchers: a group photograph of signallers of the Royal Irish Fusiliers in 1924.

was involved? How long was he at sea? Was this campaign at the beginning or end of his timespan in the Royal Navy? What sort of a record did he have? What other ships did he sail upon? At the same time, I also wished to find out the part played by his ship during the Syrian campaign.

Edward Heymer
Sutlej Medal, Aliwal reverse, clasp Sobraon.

All we have to go on is that Edward Heymer served with the 16th Lancers in the so-called Sutlej campaign - the First Sikh War, 1845-46. However, the battle of Aliwal was a notable day in the history of the 16th Lancers, when they charged and broke a Sikh square in costly fighting. So any medal to a charger on that day is exciting and, if nothing else, we can research the charge and visualize the role Heymer played in the action.

Was he a new recruit or a seasoned veteran? Did he earn any other medals? Was he killed or wounded? With no prior knowledge, research could lead anywhere or nowhere.

Henry Harvey
Afghanistan 1878, no bars.

The medal tells us that he was a captain in the 1st Battalion,

25th Regiment of Foot (The King's Own Borderers); nothing further is known. However, his commissioned rank offers good possibilities. The initial plan was to explore his role in the Second Afghan War, 1878-80. Was he awarded other medals? Was he promoted to field rank? Only time would tell. Totally unresearched medals to officers are always quite exciting, with a strong likelihood that he originated from the gentry and was well documented in his time.

Joseph Full

Egypt medal 1882-89, no bars; Khedive's Star; Long Service and Good Conduct Medal.

The Egypt medal shows Full serving with the Royal Marine detachment on board HMS *Tamar*; when the LSGC was awarded he was on HMS *Fox*; nothing further is known. With little to go on, the initial intention was simply to discover as much about him as possible. The LSGC medal indicated that he was a career marine. On the surface this group offered little potential. It is a fairly standard set of medals to the RM, and the absence of a bar on the Egypt medal indicated that Full took no active part in the land fighting. The only reason to believe something interesting might be forthcoming was the LSGC. It was possible that Full might have achieved something memorable during his long service, and that a record of it might survive.

David Boyce

22888 Pte D.Boyce, Royal Irish Fusiliers - First World War British War Medal and Victory Medal; Imperial Service Medal.

David Boyce was my maternal grandfather. I inherited his medals and the misshapen German bullet taken from his leg; I also inherited his affection for all things military. He was a slight man, with a gentle Irish accent and a mild disposition, in common with many people who have witnessed awful carnage.

Not surprisingly, a great deal was known about David Boyce prior to research. Unfortunately he died while I was a child, so much of the information came from older relatives. As a youngster I recall listening for hours, spellbound, while he recalled his time in the trenches. Alas, I remember little now. The only lasting memory is his description of lying wounded in the mud, waiting to be recovered by stretcher bearers, but fearful of being bayoneted by a German patrol. This demonstrates the benefit of recording the memories of the old; what wouldn't I give to be able to listen to his stories now?

David Boyce never fully overcame the effect of being machine gunned through the leg. He was discharged from the Army in 1921, and worked with the Post Office until retirement. His three daughters moved across to England - after two of them, including my mother, married British soldiers during the Second World War - and he moved to England to be near them.

My research began by probing relatives for information about David Boyce's military career. They knew little beyond the bare details mentioned above, although he apparently served in the same battalion as his two brothers. I wished to discover the battalion he served with and where he fought, especially where and when he was wounded.

George Reeve

Lieutenant George Reeve, Royal Irish Fusiliers. George V Military Cross and Military Medal. The medals were purchased from a fellow collector; no original documentation accompanied them.

Twice decorated for gallantry and clearly promoted from the ranks during the course of the Great War, Reeve offered enormous research potential. Research targets were fairly obvious from the outset. Where and for what he was decorated? Did he survive the war? His swift promotion indicated possible prewar service, which could be investigated. Given his apparently long front line service I also felt sure that other information would be forthcoming.

T.R.Davis

1456334 Flight Sergeant T.R.Davis, RAF. 1939-45 Star; Aircrew Europe Star; and War Medal. Purchased together with a condolence slip and original boxes of issue, giving an address in Streatham, south London. Otherwise completely unresearched, and no other information to hand.

The research targets were to discover who Davis was and find details of his operational career - in particular, to find out how and when he died and where he is buried.

CHAPTER 3: THE PUBLIC RECORD OFFICE

A visit to the Public Record Office in south-west London is a must for anyone attempting to research medals awarded to any British soldier, seaman or airman. Numerous establishments house military documents, but this single building is the resting place for the great majority of military archive material. Personnel documents are released by the Ministry of Defence administering the three services at set intervals. They are automatically transferred to the PRO, where they become available for viewing once sorted and listed.

The PRO is situated in Ruskin Avenue, Kew, Richmond, Surrey, TW9 4DU. Limited parking is available within the complex. Kew Underground station on the District Line is only a short walk away. Without a valid reader's ticket there is no access to the reading rooms, and some proof of identity is required before this can be issued. A driving licence or other form of official document showing name and address is acceptable, and the ticket is issued on the spot. After successfully obtaining a reader's ticket, coats, umbrellas and large cases must be deposited in the ground floor cloakroom. Study material brought in by readers is subject to checks by security staff before they can pass through turnstiles to the reading rooms. Scanners, mini-photocopiers and cameras are not permitted (nor are food and drinks; only pencils may be used for note-taking.

A wide staircase leads to the study area. At the top of the staircase, turn left into the Main Reading Room, dotted with octagonal desks and divided into eight individual study positions. Staff behind the large service counter present each reader with a personal bleeper and allocate a desk for the duration of their stay. The bleeper is activated whenever a file ordered by the visitor arrives at the distribution desk ready for collection.

Once settled and armed with an electronic bleeper, the researcher can begin exploring the archives. Unfortunately, early visits to the PRO tend to be rather frustrating; it takes time to come to grips with the reference system and discover exactly what type of information a given document is likely to yield. On the plus side, the Public Record Office produces various leaflets outlining material available. These are kept in pigeon-holes in the lobby on the first floor.

Military documentation forms only part of the vast PRO archive. Every conceivable type of record material is to be found stored within the premises, relating to a huge variety of topics. Many may prove useful to medal researchers - the problem is identifying those most likely to offer a chance of success. Some, like medal rolls, are obvious choices, but others are less so. There is no designated, foolproof method of undertaking

The Military Cross and Military Medal to Lt. George Reeve, now separated from the campaign medals to which he was also entitled.

research. Much depends upon the rank of the individual concerned, the service and the era in which he served. It is desirable to start with material offering potential for rapid expansion of knowledge, and hope this presents guides to further research. Particular document classes will be explained in the following chapters, but broadly speaking PRO material pertaining to military matters divides into three definable categories:

(1) Records relating to individuals

(2) Records relating to campaigns

(3) Records of ships / establishments / units.

Medal researchers are most concerned with the first, although at times the others may prove worth investigating. They provide interesting background material, and in cases where nothing about the person under the microscope can be found they may be the only source available at the PRO.

Some material can be seen on open shelves, although most has to be requested using a simple computerised system. Maps and larger papers can be scrutinised in the Map Room, situated on the second floor, where large tables give sufficient space to spread documents out. The Map Room is generally less crowded than the reading rooms and there is seldom a queue for the photocopying service, which is a definite advantage.

Medal rolls and First World War medal index cards are in the Microfilm Viewing Room. These form the starting point for research, in order to confirm entitlement to the medals in question. It should be stressed that checking entitlement is not the same as verification. Ensuring that details on the roll correspond to those on the medal does not guarantee that the medal is genuine. Medal collecting is subject to the same deception and misrepresentation as any hobby where money changes hands. Medals are renamed, sometimes by the original recipient to replace a lost medal, but more often by fraudsters seeking to present a mundane medal in a more appealing light. Familiarity with and experience in handling medals is the best protection against being deceived.

Some medal rolls are quite straightforward, others are not. Records for large campaigns contain thousands of names, handwriting is sometimes extremely difficult to read, and some rolls are very disjointed - particularly those where many supplementary sheets and late claims were added. One or two medal rolls have been lost in their entirety, and some are incomplete. In such cases muster rolls (covered later) may help to establish entitlement.

Medal rolls are on microfilm and **First World War medal index cards** are on microfiche; viewers are provided close to where the rolls are kept. Medal rolls will be explored more fully in the following chapters.

The Research Enquiries Room is sandwiched between the Microfilm and Main Reading Rooms. It forms the hub of the complex, housing a huge quantity of reference books, index cards and finding aids. The document ordering system is also located in the Research Enquiries Room. Ordering documents is easy; the hard part is identifying relevant material. Much depends upon the knowledge with which the researcher comes ready armed. Some sources of information only reveal themselves after a certain amount of experience. It is a good idea to spend time familiarising oneself with the Research Enquiries Room and browsing through the PRO Current Guide, which catalogues and describes documents held within the PRO.

Frequently up-dated, the Current Guide is a mammoth reference running to over 5,000 pages. It is divided into three parts, the third part being an index to the previous two. To identify documents of interest, start by looking the subject up in the index. This gives references to relevant sections in Parts 1 and 2. Part 2 gives a breakdown of information in each document class and makes it possible to identify classes which might be of assistance.

The PRO has produced several books to make research easier. These can be purchased from the bookshop in the foyer and are strongly recommended. They have usually been written by PRO staff, familiar with handling all the various papers on a daily basis. They help any new researcher find a route through the confusing plethora of document classes to identify those of most interest and relevance.

As mentioned above, it is possible to carry out a great deal of military research without ordering any of the documents stored within the building. Many Air Force Lists, Army Lists

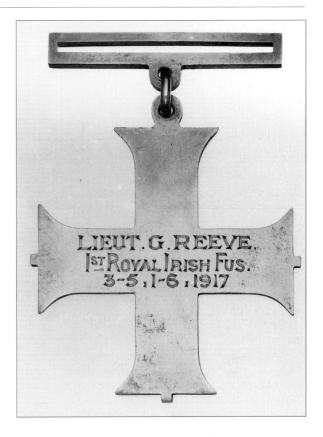

The engraved reverse of George Reeve's MC, giving his unit as 1st Battalion, Royal Irish Fusiliers, and the dates of the actions for which it was awarded.

(dating back to 1754), and Navy Lists (dating from 1754) are on open shelves. Many specialist medal reference works, published medal rolls and other reference works are also available. The Reference Room houses several nominal card indexes, created or half-created at one time or another. A large number refer to different categories of officer serving in the Army and Royal Navy. Some hold cards which display information, while most give a reference to material which can be ordered. Both types of card provide a short cut to information sought.

Archive material is broken down into different classes. Most Army records are grouped in class WO, standing for War Office. Naval documents usually appear in class ADM (for Admiralty). These letters are followed by a number to identify a particular class of documents. For example, soldier's attestation and discharge papers are in class WO 97, while disability pensions awarded between 1715 and 1882 appear in WO 116.

To order an individual document the reference number must be completed by adding a specific "piece number" applicable to the document sought. To identify the piece number, find the binder in the Reference Room with the correct prefix and class number on the spine. This is called the "class list", and describes the documents within the class broken down into alphabetical segments or divided by other criteria. Each component part of the "class" is given a further number; this "piece" number, added to the other two class numbers, forms a three-part reference to a particular item.

Supposing you wished to find attestation and discharge documents for a soldier called Dimond, who retired in 1890, the procedure would be as follows. Scan the WO binders in the Reference Room and retrieve the class list for document class WO 97 (Soldiers' attestation and discharge papers). Then flick through the pages until reaching the part covering discharges between 1883 and 1913. For this period discharge documents are stored alphabetically for the entire Army, so identify the alphabetical block containing the surname Dimond and add the number given to the rest of the reference. In this instance the complete reference would be WO 97/2667.

Now it is possible to order the required papers on one of the computers in the Reference Room. Key in the allocated seat number in the Reading Room to enter the system, and then fill in the document reference number as directed on the screen. Up to three documents may be ordered at one time. Once the spaces have been filled, the item is on its way. The time from ordering to arrival varies, but around 40 minutes is an average lapse.

When the item arrives at the distribution desk the researcher is notified by bleeper. Documents must be collected from the counter in the Reading Room, although large items are delivered to the Map Room. If more than one request arrives at a time, the researcher can select which item to view first.

The format of archive material varies from class to class. Attestation/discharge papers, given as an example above, arrive in a box file. The box contains all the papers relating to the alphabetical block in the class list, and the researcher has to leaf through the file to find the particular item required.

Some records are in books or ledgers, others are loose bundles tied with tape, and sometimes an individual sheet of paper appears. These documents are often dusty and some are in a very fragile condition. Somehow the dust and musty smell adds to the allure of the old papers, accentuating their age and imposing a sense of history. It can be quite exciting to handle the very papers signed by the man whose medals are now possessed, at the moment he embarked upon a military life. This feeling is heightened when the person is an ancestor.

Sometimes the long wait for a box of documents can prove extremely frustrating. The article sought may be missing for any number of reasons. Where papers are stored alphabetically, check the entire file - a previous reader may have misplaced the piece, or the document could have been misfiled years before. It is a good idea to keep ordering documents to ensure that a rolling supply arrives at the distribution desk. A swift glance at a document may confirm a particular point and the box is then finished with; by careful ordering it may be possible to return that batch and immediately withdraw another. Only one piece containing loose paperwork can be issued at a time, but up to three books and ledgers can be taken away for study.

Microfilm and microfiche can be copied instantaneously by the reader, using token-operated copying machines, so medal rolls do not present a problem. Copying more cumbersome documents and files must be carried out by PRO staff. There is a copying desk in the Main Reading Room and another in the Map Room. Copies can normally be collected after about an

hour. Bulk orders may be posted on to the reader. It is also possible to obtain photographs of documents. The library of photographs held at Kew may interest some researchers. Holdings include artillery panoramic views of the Western Front during the Great War; a photo of the sector where a medal recipient was killed might be desired.

After exploring the material held in the building, it is possible to set realistic research targets before subsequent visits. It is a good idea to prepare thoroughly before arrival. List class numbers which may shed light on the man in question. It may sound obvious, but actually jot down what the visit is intended to discover, then work through the list in order of priority. Don't forget to note down new research avenues which present themselves during the course of the day.

Most inexperienced readers feel a chafing sense of frustration as they leave the PRO - so little has been accomplished during a tiring day. However, as the researcher gains knowledge it becomes easier to streamline efforts and waste less time. It can be advantageous to carry out research into several medals at the same time. This ensures that there is always something to do while waiting for documents to be delivered; it also keeps a constant flow of files arriving. Sometimes research gets bogged down in a frustrating search for material on a particular man. Changing to a fresh subject and achieving immediate results helps to rekindle enthusiasm, and enables the reader to recommence research into the original person with more vigour. The more medal recipients the researcher is looking at, the more areas there are to explore; but remember, there is a tendency to become confused, particularly if researching different men from the same period, so *keep careful notes* to prevent muddled thinking. Examining the careers of several men at once usually prevents the worst possible scenario - that is, finding out shortly after arriving at the PRO that there is no scope to discover anything about the single recipient under study, so that the entire journey is wasted.

It is useful to remember that the Public Record Office keeps many other records apart from military documentation. Few are of interest in the early stages, but knowledge gained later may suggest other classes of document likely to bear fruit. A large number of organisations deposit moribund paperwork at the PRO for preservation and any of these might suddenly become relevant. For example, a newspaper obituary might mention that the individual worked for a railway company after leaving the forces. The PRO stores a selection of railway personnel records, so details of his railway service may survive. Some records for other occupations are stored at the PRO, containing various personal staff papers. These include records of Metropolitan Police officers, Customs and Excise officers, HM Coastguards and merchant seamen.

New documents are made available to public scrutiny every year, once their contents are adjudged to be no longer sensitive. For example, Army records for the Great War period have started to come into the public domain. If there has been a lapse of time between your visits, always enquire about new releases.

New technology also has a part to play, with documentation becoming available on computer and even a PRO internet station. While the general methods of document location and

One of many documents discovered at the PRO - in this case in WO 339/49015 - relevant to George Reeve's pre-1914 service as a Regular in the ranks of the Royal Irish Fusiliers. This is part of his Regimental Conduct Sheet, with details of some minor brushes with authority - see also Chapter 15.

retrieval described above remain the same, individual arrangements and procedures are steadily improved; for instance, as this book goes to press the Microfilm Reading Room has recently been reorganized on a simpler alpha-numerical basis, with a new set of reader guides to assist visitors. The next few years could be extremely interesting, with records becoming ever more accessible.

Archivists at the PRO are very approachable and more than willing to assist the novice with finding material. They have a good knowledge of document classes and what they contain, so make use of their help. It is easy to overlook extra finding aids in the Reference Room, which can save the researcher a long search through class lists. Again, PRO staff are happy to point readers towards short cuts, so don't be afraid to ask.

Research Notes

The PRO offers potential to find out details about all of the servicemen awarded the medals chosen as our research examples. Before visiting Kew it is worth spending some time examining exactly which types of document may best assist with discovering the service history of individuals.

Charles Hoggett

The Syria clasp on the Naval General Service Medal awarded to Charles Hoggett gives a starting point. Hoggett was serving with the Royal Navy off Syria in 1840. The Naval General Service medal roll should identify his ship. We can then look through ship's muster rolls to find out some personal detail

about Hoggett. After a few basic facts have been ascertained, other types of documentation may be explored, such as Greenwich Hospital pension records and Continuous Service registers.

Edward Heymer

The Sutlej medal awarded to Heymer tells us very little, except that he was serving with the 16th Lancers at a particular place and time. However, his career should be fully covered by muster and pay records. If his service records survive, they may provide pointers for further research, such as pension returns. His origins and life before and after military service are unknown; perhaps we might uncover a few clues along the way.

Henry Harvey

The Afghanistan medal roll and the Army List are the two places to start looking. The Army List will help compile his service history, and then it should be possible to start hunting through other types of officers' paperwork. At the outset I have a good feeling about this one.

POST OFFICE TELEGRAPHS.

EYRE & SPOTTISWOODE, London.

If the Receiver of an Inland Telegram doubts its accuracy, he may have it repeated on payment of half the amount originally paid for its transmission, any fraction of 1d. less than ½d. being reckoned as ½d.; and if it be found that there was any inaccuracy, the amount paid for repetition will be refunded. Special conditions are applicable to the repetition of Foreign Telegrams.

Office Star

Charges to pay   £   s.   d.

Handed in at   *Northampton*   at 5 . 5 M.,   Received here at 6 . 27

TO *Adjutant Irish Fusilier Dublin*

No longer desire to rejoin found employment. Reeve

N.B.—This Form must accompany any inquiry made respecting this Telegram.

Joseph Full

After checking medal rolls to confirm entitlement, the next stage will be to seek a service record for Full. It is important to find out which Royal Marines depot he was attached to; this is the key to retrieving relevant documentation. The Royal Marines card index in the Reference Room might assist; if not, a lot of laborious searching lies ahead.

David Boyce

The British War and Victory Medals from the Great War identified my grandfather as a private in the Royal Irish Fusiliers. He was not awarded a star, indicating that he did not serve at the front until at least 1916.

The first target of research is to establish his battalion. This may be shown on his medal index card; if not, it will almost certainly appear on the medal roll. Once this has been ascertained, we can start to examine the documentation surviving from the battalion, and try to find out when and where he was wounded. As literally millions of men served in the rank and file during the massive conflict of 1914-18 it is necessary to be realistic. Apart from the medal roll it is quite likely that we will find nothing further about David Boyce at the PRO.

George Reeve

The Military Medal and Military Cross awarded to George Reeve show that he rose from sergeant to lieutenant during the course of the First World War. Medal index cards, the Army

Even this telegram survives from 31 October 1905, in which Reeve informed the RIF that he no longer wished to rejoin the Colours despite recently seeking and obtaining War Office permission. This turned out to be a premature message. There is some confusion in the paperwork about relative dates, but it is clear that he did in fact re-enlist. (WO 339/49015)

List and officers' service papers will be the first areas to examine. Once his battalion is identified the War Diary may be of interest. As an officer, particularly one decorated for gallantry, it is most probable that Reeve will be mentioned by name. His gallantry awards will be listed in the London Gazette, and it should be possible to find a citation for the MC.

Thomas Davis

This medal group offers good scope for research and Davis' exploits should be well documented. RAF Operational Record Books may mention him by name. To begin research it is important to identify the RAF squadron with which he served. The condolence card tells us that he was a casualty; it may be possible to find further details from the Commonwealth War Graves Commission.

CHAPTER 4:
P.R.O. - ARMY OFFICERS' RECORDS

The Public Record Office holds a wide range of original Army paperwork, containing personal information about individual officers and men. Some document classes nearly always interest medal researchers and others can be informative in certain cases. Personnel records for officers commissioned up to 1920 are at the PRO; post-1920 records remain with the Ministry of Defence. At Kew, officers' records are kept in different document classes from those of the rank and file, so they will be examined separately here.

The career of an officer, by virtue of his rank and standing, was better documented than that of an ordinary soldier. Every stage was recorded, from commissioning to retirement or death in service. Many papers contain personal details and outline aspects of the officer's military life. The best way to start researching an officer is to look at the entries in the official Army List or Hart's Army List.

Army Lists

Army Lists record important events in the career of all Army officers. Facts are laid out in a standardised format, which has changed little over more than two centuries. Each volume lists every commissioned officer in the Army, with the date his commission was granted, subsequent promotions and appointments. Since 1740 the Army List has appeared in annual, monthly, quarterly and half-yearly versions. Many issues are available for scrutiny on shelves in the Microfilm Viewing Room, close to the medal roll cabinets. The career of any officer can thus be followed accurately from one volume to another, and a reasonably complete picture of his service can be established. It is possible to see where the officer was stationed throughout his service from battalion postings. Facts published in the official Army List can be supplemented from Lt.Gen. Henry Hart's unofficial Army List.

Hart's Army List was published between 1839 and 1915, and often gave information about individuals not included in the official list. Issued quarterly, Hart's List documented campaign service, which makes it extremely attractive to medal researchers. Many of Hart's Lists are on shelves in the Microfilm Viewing Room and the rest are held in class WO 211.

The next chapter describes how to follow the career of an ordinary soldier through **battalion muster rolls**. These can also be used to research an officer, as they record the whereabouts of battalion officers when each muster was compiled. Some officers spent very little time with their unit, and a glance through muster rolls can be quite enlightening.

Other important reference books in the Research Enquiries Room include the "List of Officers of the Royal Regiment of Artillery 1716-June 1914", the "Roll of Officers of the Corps of Royal Engineers from 1660 to 1898". and the "List of Commissioned Medical Officers of the Army, 1660-1960."

The next chapter describes how to check medal entitlements against **campaign medal rolls**. Medals awarded to officers can often be verified against entries in the Army List or Hart's Army List, but the roll should still be checked to ensure the facts are correct. It is good practice to check medal rolls for every medal. The roll might amplify the appointment of the officer or record wounds or secondments to other formations. Officers are usually listed in order of rank and seniority at the beginning of the medal roll for each unit. Normally the entry for an officer is no more detailed than that for a private soldier, but occasionally it includes more material. He may not be listed with his parent regiment if he was seconded to irregular troops - which was often the case, but usually this will be annotated on the regimental roll.

The PRO does not hold a copy of every medal roll. A few do not survive, others are incomplete, and rolls for some Asian campaigns are at the India Office Library. Few rolls for post-1920 campaigns have been released by the MOD.

Checking entitlement to gallantry awards has recently been made simpler; in February 1998 indexes to the Distinguished Service Order and Military Cross were moved to the PRO. The register of DSO recipients can be seen on microfilm in document class WO 390; this records all officers awarded the medal from its inception in 1886 through to 1945. Details of events resulting in the award seldom appear. An index to MCs earned by officers 1914-1938 is in class WO 389/9-24. Gazette Books recording DSOs and MCs earned during the Great War and Second World War MCs can be viewed in WO 389; records are arranged in London Gazette date order. Listings for the Great War are usually accompanied by the citation.

Some PRO document classes contain supplementary information about the more prestigious medals awarded to officers. These can be found for the VC in WO 32, WO 98 and CAB 106. Others concerning the DSO, CB and Boer War MIDs are in WO 32, WO 104 and WO 108 respectively. Officers' entitlements to gallantry medals and decorations can normally be verified through a number of sources. The Army List notes decorations for bravery and distinguished service along with other particulars. Entitlements can also be checked against lists in a number of published books. Some books specifically record officers presented a particular medal, while others, notably unit

The Afghanistan Medal, 1878-80, to Captain
Henry Harvey of the 25th Regiment of Foot, on
its crimson-edged green ribbon.

Regimental records date from 1755, although most are from the last century. They are in class WO 76, although one or two units' records have found their way into other classes, such as the Gloucesters, whose records for 1792-1866 are in WO 67. Again, a partial card index exists to regimental records, in the Research Enquiries Room. Some regimental records provide detailed information and others are sketchy. The records for several regiments have been lost.

Every officer is invested into his rank by being granted a **royal commission**. Until 1871 commissions were purchased, restricting them to the higher strata of society. Further promotion was also generally paid for, rather than earned; but promotion into a vacancy caused by a more senior regimental officer's death or disabling wounds on active service was free. The Army Purchase Commission changed the system in 1871. Before that date set prices existed for commissions, the price being dependent upon the status of the regiment. Many young gentlemen paid over the odds to guarantee entry into the regiment of their choice. A few original commissions are in class WO 43/1059, dating from 1780 to 1874. The War Office maintained **commission books** between 1660 and 1873, which are largely kept in WO 25. These were maintained for the Secretary of State for War, along with **notification books**, 1704-1858 (WO 4 and WO 25). WO 25 also contains **succession books**, recording appointments, transfers and promotions. The dates when an officer acquired and relinquished his commission are noted in the Army List. Original paperwork in document class WO 4 or WO 31 can then be retrieved. WO 4 contains indexed **letter books** spanning the years 1701-1858, and memoranda correspondence in WO 31 stretches from 1793 to 1870.

These two classes are particularly useful, furnishing personal and career details through letters of recommendation, resignations, baptismal certificates and so forth. There is a drawback, however: the papers are collected in monthly bundles, tied with red tape, and finding relevant items can be difficult. The task is not helped by the fragile condition of many of the documents. Nevertheless, it is a worthwhile chore, often introducing aspects of the individual which would otherwise remain undiscovered.

The Army Purchase Commission compiled **registers of service** for every officer serving on 1 November 1871, now in class WO 74. Ledgers list dates of promotion and whether obtained by purchase or not. Periods of home and foreign service and time spent in the ranks are indicated. The value of every officer's commission was calculated. A number of factors influenced the final figure, such as service at Lucknow or time spent on foreign service. The separate payments and allowances were added together to arrive at an individual value for each officer's commission.

Officers whose regiment was disbanded or who became inactive for one reason or another were placed upon the **half-pay list**. WO 23/68- 78 contains alphabetical lists of half-pay officers 1858-94, showing when the officer was placed on half-pay, rate of pay, payments made and often date of death. Other documents concerning half-pay officers provide little additional material. Registers in class PMG 4 provide some scant personal information from 1737 to 1921, such as the

histories, include lists of decorated officers. Citations usually appear in the London Gazette with medal announcements, and by examining entries in the Army List it is possible to bracket appropriate London Gazette indexes to consult.

After establishing the parameters of an officer's career from Army Lists and checking medal entitlements, it is possible to delve more deeply into his military pedigree.

It would be nice to think that the War Office might have collated a succinct record of each officer's service for the benefit of latterday researchers; predictably, this was not the case. Two distinct types of **service record** do exist, those raised by the War Office and others kept by the parent regiment.

Five series of War Office records were initiated, in 1809-10, 1828, 1829, 1847 and 1870-72. Returns were completed by the officer concerned, in a similar way to the naval surveys covered in a later chapter. The first series only details military service, while the others give some personal and family details. Three series are arranged alphabetically (1809-10, 1828 and 1847). The 1829 records are indexed from the 1829 Army List, and the final series is arranged by year and then regiment. All are in class WO 25. Within the same class is an incomplete record of paperwork applicable to the 1828 records but only for surnames beginning with D through to R. There is a partial card index to records within WO 25 in the Research Enquiries Room.

date half-pay ceased through death or sale of commission.
From 1837 the address of the claimant is shown, and some
later documents give date of birth. The volumes are collated
by regiment until 1841 and thereafter alphabetically. WO
25/3017-9 records half pay to officers resident abroad from
1815 to 1833; and WO 25/3232 lists officers granted permission to live abroad between the same years. They occasionally
provide some interesting information.

Many document classes contain information about officers'
and widows' **pensions**. Officers first became entitled to a pension after 1871, upon the abolition of promotion by purchase.
Until then the only financial asset possessed by a retiring officer might be his commission, which could be sold to provide
for later life. Wounded officers could claim pension payments
from 1812 onwards. Recipients 1812-1897 are listed in registers kept in WO 23/83-92. Records of payments made under
the scheme from 1814 to 1920 are in PMG 9. These two
series of documents provide little startling information, other
than confirming that a man was wounded and received a
wound pension. Correspondence between the wounded officer
and the War Office is sometimes more enlightening; some letters dating from 1812 to 1858 are in WO 4/469-93, and a
further series covering 1809-57 is in WO 43. There is a card
index to the latter in the Research Enquiries Room.

In 1708 the widows of officers killed on active service
became entitled to pension payments. Children and certain
dependents could also claim benefits from the Compassionate
Fund and the Royal Bounty in cases of need. Documents associated with these pensions and payments can be found in two
distinct types: firstly, registers of payment and secondly, applications for payment. Payment registers are not particularly
enlightening; they record payment dates, amounts, whom paid
to, and sometimes give the widow's or dependent's address.
Application correspondence is much more interesting. Birth
and marriage certificates often accompany papers in support of
a claim, together with other personal comments on the background and circumstances of the deceased officer's family.
Both types of document appear in several different PRO classes, covering varying years. The list below provides a rough
guide to papers which are likely to contain references to medal
recipients.

Payment Documents

1713-1829	WO 24/804-83	Widows in receipt of pension
1815-92	WO 23/88-92	Widows in receipt of pension
1815-95	WO 23/105-123	Widows' payment registers
1808-1920	PMG 11	Widows' payment registers
1870-82	PMG 10	Widows' payment registers
1858-94	WO 23/114-9	Compassionate List registers
1805-95	WO 23/120-3	Compassionate List summary
1812-1915	PMG 10	Compassionate List & Royal Bounty payments
1833-37	WO 54/195-6	RA & RE widows' registers
1836-75	PMG 12	RA & RE widows' payments

*Detail from a group photograph of officers of the 2nd
Battalion, 25th Regiment taken in Ceylon during
1867. Henry Harvey was serving there at the time: is
he one of them? (National Army Museum)*

Application Documents

1755-1908	WO 42	Widows' & dependents' applications
1760-c1818	WO 25/3089-197	Widows' & dependents' applications (alphabetical)
1764-1816	WO 4/1023-30	Widows' pension correspondence
1808-1825	WO 25/3073-89	Widows' & dependents' applications (abstracts - indexed in RE Room)
1818-55	WO 43	Widows' pension correspondence (indexed in RE Room)
1803-60	WO 4/521-90	Compassionate Fund letters
1812-13	WO 25/3110-4	Compassionate List correspondence

A few Army **baptism and marriage registers** are in WO 68 and WO 69 for the following units and periods:
6th Rifle Brigade, 1865-1904
Royal Horse Artillery, 1817-27, 1859-83
3rd King's Own Yorkshire Light Infantry, 1865-1904
3rd/4th Somerset Light Infantry, 1836-87, 1892-1903
West Norfolk Regiment, 1863-1908
3rd West Yorkshire Rifles, 1832-77
   Some **garrison baptismal registers** for Dover Castle, Shorncliffe and Hythe, Fermoy and Buttevant also survive in WO 156, with burial registers for Canterbury and some records for Palestine 1939-47. They provide very intermittent coverage.
   A valid Church of England **baptismal certificate** was an important prerequisite for any young gentleman taking up a commission. WO 32/8903-20 holds an indexed run of these certificates dating from 1777 to 1892. Likewise WO 42, indexed in the Research Enquiries Room, draws together a number of **birth, baptism, marriage, death and burial certificates** related to Army officers, from a range of classes. Officers were required to notify the authorities when they married, and records survive in WO 25/3239-45 for the years 1830-82, although some date back to the previous century.
   The Royal Artillery and Royal Engineers were administered by the Board of Ordnance until the time of the Crimean War. Documents referring to these two corps and their predecessors are usually found in different PRO classes from those for the rest of the Army. The Royal Engineers were an all-officer corps until the mid-19th century. Other ranks were enlisted into either the Royal Corps of Sappers and Miners or the Corps of Royal Military Artificers. The two OR branches amalgamated under the same umbrella in 1811 and all merged as the Royal Engineers in 1856. Records held at Kew are quite comprehensive and the following lists summarize what is available:

Royal Artillery

Birth/marriage registers 1817-27, 1860-77	WO 69/551-82
Officers' service records 1770-1902	WO 76
(partially indexed in Research Enquiries Room)	
Commission registers 1740-1852	WO 54/237-9
Officers' pay lists 1803-71	WO 54/946

| Half-pay lists 1810-80 | WO 23/82 |

Royal Engineers

Officers' service records 1796-1922	WO 25/3913-9
(partially indexed in Research Enquiries Room)	
Officers' service records 1828-1903	WO 25/3921-2
(Supply & Service Dept. officers)	
Officers' appointment papers 1815-46	WO 54/923-4
List of officers 1793	WO 54/701
Posting returns 1786-1850	WO 54/248-59
Commission registers 1755-1852	WO 54/240-7
Chatham RE School reports 1858-1914	WO 25/3945-54
Pay records 1805-71	WO 54/947
Half-pay lists 1810-80	WO 23/82

   Medals to Army chaplains can be fully researched at the PRO. They held commissioned status and their career details are found in the Army List with those of the other commissioned ranks.
   The PRO holds some personnel records for Army medical staff, although few relate to nurses. An indexed series of Medical Officers' Service Records are in WO 25/3896-3912, for the period from 1800 to 1840. A number of other document groups within class WO 25 also hold information about Army doctors, including some casualty returns, and registers containing details about applicants for the Medical Department. There is also, of special interest for medal researchers, a Royal Army Medical Corps Medal Book for the years 1879-96.
   Nurses' records at the PRO are somewhat sketchy. Some lists of Queen Alexandra's Imperial Nursing Service qualifications and letters of credit in support of applications survive in WO 25/3956. Other than that there are some pension records dotted around WO 23 and PMG 34 and 42. Documents supporting the applications of nurses seeking positions with medical services in the Crimea are in WO 25/264.
   A special medal, the Royal Red Cross, to be awarded for outstanding cases of care for the wounded, was created on 27 April 1883. From 1920 the medal could also be presented for exceptional bravery and devotion at the place of duty. WO 145 contains a register of Royal Red Cross awards from 1883 to 1918. Campaign medals awarded to nurses are listed on medal rolls in WO 100, alongside those for soldiers.

   The documents outlined above may present a picture of an officer's career; but most researchers yearn to find out the exact part their man played in the conduct of the campaign. Often the best hope is a published history of the regiment, battalion or campaign, but there is some limited scope available at the PRO to discover more about the role of a particular officer. Operational records for military actions prior to 1907 rarely mention officers by name, apart from very high ranking officers or persons involved in especially noteworthy actions. However, they do provide some insight into decisions made at the time. The PRO holds some private correspondence between the War Office and certain notables, which can make interesting reading.

1st Battn "The Kings Own Borderers" (late 1/25th Foot).

Roll of Effective and non Effective Officers. Non commissioned officers, and men of the above Regiment entitled to the Medal for the Afghan War.

Regimental Number	Rank at date of earning decoration	Name	Whether entitled to clasps, and for what actions &c.	If entitled to Bronze Star.	Whether serving with Service Coy or Depôt	Whether non-effective and from what cause	Remarks
"	Lieut. Col.	RUDDELL. J.A.	No	No	No	Retired	Medal sent 31.1.82
"	Major	STERRY. E.S.	Clasp for Ali-Musjid	No	No	Retired	
"		RAMSAY N.G.	No	No	Service Coy		
"	Captain	CARWITHEN. G.T.L.	No	No	1st Battn.	Serving in 2nd the Ross	
"	"	CARLETON. F.E.	No	No	Service Coy		
"	"	HARVEY. H.J.	No	No	No	Retired	
"	"	ROSS. J.L.	No	No	Service Coy		
"	"	CURTIS. F.H.T.	No	No	Depôt		
"	"	LLOYD. F.E	No	No		Retired	256444 16
"	"	McCAUSLAND. J.K.	No	No	Service Coy		
"	"	HOGARTH. J.H.H.S.D.	No	No	Service Coy		
"	"	HOPE. A.H.	No	No	Service Coy	Served 29.6.82	
"	"	DIXON. H.G.	No	No	Depôt	Adjt. 3rd Battn. West York Regiment in cont. 1.3.82	
"	"	MACKAY. A.L.H.	No	No		Serving in 2nd the Ross	
"	Lieutenant	DANDRIDGE. C.C.N	No	No	Service Coy		
"	Lieut. Adjt.	BEADNELL. A.G.S.	No	No	Service Coy		
"	Lieutenant	BECKER. C.T.	No	No	Service Coy	2nd Battalion	
"	"	CLAUGHTON. F.A.C	No	No	Depôt		
"	"	MAYNE. G.N	No	No	Depôt		
"	"	THOMPSON. J.B.	No	No		Serving in 2nd the Ross	
"	"	GIBBON. C.D	No	No		Died at Peshawar	
"	"	RETALICK. J.M.A	No	No	Probationary Staff Corps		
"	"	BRADSHAW. L.J.E.	No	No	Probationary Staff Corps		
"	"	DRUMMOND. C.J.	No	No		Died at Peshawar	16362 15
"	"	REID. J.H.E	No	No	Probationary Staff Corps		
"	"	GORDON. L.	No	No	Service Coy		
"	"	COLLCOMBE. C.L	No	No	Service Coy		
"	"	HOPE.	No	No	Service Coy	Served 29.6.82	
"	"	SPOOR. H.H.S	No	No		Died at Jegwan	
"	"	TAYLOR. D.J.O	No	No		Probationary Staff Corps Cm. C. India 1/2/82	
"	"	CORFIELD. C.J.	No	No	Service Coy		
"	"	HUTCHINSON. J.H.C	No	No	Depôt		
"	"	KEENE. C.T.P.	No	No	Service Coy		
"	"	FLEMING. J.M.	No	No	Service Coy		
"	2 Lieutenant	LOS. E.D.	No	No		Died at Jegwan	
"	"	VERNER. G. de W.	No	No		Serving with 2nd B. Ross	
"	"	TAYLOR. R.H.B.	No	No	Service Coy		
"	"	COX. H.Y.	No	No	Service Coy		
"	"	McARTHUR. C.J.E.A.	No	No	Service Coy		
"	Quarter Master	SWINEY. J.	No	No	Service Coy		
"	Paymaster	PUMFRETT. G.	No	No	Service Coy		
"	Surgeon Major	BURNETT. N.F.	No	No			Cm. C. India 4/4/82.
"	Surgeon Major	GRIBBON. G.C.	No	No			G.O. C. Portsmouth 4/4/82
"	Asst. Surgeon	LYNCH. F.	No	No		Died at camp Scinde	
"	Surgeon	TURNER. LIEUT. F.M	No	No	Depôt Company		
"	Asst. Apothecary	EDWARDES. G	No	No			
132	Sergt. Major	HOWE. J.S.	No	No	Service Coy		

The Afghanistan medal roll - in WO 100/52 - for the '1st Battn, "King's Own Borderers" (late 1/25th Foot)'. Capt. H.J. Harvey's entitlement to the medal without a clasp is confirmed - see sixth name from top.

14 Hercules Terrace
Westminster Road
Lambeth 30 January 1858

Sir

Will you have the kindness to submit the name of my
Son, — Henry James Harvey now seventeen years of age
to His Royal Highness, the General Commanding in Chief for
a Commission of Ensign without purchase in the Army

For many years I commanded the first Regiment
of Royal Guernsey Militia during which time I was at very
considerable personal expense in fulfilling the duties of
that command, & no pay or remuneration of any kind was
allowed for the same

I enclose a copy of a testimonial to that effect from
Lieut General Sir Wm Napier who was Lieut Governor of Guernsey
many years, — I served under his command during the whole
of his Administration of that Island, and you will observe
by his testimonial he was aware I was at a considerable
personal cost, & I would refer you to him as to his appreciation
of my services during the whole time of his Government

I have also the honour to enclose to you a letter addressed
to yourself by Lieutenant General Sir John Bell who succeeded
Sir Wm Napier as Lieut Governor of Guernsey and I served under
his command during the whole time of his Administration of
that Island to his satisfaction; he requested me to deliver to you
the enclosed letter in the hope that it would contribute to the
granting of my request

I shall feel exceedingly obliged to you Sir if in laying
my request before His Royal Highness you will accompany
the same with your powerful support & recommendation

I have the honour to be
Sir Your most obedient
humble Servant

John Harvey
Colonel

To
Major General
Sir Charles Yorke K C B
&c   &c   &c
Horse Guards

Units actively involved in campaigns since 1907 have been obliged to keep a **war diary** of daily events. These are an important source of information about men involved in 20th century campaigns, most of whose personal files remain with the MOD. Many officers are mentioned by name, and it is usually possible to identify the post an officer occupied within his battalion. This knowledge can then be applied to occurrences as they unfold. A reasonably full picture of his activities can be built up through diary references to company or sub-unit. First World War diaries will be covered in more detail in Chapter 15.

Second World War unit diaries are often even more detailed than those for the Great War. The 100-year restriction on the disclosure of information from the diaries does not prevent private research. Other 20th century campaigns are similarly documented, and a number of war diaries kept by units engaged in smaller conflicts are available at the PRO. The War Diary was superceded by Unit Quarterly Historical Reports in 1946; and these were replaced by Unit Historical Records in 1950. Both types were broadly similar to the war diaries which preceded them, but less detailed.

Research Notes

Captain H.J.Harvey

Two Army officers feature among our representative medals recipients, Captain Henry Harvey and Lieutenant George Reeve. PRO research into Reeve's medals is covered at the end of Chapter 15, devoted to the First World War.

The Afghanistan medal to Captain Harvey is impressed around the rim - CAPT HJ HARVEY 1/25th REGT - confirming that he held that rank and served with that regiment in the Second Afghan War between 1878 and 1880. His rank suggested that Harvey had already spent some years in the Army; promotion for subalterns was not usually rapid. Research began with Hart's Army List for 1884, to find details of Harvey's campaign service and a skeleton history of his career.

His entry stated that he "served with the 25th KOB in the Afghan War in 1878-79 with the Peshawar Valley Field Force, including the Bazar Valley Expedition under Lt. Gen. Maude". Up to 1884 Harvey had spent 26 years on full pay and six months on half-pay. His career details were shown as follows:

Ensign	June 1858
Lieutenant	1 April 1860
Captain	15 March 1873
Major	1 July 1881

So it was immediately apparent that Harvey was a career officer, whose service stretched from at least 1858 to 1884.

The surviving letter of 30 January 1858 in which Henry's father Lt.Col.John Harvey requests a commission without purchase for his son, on the grounds of the considerable personal expense accepted by Harvey senior during his command of the Royal Guernsey Militia. He cites in support two Lieutenant-Governors of the island, the first being the famous soldier Sir William Napier. The letter is among memoranda papers in WO 31/1181.

(Hart's also listed a Lt.Col.John Richard Harvey with the 25th Foot - Henry's brother.)

WO 100/52 is the Afghanistan medal roll for the 25th Foot, and Harvey is shown entitled to the medal without bars. The roll, compiled on 1 February 1882, describes Harvey as retired since the campaign. As Hart's Army List for 1884 listed Harvey on the active list, this comment about retirement was probably based upon the six-month period which he apparently spent on half-pay.

No regimental service records survive for officers from the 25th Foot. Harvey was serving when War Office service records were compiled between 1870 and 1872. They are arranged by year and regiment. The Army List showed Harvey attached to the 2/25th from 1870 to 1872. Returns for 2/25th officers are in classes WO 25/832/3, WO 25/847/2 and WO 25/861/3, one for each year. According to War Office records, Henry James Harvey was born 28 August 1840 in Guernsey. He was commissioned as an ensign without purchase into the 2nd Foot, aged 18 (sic), on 5 June 1858. He transferred to the 1/25th on 8 September 1858, and was promoted lieutenant without purchase in the 2/25th on 1 April 1860. The War Office record summarized Harvey's service as 5 years 11 months abroad and 7 years 3 months at home. Details were as follows:

Home	5/6/1858-11/4/1859
Gibraltar	12/4/1859-5/2/1860
Home	6/2/1860-27/7/1863
Ceylon	28/7/1863-20/10/1866
Home	21/10/1866-5/10/1869
India	6/10/1869 to date

All other spaces in the document were marked "Nil".

The Commissions Register, WO 25/80, lists Henry Harvey commissioned into the 2nd Foot on 4 June 1858; the document was signed by Queen Victoria on 31 May 1858 at St James' Palace.

Harvey's very informative commission memoranda papers were found in WO 31/1181. Henry's father, Colonel John Harvey, a former Commanding Officer of the Guernsey Militia, submitted his son for consideration as an ensign without purchase in a letter to Horse Guards. His application was supported by letters from two former Lieutenant- Governors of Guernsey, Lt.Gen.Sir William Napier and Sir John Bell KCB, confirming claims made by Colonel Harvey that he supplied and kitted the Guernsey Militia at his own expense for many years.

J.L.V.Cachernaille, perpetual curate of St Peter Port, gave information about Harvey's upbringing, stating that he had been under his pastoral care since his early years and confirmed into the Church of England by the Bishop of Winchester on 5 August 1855. He described Henry Harvey's moral conduct as strictly correct. In a further letter P.D.Francois, curate of St Peter Port, reiterated Henry's date of birth and enclosed a copy of his baptismal certificate, 3 September 1840. His mother's maiden name was given as Anne Sophia Grut.

Henry Harvey secured his commission vice Ensign Greene, 2nd Foot, whose letter of resignation is among the papers in the bundle. In a separate letter Lt.Gen.Pennefather reported Ensign Greene's intemperate behaviour.

The papers provided a good basis for further research. On 1 November 1871 the Army Purchase Commission compiled a record of service for every commissioned officer. Henry Harvey appears in file WO 74/179. The value of his lieutenancy was assessed at £700, with "over-regulation payment" set at £100; so on 1 November 1871 the resale value of his commission was worth a total of £800. A further allowance of £287 10s. was made for his eventual retirement in a higher rank than that held in November 1871.

The Remarks column recorded Harvey's retirement as a captain on pension on 1 January 1881 (*London Gazette* 11/1/1881). He was promoted to half-pay major on 1 July 1881, and to major, King's Own Scottish Borderers, on the same date. His promotion to half-pay lieutenant colonel on 1 July 1888 appeared in the *London Gazette* on 3 July. According to the ledger he retired on 22 August (LG 21/8/1888).

Gaps in knowledge about Harvey's career were filled from successive Army Lists. He first appeared in the Army List of 1859-60, joining the 1/25th in Gibraltar on 8 October 1858. He remained on the Rock until promoted lieutenant into the 2nd Battalion in April 1860. The 2nd Battalion were stationed at Aldershot, Shorncliffe and Edinburgh over the next three years; and embarked for Ceylon on 28 July 1863. Harvey served in Ceylon from 1863 to 1868, moving to Shahjehanpore in India in 1869 and on to Bareilly from 1870 to 1872. On his promotion to captain in 1873 Harvey returned to the 1st Battalion at Kinsale in Ireland, and moved to Buttevant in 1875.

The battalion sailed for India on 13 October 1875. From 1876 to 1878 Harvey was stationed at Fyzabad, moving up to Peshawur close behind the North-West Frontier in 1879. The 1/25th formed part of the Khyber Line Force in Afghanistan during 1880. Captain Harvey was placed on half-pay for six months before attaining his majority on 1 July 1881. He continued to serve with the 1st Battalion of the Borderers at Cherat, Umballa and Meerut in Bengal until 1887.

He disappears from the list of battalion officers in 1888. The 1890 Army List shows Harvey was promoted lieutenant colonel and retired on 1 July 1888; he was placed on half-pay on 22 August that year. Harvey's name remained on the retired list until 1916, when he was 76 years of age.

PMG 4/254 showed him placed on half-pay commencing 1 July 1888. The rate was set at 11s. per day, paid through Cox and Company, Harvey's agents. The entry was cancelled on 21 August 1888 when he went to retired pay. The War Office record in WO 23/72 gives much the same information, but shows Harvey in receipt of retirement pay at a rate of £300 per annum.

Regimental musters around the time of the Second Afghan War were consulted; WO 16/1584 runs from 1 April 1877 to 31 March 1879. The battalion was initially based at Fyzabad, but from January to March at Lundi Kotul in Afghanistan. The 1/25th were affected by a cholera outbreak during 1879, revealed by the next muster roll (WO 16/1585): 39 men died during the month of June. On 8 November 1879 Harvey set sail for England, and next appeared on the York Depot muster from January to September 1880.

Harvey next appeared on muster WO 16/1586 as a major in July 1881. The 1st Battalion was shown at Ludianna, but Harvey served with the 2nd Battalion until September 1881. In October he rejoined the 1st Battalion, where he remained.

At this point it was felt that most avenues of enquiry were exhausted, and PRO research into Harvey ceased.

CHAPTER 5:

P.R.O. - ARMY OTHER RANKS' RECORDS

There is plenty of scope for researching ordinary soldiers awarded medals at the PRO, although they are less well documented than officers. Many different documents contain information about other ranks, and a reasonable sketch of their career can be drawn. There is no Army List to provide shortcuts, but there are unit musters, description books, attestation documents, discharge papers and many other sources. Medal rolls list other ranks awarded campaign medals in the same way as officers.

Medal rolls are on microfilm in the Microfilm Viewing Room. There is no waiting time, which makes consulting them an attractive prospect while you are waiting for documents ordered via the computer. Each roll is individually boxed within a row of filing cabinets, and index binders lie on top of the cabinets. To find the required roll of microfilm it is usually necessary to know the recipient's regiment.

On most medal rolls, names are listed in rank order and then alphabetically. The titles of different clasps often lie along the upper horizontal axis, and ticks against the man's name indicate the clasps he was entitled to. However, the format of each roll varies and some are designed very differently. Various supplementary sheets correct mistaken entries made on the original sheet, or add names omitted when the document was first compiled.

Apart from confirming entitlement, medal rolls sometimes provide further information. A footnote might appear against a man's name indicating death or wounds, accompanied by date or place. Occasionally a note mentions that medals were forfeit.

The medal roll might indicate other interesting features. Perhaps that medal was only issued to a handful of men from a particular regiment, making an example more valuable than first thought. A certain clasp may be rare to the unit, suggesting an attachment to another formation or an unusual duty performed, maybe as a senior officer's batman. There are many possibilities. Apart from medal rolls in WO 100, there are several files in class WO 32 containing recommendations for awards, usually connected to smaller campaigns.

Do-it-yourself microfilm photocopiers are situated in the Viewing Room. Pre-pay cards can be purchased, allowing the dubious pleasure of spending half an hour wrestling with one of the fairly complex machines dotted around the room. They are just complicated enough to let the researcher forget how to use them by the next visit, so he can go through the learning process again ....

Long Service and Good Conduct Medal rolls are in class WO 102, covering the years between inception and 1953. WO 101 lists men entitled to the Meritorious Service Medal from 1846 to 1919. A record of payments made to MSM and LSGC recipients 1846-79 can be seen in WO 23/84.

There are no rolls, as such, listing gallantry awards to other ranks apart from the period of the First World War. (Great War awards are covered separately in Chapter 15.) Names of men presented with medals for bravery and meritorious service appeared in the **London Gazette**, and copies of this will be found in document class ZJ 1.

The approximate date of an award can usually be identified through printed works or unit histories. Gallantry medals awarded to other ranks nearly always bear personal details and unit. Before the Great War records of gallantry awards are scattered across various classes. DCM submissions and some citations are in WO 146, and some other DCM records are in WO 32. Boer War MIDs are in WO 108/142.

Once medals have been verified and any extra information

The Sutlej Medal to Pte. Edward Heymer of the 16th Lancers, on its crimson-edged blue ribbon with clasp SOBRAON. This medal for the Sikh War of 1845-46 bore on the reverse ARMY OF THE SUTLEJ and the name of the action for which it was awarded, in this case ALIWAL 1846. If the soldier took part in a subsequent action he was awarded the relevant clasp.

An impression of the charge of the 16th Lancers on 28 January 1846 at Aliwal, where Edward Heymer and his comrades faced a formidable Sikh army equipped and trained along European lines. The enemy's massed musketry and strong, well-served artillery were comparable - in the opinion of veterans - to the opposition they had faced in the Napoleonic Wars. From a morning strength of 530 all ranks the 16th Lancers lost that day 59 killed and 83 wounded, but 30 of the latter would died of their wounds. The regiment's losses represented about a quarter of the total British casualties at Aliwal, from an army of some 10,000 men. A campaign medal to a survivor of such an epic action is obviously of much greater interest than those to units less bloodily engaged.

gleaned from the medal roll/s, it is time to investigate other documentary research sources available at the PRO. The best place to start looking is WO 97 - **attestation and discharge papers** for soldiers of all units between 1760 and 1913. These varied slightly in format between different regimental depots and as amended over the years, but the basic information recorded changed little, though later papers give more particulars about family background and next-of-kin.

The front page generally gives personal information about age, place of origin, trade and a physical description. Inside pages record service history - usually listing medals and clasps awarded, promotions achieved, examinations passed, demotions, courts martial, punishments, wounds, and an assessment of conduct.

Documents within WO 97 are stored in four different segments according to date of discharge. Documents for 1760-1854 are stored alphabetically by regiment, so it is imperative that the researcher knows which regiment the soldier served with. These papers have been microfilmed and are available in the Microfilm Viewing Room. The next series, covering discharges between 1855 and 1872, are arranged identically to the first. From 1873 to 1882 soldiers' documents are sorted alphabetically into cavalry, artillery, infantry and corps. At this stage a researcher can contemplate searching for documents where the unit remains unknown. After 1883 all attestation and discharge papers are in alphabetical order for the entire Army.

There is one major problem, however: paperwork for men who died during service has been destroyed - WO 97 only holds material relating to men who survived their time in the Army. Research into medals awarded to men who died from any cause is therefore quite frustrating. In such cases it is necessary to fall back on material originated at regimental level instead of being able to draw upon a condensed history of the soldier from discharge records. Up until 1898 it is sometimes possible to follow a casualty's career through regimental muster rolls, but there is little hope of tracing any reference to men serving between 1898 and 1913 at the PRO, apart from a brief mention on medal rolls.

The PRO holds a quantity of **muster books and pay lists** maintained by regiments and depots. They were up-dated periodically to account for victuals and expenses. To commence searching for muster books, the unit must be known. By using the medal campaign date as a starting point it should be possi-

ble to find the man in regimental records.

Each muster normally covers one year, and gives an insight into the daily routine of Army life. Men are shown sick in hospital, on furlough, recruiting, despatched to collect prisoners, and engaged on all manner of other tasks. Even the briefest mention is worthwhile if it proves the man was involved in a particular action. Account sheets list expenses incurred on route marches or while on detached duty. Large numbers of men are often listed as awaiting court martial or in detention for a range of offences; it quickly becomes apparent that the soldiers of yesteryear were no angels.

The first and last entries for any given soldier often show the most information. On recruitment the entry normally indicates age, trade and where he enlisted. Death and discharge are recorded under the list of men becoming "non-effective". This entry reiterates trade, confirms date of enlistment and gives place of origin. Later muster documents give details of marriages and offspring if the family moved into Army married quarters. The wife's name is shown, together with the ages of children in years and months. There is also a column detailing reasons why particular wives were struck from the "married roll".

Most muster and pay lists are in WO 12, spanning the years 1732-1878. Records for later years until 1898 are in WO 16, including musters for regiments in India 1883-89. However, the material for each unit in this class is sporadic and disjointed.

Muster volumes for engineers, artillery and militia/volun-

teers are held within different classes, covering different years. Engineers' musters are in WO 11 (1816-78), artillery WO 10 (1710-1878), and militia/volunteers WO 13 (1780-1878). No musters survive for engineers or artillery in India.

From 1825 a description of every soldier was entered into a **description book**. These were compiled to prevent fraudulent re-enlistment (joining up for a bounty, then immediately deserting and re-enlisting in another unit, has been a popular way for an active rogue to make money for many centuries past). The books record physical characteristics, with brief service details, age, place of birth and trade. A description was first taken when recruits arrived at the depot and a regimental book documented men joining each battalion. Early records are fragmentary. Some descriptions of the oldest and most senior men date from the latter years of the 18th century, but the most are for the 19th century. PRO holdings vary, so be prepared for many gaps in the series. Regimental books run from 1778 to 1878 in WO 25/266-688, while depot books span 1768-1908 in WO 67. These latter are generally the most accurate.

Description books are arranged alphabetically by initial letter of surname, or by enlistment date. If a record cannot be found it is possible to estimate enlistment date from the **regimental number**. Before the First World War individual units allocated their own numbers, so the service of the medal recipient can be guesstimated from comparison with other men shown in the musters. Note that men acquired completely new

numbers when they transferred from one unit to another, which was often the case.

Regimental **casualty records** are another source of information when researching deceased soldiers. They were compiled monthly and quarterly from 1809 to 1875, though some contain later entries up to about 1910. Each records the date and place the man met his fate, and how, with standard information on name, rank, place of birth and trade. Next-of-kin are identified, and very occasionally the entry is accompanied by wills and other correspondence. Regimental casualty returns are in class WO 25/1359-2410 and 3251-3260. They are indexed by pieces 2411-2755 and 3261-3471. Records cover absentees, deserters and discharges as well as dead and wounded. There is an alphabetical list of payments made to next-of-kin from credits owing to fallen soldiers in class WO 25, spanning the years 1810-1881. Some list property belonging to the dead man and others give personal details about next-of-kin.

Pension records can supplement information from discharge papers in WO 97. Pensioned soldiers fell into two distinct

OVERLEAF *Part of the muster roll of the 16th Lancers after Aliwal, in WO 12/1279. No.1526 Heymer, Edward, is the twelfth name up from the bottom - just above the unfortunate Pte. John Holland, No.1476, who is marked as "Killed in Action at Alliwall".*

Muster for the Month, ended the 31 of January 1846

Medals A S	No. entitled to higher Pay from length of Service, after 17 years	Regimental Number	† Privates.	Effective and belonging to the Corps. Periods — From	To	REMARKS, explanatory of the Reasons and Durations of Absence, and Causes of broken Periods; also specifying the precise Dates of Inlistment of Recruits, and the Date on which each Man ceased to be effective as belonging to the Corps.
1-1	156	1205	Greenhalgh James	1 June 4	31 Jan y	
1-1	158	1430	Gray William	"	"	
1-1	157/6	523	Greanes Henry	"	"	
1-1	160/27	405	Grieve Ralph	"	"	
1-1	161/28	531	Grundell John	"	"	
0-0	149	1505	Gain Henry	"	21 "	Killed in the Skirmish at Buddowoll
		969	Griffiths Robert			
1-1	185/29	464	Hughes Michael	"	31 "	Farrier
1-1	186/30	373	Hall John	"	"	
1-0	187	855 1417	Harding Anthony	"	"	Genl Hospital Loodianah
1-1	444	1546	Harding Henry	"	"	
1-1	188	768	Haywood William	"	"	
1-1	189	1093	Hicks George	"	"	
		1573	Hegarty James	"	"	At Meerut
		1124	Hunt George	"	"	Invalid at Calcutta
1-0	177	692	Hawksley John	"	28 "	Killed in Action at Alliwall
1-1	178	886	Hepper Henry	"	31 "	
1-1	184	831	Hart Henry	"	"	Rough Rider
		1574	Hegarty Samuel	"	"	At Meerut
1-0	191/31	576	Harris John	"	"	Genl Hospital Loodianah
1-1	190	1548	Halsell William	"	"	
1-1	168	705 Cpl	Harvey Samuel	"	"	Good Conduct Pay R Rider
1-0	169	607 Cpl	Hawkins Thomas	"	"	Good Conduct Pay Genl Hospital Loodianah
1-1	170	1111	Hawkins William	"	"	
1-1	724	703 1406	Halstead John	"	"	
1-1	171	1526	Heymer Edward	"	"	
1-0	167	1476	Holland John	"	28 "	Killed in Action at Alliwall
1-1	732	530	Halliwell William	"	31 "	
1-1	180	1542	Harrison William	"	"	
1-1	181	638	Hanbrey William	"	"	
1-1	183	1100 Cpl	Head Henry	"	"	Good Conduct Pay Corpl
1-1	182	741	Hewitt Thomas	"	"	
1-0	173	627	Haken George	"	"	Genl Hospital Loodianah
1-1	192	1246	Halligan Charles	"	"	
1-0	174	981 1346 Cpl	Hutchins George	"	"	Good conduct Pay Genl Hospital Loodianah
1-1	175	1272	Hyde George	"	"	
1-1	176	1249	Hyde William	"		

Muster for the Month, ended the 28 of February 1846			Muster for the Month, ended the 31 of March 1846		
Effective and belonging to the Corps — Periods		**REMARKS, explanatory of the Reasons and Durations of Absence, and Causes of broken Periods; also specifying the precise Dates of Inlistment of Recruits, and the Date on which each Man ceased to be effective as belonging to the Corps.**	**Effective and belonging to the Corps — Periods**		**REMARKS, explanatory of the Reasons and Durations of Absence, and Causes of broken Periods; also specifying the precise Dates of Inlistment of Recruits, and the Date on which each Man ceased to be effective as belonging to the Corps.**
From	To		From	To	
1 Feby	28 Feby	Volunteered to H. M. 3rd Light Dragoons			
"	"		1 March	31 March	
"	"	Volunteered to H. M. 3rd Light Dragoons	"	"	
"	"	L. Corporal	"	31 "	Volunteered to H. M. 3rd Lt. Dgs.
12 "	"	From Corporal C. Volunteered to H. M. 3rd Light Dragoons			
1 "	"	Farrier	"	31 "	Volunteered to H. M. 3rd Lt. Dgs.
"	"	Volunteered to H. M. 3rd Light Dragoons	"	"	
"	"	At Loodianah	"	"	Rejoined 8th inst
"	"		"	"	
"	"		"	"	
"	"		"	"	
"	"	At Meerut	"	"	Rejoined 26th inst
1 Nov	8 Jan	Invalid embarked for England			
1 Feby	28 Feby		"	"	
"	"	Rough Rider Volunteered to H. M. 3rd Light Dragoons			
"	"	At Meerut	"	31 "	Rejoined 26th inst, and Volunteered to H. M. 3 Lt. Dgs.
"	"	At Loodianah	"	"	At Loodianah
"	"		"	31 "	Volunteered to H. M. 3 Lt. Dgs.
"	"	Good Conduct Pay. R. Rider	"	31 "	Volunteered to H. M. 3 Lt. Dgs.
"	"	Good Conduct Pay. At Loodianah	"	"	Good Conduct Pay Invalid proceeding to Bombay
"	"		"	"	
"	"		"	"	
"	"		"	"	
"	"	Volunteered to H. M. 3rd Light Dragoons	"	"	Farrier
"	"	Volunteered to H. M. 3rd Light Dragoons			
"	"	Good Conduct Pay. L. Corpl.	"	"	Good Conduct Pay. L. Corpl.
"	"	Volunteered to H. M. 3rd Light Dragoons			
"	"	At Loodianah	"	"	Invalid proceeding to Bombay
"	"		"	"	
"	"	Good Conduct Pay. At Loodianah	"	"	Good Conduct Pay. Invalid proceeding to Bombay
"	"		"	"	
"	"	Volunteered to H. M. 3rd Light Dragoons			

groups: so-called *in-pensioners* and *out-pensioners*. In-pensioners resided at the Royal Hospital, Chelsea, or the Royal Hospital, Kilmainham, in the case of Irish soldiers until 1929. Out-pensioners received a monetary income and lived within the civilian community. Irish out-pensioners were administered from Kilmainham up to 1822. Pension paperwork assists with research into life after a military career.

Several different categories of pension paperwork survive at Kew, and provide useful information if the soldier awarded medals is thought to have completed his term of service. WO 121/1-136 contains pensioner's discharge documents for the years 1787-1813; these include similar details to WO 97. Compiled for submission to the board of the Chelsea Royal Hospital Chelsea, they are organized by the date the papers went before the board. Discharge documents for Kilmainham pensioners from 1783 to 1822 are in class WO 119, indexed by WO 118.

Each regiment maintained a list of men discharged to Chelsea pension from the early part of the 18th century until the mid-19th century. An incomplete index covering the years 1806-38 is held in the Research Enquiries Room. The registers are in class WO 120, on microfilm. The early ledgers give some personal particulars of each pensioner, including age, where born and an abridged service record. After 1843 they contain information about the pension awarded to each man and identify the establishment administering its payment. Regimental registers continue until 1876 in WO 23/26-65. Date of death is shown in registers dating from 1812 to 1877. Knowledge of the pension office handling payments, from WO 120, can be extremely useful. Records of district pension office payments 1842-83 are in WO 22, and enable a researcher to follow the pensioner through later life. Entries for soldiers are made in blue/black ink and show date pension commenced, with the rate awarded. Returns are divided into separate sections for men moving into or out of the district, changes in payment, and cessation through death. This last column shows the age of the deceased, date of death and remarks.

In- and out-pensioner admission papers for Chelsea and Kilmainham are generally by regiment in discharge date order. Although records are unindexed, it is feasible to use the date of discharge from the Army to narrow down the likely period of examination for pension. Admission papers give description, age, years spent in each rank, foreign service, character, good conduct badges, place of birth and trade. They also show the reason for discharge, which can be interesting - though often simply "worn out". Kilmainham records for in- and out-pensioners are in a single series, WO 118, 1704-1922. Chelsea records are divided into long service awards and disablement pensions, WO 117 1823-1913 and WO 116 1715-1913 respectively. Royal Artillery pension returns are stored separately in WO 116/125-85 for the years 1833-1913.

If the medal recipient was a Chelsea in-pensioner, class WO 23 may repay some scrutiny, for supplementary information about hospital residents such as lists of pensioners, muster rolls and so on. WO23/133 and 163-72 are in-pensioner admission books, which are particularly informative. They show standard information about age, regiment, date pension commenced, as well as comments about the reason for discharge and home address. They are unindexed, so the researcher must narrow down likely dates of admission before drawing books to browse through. The period between 1858 and 1933 is indexed by WO 23/173.

For a lucky few researchers there is a rich seam of information in class PIN 71, although it only relates to approximately 5,000 men **disabled prior to the First World War**. Records are held alphabetically, and information given includes descriptions of how the injury happened and medical documentation. The papers also offer a great deal of genealogical information.

Other classes provide information regarding pensions and pensioners, but to go into any greater depth is beyond the scope of this book. The PRO Current Guide lists categories of paperwork, and it is a matter for the individual researcher to decide how far to go. Some documentation connected with **Army boarding schools**, set up for the children of serving or deceased soldiers, is held at Kew. Unfortunately, although the information given in various admission and discharge registers is quite comprehensive, it is difficult to tie down the relationship between a particular child and parent. The papers span 1803-1923 for boys attending the Royal Military Asylum at Chelsea, later the Duke of York's Military School. Girls were admitted until 1840 and records relating to them are more detailed, showing parents' names. Boys were recorded in chronological order of admission and entries are not indexed, apart from the periods 1804-1820 and 1910-58 which are found in WO 143. A register of boys admitted to the Royal Hibernian Military School in Ireland was compiled in 1863. The register in WO 143/27 includes details of pupils spanning from the early 19th to early 20th centuries. Few other records for the Royal Hibernian School survive. Unless other documentation indicates that offspring attended a military school at a given time, searching the records is a pretty thankless task. If the soldier under research attended one as a child, details are usually shown on attestation papers.

Sometimes the medal recipient was unfortunate enough to be taken **prisoner of war**. POW records at the PRO are sketchy and the amount of material available varies. Little paperwork survives from before the First World War, apart from some incomplete lists of names and lists of captured officers from the Crimean and Boer Wars. Several types of document provide information about men taken prisoner during the two World Wars, although by far the most extensive POW records relate to the Korean War 1951-53, in WO 208/3999.

As mentioned in the previous chapter, records for the Royal Artillery and Royal Engineers are stored in separate classes to those for the rest of the Army. Usually the documents are virtually identical to standard Army forms. Paperwork available may be summarized as follows:

Royal Artillery

Service Records 1791-1855 ... WO 69
Arranged by last unit served with; this can be
found by reference to WO 69/779-782, 801-39.
Muster Rolls 1708-1878 ... WO 10/16
Few records for India.
Soldiers' documents 1760-1854 ... WO 97
Discharge/transfer/casualty registers 1740-1858 ... WO 5

Casualty returns from 1850 ... WO 25
Battalion description books 1749-1859 ... WO 54/260-309
Depot description books 1773-1874 ... WO 69/74-80
Pensions admission books ... WO 116/127-185
Pension registers ... WO 54/338-452,470-80
Miscellaneous records 1692-1876 ... WO 54/672-755
RHA births/marriages 1859-83 ... WO 69
RHA description books 1776-1821 ... WO 69/1-6
RHA service records 1803-63 ... WO 69
RHA applications 1820-51 ... WO 54/927

Royal Engineers

Discharge/transfer/casualty books 1800-59 ... WO 54/329-35
Soldiers’ papers 1760-1854 ... WO 97/1148-52
1855-1872 ... WO 97/1359-64
Musters 1816-78 ... WO 11
Deceased soldier register 1824-58 ... WO 25/2972
Pension Registers 1834 ... WO 23/141-5
Created 1834, but records date back several years.

Before 1859 the Indian Army was administered by the East India Company, and most EIC records are at the India Office Library. Service records for post-1859 British Indian Army personnel are usually with those for British units. However, some paperwork connected with discharge back to the UK does appear in separate classes.

Campaign medals to civilians often appear on the market, particularly to the Commissariat Branch, which supplied the Army in the field. A full range of personnel documentation for members of the department survives at the PRO, including applications, full and half-pay returns, pension records and description books.

The documents outlined above are the main sources for information about soldiers who were awarded medals. There are many others, such as those connected with deserters and courts martial. Facts uncovered by looking at the papers listed will naturally lead on to other areas of research. Relevant paperwork can then be found from the PRO Current Guide or by a request for assistance at the desk in the Research Enquiries Room.

Research Notes

Edward Heymer
Medal rolls for the Sutlej campaign are at the India Office Library, so the starting point at Kew was to hunt for Heymer’s service papers in WO 97, Soldiers’ Attestation and Discharge Papers.

These are arranged in batches by date of discharge. Not knowing when Heymer was discharged, it was necessary to try and deduce where to start looking. No rank is shown on the medal to help estimate his length of service at the time. He could have just enlisted or been approaching the end of his service. Prior to 1872, WO 97 is arranged by regiment and then alphabetically. Records in WO 97/1-1271 cover the years 1760-1854 and WO 97/1272-1721 from 1855 to 1872; Heymer could appear in either batch.

His papers were found in class WO 97/1287. They con-

tained a good deal of personal information and an outline of his service career. He enlisted into the 16th Lancers on 15 September 1841, aged 17 years - five years before the First Sikh War. He was discharged in the rank of troop sergeant major on 21 September 1865, after 24 years and seven days service with the Colours. Three years and nine months were spent in “the East Indies” - i.e. the Indian sub-continent.

TSM Heymer was never entered into the regimental defaulter’s book. He earned his first good conduct badge after five years’ service and a second at the ten-year point. On 17 January 1852 Heymer was promoted to corporal, and to sergeant in August 1855. Five years later he was made a troop sergeant major, but resigned to sergeant in April 1864.

The documents verified Heymer’s entitlement to the Sutlej medal for Sobraon and Aliwal, but also indicated that he was awarded the Maharajpoor Star and the Long Service and Good Conduct Medal. The Maharajpoor Star was awarded to troops present at the battle of that name, in the state of Gwalior, fought on 29 December 1843. British forces under Sir Hugh Gough routed the entrenched Gwalior army at a cost of about 800 casualties. So Edward Heymer took part in two very bloody battles within five years of enlistment, although the rest of his service was relatively peaceful. Heymer’s Long Service and Good Conduct Medal is listed on WO 102/2; it was issued on 30 June 1865.

Edward Heymer was described on discharge papers as 5ft 10ins tall, with a sallow complexion, hazel eyes, dark brown hair, and a small scar on the left of his chin. His place of birth was given as Shoreditch, so he was a Cockney; but he enlisted at Maidstone and discharged at Canterbury, indicating a move down the Thames to Kent before he enlisted; his trade was given as porter. His discharge address was 36 Nine Elms Grove, Gravesend, Kent.

A full set of muster rolls survive for the duration of Heymer’s service with the 16th Lancers. From these it is possible to establish a complete record of Heymer’s career. One of the first things to strike anyone reading muster returns is the large number of enlisted men awaiting court martial, in prison, forfeiting pay and undergoing various forms of punishment. Men serving in the ranks during the last century were often ill-educated, drunken, undisciplined and undesirable in almost every way. Men like Heymer, who kept themselves out of trouble and made progress through the ranks, must have been exceptional, managing to sustain their self-respect and personal standards amid the violent life of the barrack room.

Edward Heymer first appears on the regimental depot muster in WO 12/1276 after recruitment. He embarked to join the regiment in India on 23 July 1842. The regimental muster first lists him on the regimental strength on 4 November 1842; it records, “2 recruits landed from England 4/11/42. On the way to join on board the *Zemindar*”. He finally joined the regiment on 23 March 1843 at Meerut, 18 months after he enlisted. Heymer remained as a private soldier with the regiment throughout muster WO 12/1278, covering 1 April 1843 to 31 March 1845. The regiment was in camp at Dunailla during the last quarter of 1843, when

HER MAJESTY'S _16th_ REG. OF _Lancers_

Whereof _Lt. General The Honble Sir E. Cust KCH._ is Colonel.

[Place and Date] _Canterbury 21st Sept_ 1865.

PROCEEDINGS OF A REGIMENTAL BOARD, held this day, in conformity to the Articles of War, for the purpose of verifying and recording the Services, Conduct, Character, and cause of Discharge of No. _1526, Lce Troop Serj Major Edward Hymer_ of the Regiment above-mentioned.

President.

Lieut Colonel E. Tomkinson, Cavalry Staff

Capt Dumbleton 21st R. Members. _Capt Riddell 16th Lcs_

THE BOARD having examined and compared the Regimental Records, the Soldier's Book, and such other Documents as appeared to them to be necessary, report that after making every deduction required by Her Majesty's Regulations, the Service up to this day, which he is entitled to reckon, amounts to _24_ years, _7_ days, as shown by the detailed Statement on the 2nd page; during which period he served abroad _3 9/12_ years, viz. :

at _____ years,

in _The East Indies 3 9/12_ _____ years ;

" _____

and further, that his DISCHARGE is proposed in consequence of

[Here state whether—Completion of period, at his own request, or as unfit for further Service.] _his own request, free, with pension, after 24 years Service_

With regard to the CHARACTER and CONDUCT of _Edward Hymer_ , the Board have to report that upon reference to the Defaulter's Book, and by the Parole testimony that has been given, it appears that _they have been Good, & he was when promoted in possession of two (2) Good Conduct Badges, & would had he not been promoted, have been now in possession of five (5) Good Conduct Badges. — He has the Medals for "Maharajpore" and "Aliwal" and has been recommended for a medal "For Good Conduct & Long Service" with a gratuity of Ten (10) pounds._

[Insert opposite—the man's Character, the number of Good Conduct Badges in his possession, and all Badges of Merit, or gallant conduct in the Field, conferred upon him.]

[Insert the number of times his Name appears in the Defaulter's Book, and that he has been tried by Court Martial.

The charge, finding, and sentence, on each occasion, is to be recorded on a separate sheet, which is to accompany the Discharge Documents.

If never tried or entered in the Defaulter's Book, state so.] _Never tried or Entered in the Regimental Defaulters Book_

If this man received Wounds, &c.,

OPPOSITE *Part of Sgt.Maj.Edward Heymer's discharge papers, in WO 97/1287. This confirms (see lower right) his entitlement to the medals for Maharajpore and Aliwal, and his recommendation for the LSGC.*

Edward Heymer being asked to what date he has been paid, answered, that his Account is balanced up to the latest period required by the Regulations; and being further asked whether he has any claim on the Regiment for Arrears of PAY, ALLOWANCES, or CLOTHING, answered that he has received all just demands, from his entry into the Service up to the **21 September 1865** and in confirmation therefore, affixes his signature hereto.

I acknowledge this to be true *E Heymer*

Witness *Middlehalt*

Commanding the Corps to which he belongs.

THE Board have ascertained that *Edward Heymer's* Soldier's Book is correctly balanced, and signed by the Officer Commanding his Company, and they declare, that they have impartially inquired into, and faithfully reported upon, all the matters brought before them, in accordance with the Regulations and Instructions issued by Her Majesty's Orders.

President.

Members.

Detailed Statement of the Services of *N. 1526 Edward Heymer*

Regiment	Promotions, Reductions, &c.	Rank	Period of Service in each Rank		Amount of Service	
			From	To	Years	Days
16th L.co	————	Private	15. Sep 1841	16 Jan 1852	10	124
	Granted 1st G. Pay		15. Sep 1846.			
	Granted 2d ———		15. Sep 1851.			
	Promoted Corporal	17. Jan 1852	28. Aug 1855	3	224
	Promoted Serjeant	29. Aug 1855	5. June 1860	4	281
	Promoted Troop Serjeant Major	6. June 1860	11. Apl 1864	3	310
	Resigned Serjeant	12. Apl 1864	21. Sep 1865	1	163

* Further Service from the **22nd Sept** to the **3rd Oct 65**

Total of the foregoing Statement **24 72**
when finally discharged ... ...
Total Service allowed to reckon to the day of final discharge **24 19**

* To be erased, when not required, by drawing the Pen through the Lines.

I have carefully examined the Proceedings of this Board in all its details, and I find them in every respect correct. Commanding *Cavalry of Depot*

RIGHT *On this page Heymer's signature at the top confirms that he has received his full pay and allowances up to 21 September 1865. His promotions, and years and days of service in each rank, are listed below.*

No. *1526* *Edward Heymer* referred to in the preceding pages, by Trade a *Porter* was born in the Parish of *Shoreditch* near the Town of *London* in the County of *Middlesex* and attested for the *16th L.* Regt. at *Maidstone* in the County of *Kent* on the *15th September 1841* at the Age of *18 12 years* His final description, &c., when discharged from the Service, at *Canterbury*

this ___ day of ___ 18*65*. Age *42 12 years* Height *5* Feet *10* Inches, Complexion *sallow* Eyes *hazel* Hair *dark brown* Trade *Porter* Marks or Scars upon the face, or other parts of the body *small scar on left side of chin.*

Intended Place of Residence *36 Nine Elms Grove Gravesend.*

This section of his discharge papers includes details of Heymer's origins, enlistment, final appearance, trade and intended future residence. (WO 97/1287)

the battle of Maharajpoor was fought. WO 12/1279 is the muster covering the Sutlej campaign and the battle of Aliwal. Edward Heymer was present throughout the period, and the muster confirms his entitlement to the medal for Aliwal and Sobraon.

The regiment embarked for England on 12 August 1846 on board the transport ship *Marion*, arriving on 29 December. Heymer was awarded his first Good Conduct Badge on 15 September 1846. The following muster returns record the life and times of the 16th Lancers at various postings across the British Isles. Heymer's name is always present, although he seemed to be in poor health, spending regular periods in hospital. As already established, he was promoted to corporal on 17 January 1852, vice Corporal Hodgson, who was reduced to the ranks by court martial; he was made sergeant on 29 August 1855, and troop sergeant major on 6 June 1860. Muster WO 12/1292 shows Heymer in that rank until 12 April 1864, when he reverted to sergeant. No explanation is given, but his pay was cut from 3s.2d a day to 2s.4d. He remained with the regiment until 16 December 1864, when he was listed sick on furlough. The earlier demotion was probably linked to recurring health problems.

He returned to the regiment in April 1865, but was again placed on sick furlough from 8 June, and transferred to the depot troop on 20 June. The regiment embarked for Madras on 28 June, leaving Heymer behind. His long career with the 16th Lancers was at an end, apparently shortened by ill health.

Heymer's discharge documents noted that he was entitled to a pension. He appeared successfully before the Chelsea Pension Examination Board on Tuesday 3 October 1865, as recorded in WO 117/13. He was awarded a pension of two shillings per day; the papers reiterate his service details. Heymer was listed in Regimental Out-Pension Register WO 23/62 for Woolwich Pension District. This confirmed his payment of 2s. a day dating from 3/10/1865. The register also gave his date of death, on 21 December 1866, just over a year after leaving the army.

From the documents viewed at the Public Record Office, we now know that Heymer was a career soldier who rose to the rank of sergeant major. He spent his entire unblemished service with the same regiment, and fought in two bloody battles in India. His final years in the Army were plagued by ill health; and after 24 years' service he died in his early forties, soon after retirement.

CHAPTER 6:

P.R.O. - ROYAL NAVY OFFICERS' RECORDS

A huge variety of documents recording information about naval officers are housed within the Public Record Office. Unfortunately, material is scattered somewhat haphazardly across a range of document classes, making research into naval medals a little difficult. There is no clear-cut route to be followed. Unlike British Army personnel, who usually remained with a regiment for most of their service, Royal Navy officers were brought together for the commission - the specific voyage or period of operations - of a particular ship, and then went their separate ways. However, by patient research it is possible to build up a picture of their service and establish how they came by their medals.

The best source of reference to naval documentation at Kew is *Naval Records for Genealogists* by N.A.M.Rodger, reprinted by Her Majesty's Stationery Office in 1998. This is essential reading for anyone contemplating research into the career of a naval officer, and thoroughly analyses all types of documentation at the PRO.

Apart from looking at the officer himself, it is interesting to discover the role his ship played in the action resulting in a medal. This can be pursued through printed works and also by studying ships', masters' and captains' logs in ADM 51-53.

The first step in researching a naval officer at Kew is the same as for Army officers. The **Navy List** offers similar potential to the Army List, documenting the officer's career and highlighting promotions. The dates of medal actions make it a simple task to find him in the alphabetical list for the appropriate years. The Navy List was originally called Steele's Navy List, first printed in 1782. It has been produced quarterly since 1814 and copies are available on open shelves in the Microfilm Reading Room at Kew (with the exception of classified editions printed during the two World Wars) in class ADM 177. Apart from listing officers, there is another useful feature: all naval vessels are recorded, with their complement of officers. This assists with following an officer from volume to volume and identifies successive appointments.

There are some other useful books in the Research Enquiries Room. *Commissioned Sea Officers of the Royal Navy 1660-1815*, published by the National Maritime Museum, lists officers, giving their seniority. The *Naval Biographical Dictionary* by W.R.O'Byrne (1849) outlines the service of all RN officers still alive in 1846. The *Royal Naval Biography* compiled by J.Marshall, London, 1823-35, can also be seen.

Once the outline of the officer's career has been established from the Navy List, the next step is to check that he was entitled to the medal. Naval medal rolls are on microfilm in class ADM

171 in the Microfilm Vviewing Room. Naval medals are often difficult to verify. Medal claims are sometimes scattered across a spool of microfilm and original handwriting can be hard to decipher. Names are usually listed according to the ship upon which the officer served. Medal rolls have been published for several campaigns, saving research time. The Naval General Service Medal 1793-1840 provides a good example; the PRO holds a copy of the Douglas-Morris roll for that medal, making life easy for the researcher. Having said that, always double check the information given on a published roll - errors are not unknown.

After medal entitlements have been checked the search can be widened. Paperwork available depends upon when the officer served, and documentation held at Kew is broken into confusing lists of dates and types. A minority of medal researchers are concerned with officers' documents originating prior to 1793, when the earliest Naval General Service Medal actions took place, so these are not covered here. Not all types of record outlined below will apply to every naval officer awarded a medal. Knowledge gained as research proceeds will dictate which document classes are worth scrutinising and which may be discarded.

Service records break down into two categories. Some documents summarize the man's entire career, like certificates of service, and others detail a single aspect of a naval life, such as passing certificates. After a time the information revealed may become repetitive and add nothing to what is known. How thoroughly to search is a matter for the individual.

Certificates of service give an opportunity to obtain full career details of an officer. They were compiled retrospectively from pay records for a specific purpose, usually to support a claim by showing qualifying service. They list ships served upon, showing rank and relevant dates. The sketchy details provide a sound basis for further research. Officers' service certificates are scattered across several different document classes. They accompany applications for children to attend Greenwich Hospital School in ADM 73, and pension claims in many different PRO classes. Certificates for prospective lieutenants are in ADM 107/71-75, spanning 1802-48. Others are often lodged with lieutenants' passing certificates in ADM 6, 107 and 13.

Service registers were volumes specifically designed to record contemporary details of an officer's career as it progressed, kept by different branches and containing information for their particular needs. They were intended to record an officer's entire career from entry to discharge, retirement and/or death, but many were left incomplete. They began in the mid-19th century, although they often include details of earlier service. In many cases surviving registers overlap, giving similar details, but where some are missing one can fill gaps left by another. Service registers became more thorough as the years went by, and later records give many personal details, such as dates of birth, marriage and death, wives' and parents' names, pay and pension particulars. They also detail incidents involving the officer and contain reports by senior officers on his conduct and capabilities.

The earliest registers were assembled from existing certificates and documents pertaining to the officer; they were therefore more organised, although frustrating gaps frequently exist. Some began on commissioning and continued throughout an officer's career - these are the most helpful to a researcher. Others were maintained for a specified duration or until a book was full. Officer's service registers are in class ADM 196, divided into several series. Most are well indexed in the Research Enquiries Room, although sometimes they are extremely confusing.

Officer's surveys were completed by individual officers in response to letters from the Admiralty asking about their experience and details of service. Given the fact that the Royal Navy was trying to cut down the numbers of officers employed and wished to retain those with the most impressive credentials, it is likely that some were tempted to embroider their career. Surveys were carried out in 1816-18, 1822, 1831 and 1846, although not all officers replied. Admirals completed a separate survey in 1828. A completed document shows rank, ships, date of entry and discharge for each ship, station of employment, summary of services performed, date of passing examination for lieutenant, age, other qualifications, and - best of all - letters or reports from superior officers in which an individual's services are noted. Some officers completed the summary of services performed in great detail, mentioning every possible noteworthy deed. Others were able to furnish numerous letters of commendation. Surveys are in classes ADM 6, ADM 9 and ADM 10. There are indexes to those of 1816-18, 1828 and 1846, but not for 1822 and 1831.

Some of the information from surveys was collated into **analyses**; these were documents drawn up to assist the Admiralty select officers. They enabled comparisons to be made between officers in terms of service, age and experience. Some give a breakdown of individual officers' service. They were compiled in 1844, 1847, 1848 and 1893-1900; and are to be found in ADM 11/64, ADM 6/174, ADM 11/10 and ADM 11/80 respectively.

Ships' musters recorded the full complement of a ship at regular intervals and include the names of officers. Using details from the Navy List, it is possible to follow the officer's career from ship to ship and to see where he travelled and what duties he undertook.

Class ADM 24 contains **full pay registers** from 1795. A separate register was maintained for each commissioned rank by the Naval Pay Office until 1830; from that date a register for all ranks began. The PRO holds registers covering 1795-1872. The registers give name, rank and dated successive appointments. Indexes are available to each type. They provide an accurate record of an officer's career, in a similar way to certificates of service, originally compiled from these registers. The Navy List can

be used to ascertain whether the officer whose medals are being researched was on full or half-pay at a given time.

Whenever the Royal Navy was overstrength, surplus officers were placed on half-pay. Their names were listed in **half-pay registers**, and they were retained in case a need for their services arose. Half-pay supported (at a beggarly level) many officers in the absence of a superannuation system, and the system persisted until 1938, although from the late 19th century only for officers who were between ships. Half-pay registers merely list names and payments. They sometimes show an officer's address and are thus useful in completing a full record of an officer's career, as they were once used, together with full pay registers, to complete certificates of service by the pay branch.

The earliest half-pay registers of interest to medal researchers are in ADM 25/1-255 covering the long period 1697-1836. Others in PMG 15 run from 1836 to 1920, and are either indexed or in alphabetical order. A second series is in ADM 23 and ADM 25 in alphabetical order, covering 1867-1924.

Officers who became **casualties** are listed in several different document classes. There is a card index in the Research Enquiries Room, ADM 242/1-6, listing all First World War officer casualties from every cause, from 1914 to 1920. Each card gives name, date of death, cause, place and/or ship. ADM 242/7-10 lists place of burial, date of birth and name and address of next-of-kin. ADM 104/109-121 records naval deaths between 1893 and 1956 which did not result from enemy action; this series is known as *Registers of Reports of Deaths: Ships*. The record shows name, rank, date, place and cause of death. Registers are indexed by ADM 104/102-108; ADM 104/120-21, covering 1951-56, are self-indexed. Registers are closed for 75 years.

ADM 104/144-149 gives details of all ranks killed or wounded in action between 1854 and 1929. ADM 104/140-143 act as the index to 146-9; 144 and 145 contain indexes. Of special interest to medal researchers are the columns concerning date and nature of wound - information which is normally hard to come by.

Claims by next-of-kin for deceased officers' **back pay**, 1830-60, are in ADM 45, part of which is indexed in the Research Enquiries Room. Such claims were frequently supported by wills, birth and marriage certificates.

Numerous documents record information associated with **officers' pensions**. An analysis of the qualifying criteria required for each type is outside the scope of this book; it is merely necessary for the medal researcher to know which pension documents might be applicable to the officer of interest and what information they provide. The notion of a guaranteed retirement pension for naval officers was not conceived until the mid-19th century. From 1836 onwards the idea was gradually adopted, subject to officers meeting stipulated conditions.

The main set of documents recording officer's retirement pensions from 1836-1920 is PMG 15/1-174, which are either alphabetical or internally indexed. Further records are in classes ADM 23/33-41 and ADM 22/488-522, covering 1867-1934. They are alphabetical, and give few details other than name and rate of payment.

Prior to 1836, three different types of pension existed: Widows' and Orphans' Pensions, Wounds Pensions, and Admiralty Pensions to certain deserving officers by virtue of their seniority. Pensions paid to the widows of officers killed in action or as a result of their service are in classes PMG 16/2-14 (1836-70), and PMG 20/1-23 (1870-1919). The large volumes show date and amount paid. Incidentally, these classes also document pensions applicable to holders of the Victoria Cross. A scattered group of registers in ADM 23 covers widows' pensions from 1866-1932.

After 1809 the Admiralty administered a Compassionate Fund payable to orphans and dependents of officers killed in action. Payments in respect of appeals to the fund are recorded in ADM 22/239-250 for the years 1809-36 and in PMG 18/1-38 for 1837-1921. Alphabetical records of dependants in receipt of the Compassionate Fund between 1867 and 1926 are held in ADM 23/4244, 96-100 and 200-205. Some files contain particulars of the deceased officer and the claimant.

Officers contributed through their salaries to the Charity for the Payment of Pensions to the Widows of Sea Officers, which made payments to widows irrespective of the cause of their husband's death. The fund was only payable where the widow was adjudged a needy case. Registers of payments 1836-1929 are in PMG 19/1-94; each volume is alphabetical. Various registers providing similar information are in ADM 23, covering 1836-1932 minus the years 1840- 66.

From 1862 officers were required to leave copies of their marriage certificates with the authorities if they wished to guarantee their wife a widow's pension in the event of their death. A card index in the Research Enquiries Room lists surviving examples; these certificates are in ADM 13, running from 1806 to 1902.

Records of wounded officers eligible for pension payments can be of interest to medal researchers. Documents in ADM 22/17-30 cover the years 1793-1821; ADM 181/1-27 contains similar records from 1708 to 1818. Ledgers of later wound pension awards were maintained by the Paymaster General's Office and accounts dating from 1836 to 1920 can be seen in class PMG 16/1-31. Admiralty registers for 1866-70 are in ADM 23/32.

Before retirement pensions were introduced in 1836 a small number of long-serving officers were already entitled to a superannuation pension in recognition of their service. They included the 30 most senior lieutenants, flag officers, and certain senior captains who were appointed rear admiral for pensionable purposes in exchange for terminating their careers - known as the "Yellow Admirals". Pension records for this select band are generally found among those for wound pensions and widow's pensions. The earliest documents applicable to possible medal recipients are in ADM 22/1-5 and ADM 22/17-30, documenting the period between 1781 and 1821. Similar information can be found in ADM 181/1-27. Other details can be found in ADM 22/31-36. Later records are among the documents of the Paymaster General's branch in PMG 15, starting in 1836.

All of the documents listed above offer opportunities to discover the service details of a naval officer, but few give an insight into his personality, abilities or deficiencies. The following records offer the chance to find out what sort of man he was. The scope for research is determined by the amount of information already discovered. The above sources should be looked at first, and may lead on to those listed below.

Officers customarily applied in writing for favourable positions or promotion. Often this was done on their behalf by a sponsor. Senior officers could also make application for officers they wished to employ. The **applications** were recorded, and frequently the original letter, outlining noteworthy service or explaining why the officer considered himself suitable for the post, accompanies the entry. ADM 6/170-172 contains indexed applications for the post of lieutenant for the period 1799-1818; the result of the application is given, with a record of service, and home addresses are recorded. Applications made by various commissioned officers from 1842 to 1858 are in ADM 6/1-2. Similar records survive for promotion candidates or young men applying for cadetships. Most record basic service details, or in the case of potential cadets, some information about their background. Frequently comments are made about the character and aptitude of the applicant. Documents are in ADM 6, 7 and 11.

A **confidential report** on each officer ranked captain or above was prepared annually by commanding officers, outlining their performance and potential. The reports assisted the Admiralty to select suitable officers for vacant posts. Records are held in registers, covering the years 1893-1944. They are in class ADM 196/86-94. ADM 196/86-88 holds reports on lieutenants and commanders. Entries are listed in order of seniority, so the Navy List may be used as an index.

The ability of an officer can be judged - to some extent - from his **examination results**, which survive from the last century onwards. Often it is possible to see the score attained by the candidate in various subjects. As naval service grew more technical, it became necessary for naval officers to pass examinations in more subjects. Sometimes extra information is given, particularly in the case of young officers attending Royal Naval College. Occasionally this includes interesting notes about the student's personality and behaviour.

Passing certificates testified that the young officer concerned had passed the necessary seamanship exam to obtain a commission. There is seldom further information, other than the date of the exam, but sporadically there may be certificates of service or other supporting paperwork. A very few pass comment upon the candidate.

A range of examination results for 1816-1957 are held in ADM 6,7,11 and 203; some are indexed, some are not. Passing certificates are spread across classes ADM 1, 6, 11, 13, 30 and 107, intermittently covering the years 1691-1902. Some series are indexed, some run alphabetically, and some are indexed on cards in the Research Enquiries Room.

It is possible to delve into further types of document, but few add to the material available in those shown above. Seniority lists, disposition lists, succession books and commission documents can be seen, but the same information can be found more easily from the Navy List. There are other, slightly more obscure document classes at the PRO, but they are beyond the realms of this book. Some may become relevant to an individual by virtue of information gained along the way. In the majority of cases they repeat facts seen elsewhere.

CHAPTER 7:
P.R.O. - NAVAL RATINGS' RECORDS

The term "ratings" refers to all enlisted men in the ship's company, including volunteers, pressed men and ship's boys. Researching naval ratings is seldom as straightforward as researching officers - their names do not appear in a helpful publication like the Navy List. However, it is still possible to discover a considerable amount about them.

Between the commissioned ranks and ordinary seamen lay an intermediate group - the warrant officers. Each warrant officer headed a branch of tradesmen and enjoyed special status. They included masters, boatswains, carpenters, surgeons, pursers and gunners. Warrant officers were educated men, professional seamen who had served apprenticeships or passed examinations to attain their post. They were not executive officers, although answerable directly to the captain for their particular trade.

Naval ratings were not career seamen until the mid-19th century. They were signed up or pressed into service for the duration of a ship's commission. After that their future was uncertain. Many sailors sailed with both the fighting and merchant service intermittently. Some were paid off and left to their own devices when their ship docked in England, others transferred - voluntarily or otherwise - to another ship. Prior to 1853 it is difficult to research the life of a rating without knowing the name of a ship on which he sailed at a given time. Few centralised sailors' records existed; only ships' musters and pay books recorded the service of individual seamen. Many musters survive, however, and can be seen at the PRO in ADM 36-39.

Without knowing a ship and date, research entails a tedious search through dozens of muster rolls. Even then, if the seaman was blessed with a common surname it may be difficult to identify him. Medals can be the key. Sometimes the name of the recipient's ship was impressed around the rim of the medal, establishing an approximate date when the rating was aboard a particular vessel. By consulting the ship's muster around the dates of the medal action the man's name should be found listed among the ship's company.

If the name of the ship is not impressed upon the medal and many ships were engaged in the action, it is advisable to search through **medal rolls** to identify the ship the man served upon rather than ordering the musters for every ship involved. Scrutinising a medal roll is quicker than searching through musters, but even then finding an individual name is a difficult task. In any case, it is good practice to verify medal entitlements before doing anything else. As explained in the previous chapter, medal rolls can be viewed on microfilm at Kew. Naval rolls are in ADM 171, filed adjacent to the Army medal rolls.

(First World War naval medals are dealt with in Chapter 15.)

After verifying medals and identifying a ship, **musters** can be consulted. Class lists for musters in ADM 36-39 list ships alphabetically within different time periods. Musters in ADM 36 run from 1688 to 1808, ADM 37 from 1792 to 1842, ADE 38 from 1793 to 1878, and ADM 39 from 1667 to 1798. Where the sought-after muster roll has not survived, the ship's **pay book** might be found in classes ADM 32-35. Pay books duplicate much of the information from the original muster.

Musters were kept to account for wages paid and victuals consumed during the period of a ship's commission. They were not compiled for the benefit of latter-day medal researchers; that said, they do give some interesting information. Details are spread across several headed columns. What can be found out depends upon how many columns were completed for the man under research. The books were gradually modified, and later musters tend to give more information than their predecessors. At Kew, each volume usually contains a six-month run of musters. "Open lists" were also created, for an entire year, although they only recorded presence or absence for wages and victualling purposes. "Complete books" covered the entire commission of the ship.

Muster books normally record the man's unique number, the date he was entered onto the books, whether he was a volunteer or pressed man, and whether he allotted wages to relatives. His age on joining the ship and place of birth were also recorded, although the accuracy is debatable. Wage deductions for negligence, slops (clothing), soap, tobacco, venereal disease treatment, trusses and beds were listed. A further column showed if he was discharged, died or went absent. The destination of discharged men is usually annotated. Separate narrow columns, one for each week of the muster, record periods when the man was not present and the reason.

The muster should record the name of his previous ship and it may occasionally name a vessel he was discharged to. This feature enables the researcher to track a sailor backwards from one ship to another, establishing a complete record of service. The more medals in the group naming ships at different times, the less this process has to be relied upon.

There is a table at the beginning of each book recording the location of the ship on a fortnightly basis, revealing the voyage undertaken during the period of the muster. Place names have changed, but it is normally possible to deduce the route taken.

Captains kept **description books** of all men in the crew. Few survive, but where they do, they are generally found within

Postcard photograph of a sailor and his lady from the 1914-18 period; his cap tally and sleeve badge identify him as a torpedoman on HMS Hornet.

new recruits. It is worth checking the index for any man who joined the navy after 1830, in case he was still at sea in 1853. Such a discovery can save a lot of time searching through ship's musters. ADM 188 takes in the full naval careers of recruits from 1873 to 1923. The records of ratings who enlisted after 1923 remain with the Ministry of Defence.

Documents in ADM 139 and ADM 188 resemble soldiers' attestation papers; they give name, date and place of birth, description and date of enlistment. Where a rating was already serving and signed on for continuous service, his rate, ship, badges, certificates and previous service with the Royal and Merchant Navy are recorded. A more detailed summary of service appears within. There is also a **certificate of fitness**, which the sailor signed or made his mark on. Boys could not be enlisted without their parents' consent in writing and a certificate to this effect should accompany enlistment papers. Boys agreed to serve for ten years from their eighteenth birthday.

Certificates of service are another short cut to finding details of a seaman's service. They were completed in a similar way to officers' certificates of service, with information taken from muster and pay books. If a man applied for a medal, a Greenwich Hospital pension, places for his children at Greenwich Hospital Schools, or sought a gratuity, he needed a certificate of service issued by naval pay authorities in order to press his claim. The document gave a resumé of the seaman's career, listing his ships and relevant dates. After 1853 continuous service documents recorded the information at the time, instead of years later. Certificates of service are in ADM 29 and ADM 73. There is a semi-alphabetic index to ADM 29 in the Research Enquiries Room. Index volumes, numbered ADM 29/97-104, are difficult to read, but give a piece reference and page number in ADM 29. The appropriate document may then be ordered. If the seaman only served post-1853 on a continuous service engagement, the index gives his CS number. This can be used to retrieve his papers as shown above.

Class ADM 73 contains a wealth of documents, mostly connected with **Greenwich Hospital pensions and schools**. They are a good source of certificates of service, compiled to support pension claims or applications for school places, so ADM 73 is well worth exploring. As with the Army's establishment at Chelsea, Greenwich Hospital pensioners received either in- and out-pensions. In-pensioners resided within Greenwich Hospital; out-pensioners received a monetary pension and lived in the community. In-pension documents can be categorized as application papers, entry registers, and records compiled during the time spent at the hospital. Sometimes all three types refer to the same man.

Applications to Greenwich Hospital between 1790 and 1865 are grouped alphabetically in class ADM 73/1-35. Applications for 1737- 1859 are in ADM 6/223-266, some of which are card indexed in the Reference Room. In-pensioner admission papers are in several series, some of which overlap. Records in ADM 73/36-41 are indexed, and record the date of entry for each pensioner in the period 1704-1846, with the discharge date if applicable. An unindexed set of entry registers for 1704-1863 in ADM 73/51-62 provide more interesting biographical information, such as marital status, place of residence

the pages of an open list or complete muster book. The PRO class list indicates muster books which contain a description book. They provide a physical description, noting distinguishing marks, place of residence and marital status. Previous ships are sometimes noted. Pay books were copied from musters. If wages were made over to the seaman's next-of-kin, details are sometimes recorded in the "To whom paid" column.

The introduction of continuous service in 1853, whereby seamen signed on for a term of years like soldiers, brought a better record- keeping system. Every seaman was allocated a continuous service number, which he retained throughout his service. At discharge, each seaman's career was summarized and a record was compiled, showing service on each ship.

Researching post-1853 seamen is therefore relatively easy. **Continuous service records** are in ADM 139 and ADM 188; there are semi-alphabetic indexes (ADM 188 245-267) to both classes on shelves in the Microfilm Viewing Room. The indexes list names and continuous service numbers. Documents in both classes are in order of service number, so after finding the man's unique number from the index it is quite straightforward to identify the correct piece number and order the seaman's papers. ADM 139 covers 1853-1872 and includes existing seamen who elected to sign on under the new system, as well as and trade. The date of entry from the first series makes it possible to track down the same individual in the second.

While at Greenwich in-pensioners were listed in a register, recording details about the pensioner's family and state of health, any disablements, and the hospital ward where he stayed. Two series of documents survive, from 1779 to 1866 partially indexed in ADM 73/42-50, and a second covering 1764-1865 in ADM 73/65-69.

Out-pensioner records are less informative. Pay ledgers in ADM 22/254-443 run in alphabetical order for 1814-46, recording payment date and place. Other books include more details. A series of volumes in ADM 6/271-320 record judgements made on men's eligibility for in- and out-pensions; these give varying amounts of information on individual applicants, but normally indicate age, length of service, and amount and duration of annual pension awarded. From 1789 to 1859 they run in chronological order of the examination dates. Although unindexed, it is possible to narrow down the period when the man was most likely to apply - usually immediately after discharge - and examine likely books. They are reasonably easy to flick through quickly. For each examination there are three lists: seamen, marines, and those awarded in-pensions.

After 1842 out-pensions were administered by the War Office, and registers in WO 22 record payments made 1842-1862, arranged in geographical pension districts. To use these it is important to have some idea where the medal recipient lived. They are a useful way of tracking a pensioner through later life. All the registers give name, the date the pension commenced, and rate of pension. War Office returns list naval pensioners in red ink. They are divided into several sections, listing men who transferred in and out of the district, new pensioners, changes of pension, and cessation through death. The list for deaths is accompanied by columns for age, date of death and remarks. From the registers it is possible to see when the pensioner moved area; following him from district to district is particularly useful for those interested in investigating the man's family background through genealogical sources. If he died before WO 22 records ceased, then his date of death can also be established.

Many naval ratings applied for places at one of the Greenwich Hospital Schools on behalf of their children. The largest group of **school applications** are in class ADM 73/154-389, spanning 1728-1861. Each bid was accompanied by a certificate of service, often the original of one copied into class ADM 29 outlined above. Admission papers for children are arranged alphabetically. Each document box contains bundles of folded admission papers in alphabetical stacks. These can be a goldmine to the researcher. Apart from details of the father's service and reasons for his discharge, many contain birth and baptismal certificates and full details of the parents, often including marriage particulars. These documents are easy to locate, can be quickly checked through, and provide a lot of information.

Three other series contain material about Greenwich Hospital Schools. Applications for boys to the Upper School, 1832-81, are in ADM 73/415 and 398, also ADM 161/2. Lower School applications, 1803- 1930, are in ADM 73/391-7,

The Naval General Service Medal, 1793-1840, on its blue-edged white ribbon with clasp SYRIA, to Charles Hoggett.

ADM 161/1 and 3-19. Applications for girls to the Royal Naval Asylum are in ADM 73/391-2 and 440-41. The majority of papers are indexed.

The Public Record Office holds several types of paperwork concerned with naval deaths. Many are of interest to medal researchers, enabling them to verify whether the man was a casualty in a particular action.

Sailors' wills 1786-1882 are in ADM 48, generally from claims in respect of back pay. They are indexed by ADM 142, a series of large, heavy alphabetical volumes showing the sailor's ship and date of death. Further papers concerned with claims for deceased seamens' back pay between 1800 and 1860 are in ADM 44, indexed by ADM 141. They often contain paperwork verifying the claimant's relationship to the deceased in order to uphold the application. The amount of information given varies from one case to another, but they normally identify next-of-kin and sometimes provide clues to home and family background.

The **death** of any rating 1802-1878 is recorded in alphabetical registers ADM 141/1-9 and ADM 154/1-9; next-of-kin details are shown. Deaths with no connection to enemy action between 1893 and 1956 are in class ADM 104/109-121, largely indexed by ADM 104/102-108. They record cause of death, where it occurred and when. Deaths as a result of enemy action from 1854 to 1929 are in ADM 104/144-9, which are all indexed; these ledgers also record wounds received. A series of alphabetical registers in ADM 104/122-126 also show deaths caused by enemy action. First World War burial places for all ranks are listed alphabetically in ADM 242/7-10; next-of-kin particulars are given, with date of birth, and date and place of death. Other ranks' deaths during the Second World War are listed alphabetically in ADM 104/127-139, with details of ship served upon, date and place of death, date and place of birth and cause of death.

Some men elected to allocate a proportion of their pay for the support of kinfolk at home while they served at sea; this was known as an allotment. **Allotment records** are a good source of information for researchers keen to discover family background. The date of the arrangement is normally shown on the ship's muster, giving the researcher a starting point. Allotment records for 1795-1852 are arranged very haphazardly in ADM 27 and it is pointless to search blindly without knowledge of such an arrangement. The allotments index is arranged by ship and date, but the index is handwritten and hard to decipher. Allotment book pages are arranged in no apparent order; within each volume it is difficult to locate the record page relating to the ship sought. A single allotment book may contain several scattered pages pertaining to a single ship. Each entry gives the name and rate of the sailor making the allotment, the name of the person to whom it should be paid, relationship, number of children - indicating boys and girls by B/G - place of residence, amount, signature or mark, date, and finally to whom and where to be paid.

Remittances also ensured that families received a proportion of a man's pay, specifically by six-monthly payments. Again, muster books usually identify whether a man arranged to make a remittance and when. **Remittance books** in ADM 26 are better organised and easier to search through than allotment books. Many of the bulky volumes are indexed or arranged alphabetically; they contain similar details to allotment books.

The documents listed above are the main sources of information about naval ratings available at Kew. There are many others. Much depends upon information gathered along the way, indicating new areas to investigate. There comes a time when the researcher must accept he has found all he can about a given rating; to proceed past this point incurs long, usually fruitless, searches, turning up repetitious material. There are always other places to look.

Warrant Officers

Medals awarded to naval warrant officers are particularly interesting to research. Their unique position, between the commissioned ranks and the forecastle hands, means that their documents can be found within a wide range of classes applicable to their own rank, as well as those of the other two groups. Many papers connected with warrant officers are directly concerned with their branch or trade, making it easier to locate sought-after material.

Each warrant officer was the head of a branch of ships' tradesmen, responsible to the captain for the efficient performance of the tradesmen under his control. Over the years the status of different types of warrant officer changed, but there is insufficient space in a book of this type to explore the evolution of the various ranks. For our purposes the ranks included under the term are the following: master, mate, surgeon, purser, boatswain, gunner, carpenter, engineer, master at arms, cook and chaplain. The chief types of record applicable to warrant officers are listed below. Many are similar in format and contents to those already outlined for commissioned officers and ratings above. For easier reference, a list of classes applicable to all warrant officers precedes those relating specifically to named ranks. In some instances classes listed below duplicate those mentioned above.

Papers applicable to all Warrant Officers

Warrants 1695-1815	... ADM 6/3-32	
1774-1798, 1832-49	... ADM 6/33-38, 46-49	

Records are chronological, giving name and ship.

Certificates of service 1836-94	... ADM 29
1728-1861	... ADM 73/154-389

Compiled to support applications for Greenwich Hospital Schools, the second series contains the original certificates and is alphabetical. The first series is indexed by ADM 29/97-104. Many applications concern children of deceased men.

In-pensions 1703-1846	... ADM 73 (various)
1737-1859	... ADM 6/223-266
1824-66	... ADM 73/42-9
1764-1865	... ADM 73/65-9

Greenwich Hospital in-pensioners' applications and admissions. Some indexed, some chronological; many give details of service, family, wounds, etc.

Decision books 1789-1859	... ADM 6/271-320

Chronological records of Greenwich Hospital Examination Board.

Out-pensions 1814-46	... ADM 22/254-443

Alphabetical volumes recording payments made to out-pensioners.

Wound pensions 1836-1919	... PMG 16

Wound pensions from 1866 and superannuation from 1836.

Widows' pensions 1836-1919	... PMG 16, PMG 20
1836-1932	... ADM 23
Widows' charity 1864-1929	... PMG 19/1-94
1797-1829	... ADM 6/335-384
1808-30	... ADM 6/385-402

The first lists payments made to needy widows from the Charity for the Relief of Officers' Widows. The second and third cover applications for relief. There is a card index to the second series. Warrant officers' widows did not qualify from 1830 to 1864 unless their husband was killed in action.

Compassionate Fund 1885-1921	... PMG 18

Details dependants in receipt of monies.

Superannuation 1793-1821	... ADM 22
1836-1924	... PMG 15, 16, 69
1867-1931	... ADM 23

The Royal Yacht, HMS Victoria and Albert, *in 1855; and another engraving of her passing men-'o-war in review.*

The first series relates to superannuation paid to senior warrant officers. The second two record payments made to warrant officers after 1836.

Supplementary pensions
1871-1961   ... ADM 165/1-6, 9
Supplementary pensions paid to deserving cases after the closure of Greenwich Hospital.

Pension payments 1842-83   ... WO 22
Records of out-pension payments arranged by geographical location; no indexes.

Schools papers   ... ADM 73 (various)
Numerous documents concerning Greenwich Hospital Schools applications/admittance/discharge. Some alphabetical, some indexed, some not.

Leave books 1804-46   ... ADM 6/200-205
Alphabetical records of leave granted.

Marriage certificates 1891-1902   ... ADM 13/191-2
Copy certificates for a few warrant officers.

Full pay registers 1795-1872   ... ADM 24
Separate registers for separate ranks until 1830, giving complete records of service. Mostly indexed.

Half-pay registers 1867-1924   ... ADM 23, 25
Alphabetical by volume. Boatswains, gunners, carpenters to 1881.

Succession books 1780-1848   ... ADM 11/65-71
              1872-96   ... ADM 23
The second series is largely indexed.

Documents relating to individual trades: Boatswains

Certificates of service 1817-73   ... ADM 29/4, 23, 121
Internally indexed, and also indexed in ADM 29/97104.
Compiled for pension applications.

Service registers 1848-55   ... ADM 196/74-76
               1855-90   ... ADM 196/29-32
               1860-1912   ... ADM 29/16/119
First and third series alphabetical by volume, second indexed by ADM 196/33. Third series includes other paperwork.

Full pay registers 1854-74   ... ADM 22/458-64
No indexes; by date of entry.

Applications 1770-95   ... ADM 6/187-9
No indexes; applications for promotion and appointments, sometimes requests by senior officers.

Surveys 1816-18   ... ADM 11/35-37
Unindexed; surveys were completed by senior officers and sometimes contain opinions about men's qualities.

Succession books 1764-1831   ... ADM 106/2898, 2902-6
               1800-39   ... ADM 6/192 ADM 11/31-3

Seniority lists 1810-44   ... ADM 118

Gunners

Certificates of service 1817-73 ... ADM 29/3, 24, 121
As for boatswains.
Service registers   1848-55 ... ADM 196/74-76
                    1855-90 ... ADM 196/29-32
As for boatswains.
Full pay registers 1854-72 ... ADM 22/469-74
No indexes; in order of entry.
Applications 1770-95 ... ADM 6/187-9
As for boatswains.
Surveys 1816-18 ... ADM 11/35-37
As for boatswains.
Passing certificates 1731-1812 ... ADM 6/123-9
Mainly alphabetical.
Succession books   1764-1831 ... ADM 106/2898, 2902-6
                   1800-39 ... ADM 6/192, ADM 11/31-3
Seniority lists 1810-44 ... ADM 118

Masters

Dockets 1800-50 ... ADM 6/135-268
Alphabetical; each docket contains a variety of paperwork.
Service registers   1843-c1850 ... ADM 196/1
                    1852-1922 ... ADM 196, ADM 6
First series indexed by ADM 196/7, second variously indexed.
Certificates 1660-1830 ... ADM 106/2908-50
Alphabetical; masters' certificates, sometimes accompanied
by other paperwork. Sometimes more than one for a single
master.

Surveys 1851 ... ADM 11/7-8
Indexed by ADM 10/6-7.
Leave books 1814-47 ... ADM 6/207-11
Alphabetical; leave granted for men on half-pay to travel
abroad or take employment in the merchant fleet.
Superannuation 1672-1920 ... PMG 15 & various
Indexed or alphabetical.
Half-pay registers 1674-1920 ... PMG 15, ADM 23,
                                 & various
Indexed or alphabetical.
Succession books 1733-1807 ... ADM 106/2896-2901
Seniority lists 1780-1846 ... ADM 118

Mates

Certificates of service 1744-1818 ... ADM 6/86-118
Alphabetical each year. Issued with passing certificate for
lieutenant's exam. Sometimes with other paperwork.
Service registers 1843-c1850 ... ADM 196/1
Indexed by ADM 196/7.
Candidates 1802-48 ... ADM 107/71-75
Indexed by volume. Service details of candidates for
lieutenant's exam.
Candidate reports 1814-16 ... ADM 6/176-80
Unindexed. Summaries of service of candidates for
lieutenant, including reports on personal qualities.
Examinations 1829-60 ... ADM 11/22
Indexed by volume. Records results of lieutenant's
examination giving scores obtained.

Half-pay registers 1840-1920   ... PMG 15

Pursers

Service registers   1843-c1850   ... ADM 196/1
                    1852-1922   ... ADM 196 & 6 (various)
                    1873-1882   ... ADM 196/80-1
First series indexed by ADM 196/7. The second refers to
registers compiled by the civil branch, variously indexed.
The third series is alphabetical.
Applications 1770-95   ... ADM 6/187-9
As for boatswains.
Passing certificates 1851-89   ... ADM 13/79-82, 247-8
Superannuation 1672-1934   ... PMG 15 & various
Indexed or alphabetical.
Leave books 1814-47   ... ADM 6/207-11
As for masters.
Half-pay registers 1814-1920   ... PMG 15, ADM 25
Succession books 1764-1831   ... ADM 106/2898, 2902-6
                  1800-39   ... ADM 6/192, 11/31-3
Seniority lists 1810-46   ... ADM 118

Carpenters

Certificates of service 1817-53   ... ADM 29/5, 6, 121
                         1870-73   " " " "
Indexed by volume and by ADM 29/97-104.
Service registers   1848-55   ... ADM 196/74-6
                    1855-90   ... ADM 196/29-32
First series alphabetical. Second series indexed by
ADM 196/33.
Applications 1770-95   ... ADM 6/187-9
As for boatswains.
Surveys 1816-18   ... ADM 11/35-37
As for boatswains.
Full pay registers 1853-74   ... ADM 22/465-8
Includes details of service.
Succession books 1764-1831   ... ADM 106/2898, 2902-6
                 1800-39   ... ADM 6/192, 11/31-3
Seniority lists 1810-44   ... ADM 118

Chaplains

Service registers 1891-1922   ... ADM 6/443-4, 196/85
Partially indexed by ADM 6/442.
Applications 1793-95   ... ADM 6/188-9
As for boatswains.
Half-pay registers 1817-1920   ... PMG 15, ADM 25
Succession books 1699-1824   ... ADM 6

Surgeons

Confidential reports 1817-32   ... ADM 105/1-9
Indexed by volume. Reports fully on the qualities of
individual surgeons.
Reports 1845-1926   ... ADM 104/45-50
        1822-32   ... ADM 105/10-19
Indexed by volume. Similar to the above.
Certificates of service 1815-22 ... ADM 104/30
Service registers 1774-1886   ... ADM 104/12-29
                   1840-95   ... ADM 196/8-10

1843-c1850   ... ADM 196/1
1829-93   ... ADM 104 & 105 (various)
1881-91   ... ADM 196/82
1873-82   ... ADM 196/80-81
First series largely indexed by ADM 104/11. Second series
indexed by volume or ADM 196/26-28. Third series indexed
by ADM 196/7. Fourth series individually indexed,
occasionally yields some extra paperwork. Fifth indexed
by ADM 6/442. Sixth series is alphabetical.
Applications   1829-33   ... ADM 6/186
               1844-50   ... ADM 6/2
The first series records applications to serve upon
convict ships.
Candidates   1838-66   ... ADM 105/37-39
               1870-1902   ... ADM 6/468
Passing certificates 1700-96   ... ADM 106/2952-63
Alphabetical. There is a card index to the contents of
certificates.
Analyses 1808   ... ADM 11/40
Black books 1741-1814   ... ADM 11/39
Details surgeons who were not to be employed, with reasons.
Leave books 1814-47   ... ADM 6/208-11
As for masters.
Compassionate Fund 1809-36   ... ADM 6/323-8
As for masters.
Superannuation 1672-1920   ... PMG 15 & various
Indexed or alphabetical.
Half-pay registers 1729-1920   ... PMG 15, ADM 25
Succession books 1870-1924   ... ADM 104/88-94
Seniority lists 1780-1886   ... ADM 104, ADM 118

Engineers

Service registers 1837-79   ... ADM 196/71, 29/105-111
                   1856-86   ... ADM 196/23-25
First series indexed by volume and largely by ADM 29/131.
Second by ADM 196/26-28.
Passing certificates 1863-1902   ... ADM 13/200-5
Alphabetical by year. Also give service details.
Full pay registers 1847-73   ... ADM 22/444-57, 29/113
Mainly unindexed. Give details akin to those in a service
register.
Half-pay registers 1856-1920   ... PMG15

Research Notes

Charles Hoggett

The Naval General Service medal with clasp "Syria" awarded to
Charles Hoggett only bears his name. To find his ship it was
necessary to consult the Naval General Service Medal Rolls,
ADM 171/1-8. Medals for Syria are hard to verify, as nearly
7,000 were issued and recipients are listed in several different
batches. Only one Charles Hoggett appears on the roll, listed
on ADM 171/3, with HMS *Edinburgh*. HMS *Edinburgh's*
muster, ADM 37/9059, includes the period of the Syrian
action in November 1840. Charles Hoggett was recorded as an
Able Seaman, 417 on the Ship's Company list. He was aged 22
years when he joined the ship, and was born in Portsea. The
muster states that he was previously on HMS *Apollo*, until 25

21

Wages Office
ACCOUNTANT GENERAL
OCT. 15
1853
OF THE NAVY

S. Victoria e Albert

July 1853

3835

No. 95.

When Men or Boys enter for Continuous and General Service, (C.S.) Commanding
Officers are immediately to fill up this Form and transmit it to the Accountant
General of the Navy.

Christian and Surname in full .... *Charles Hoggett.*

Where Born .... *Portsea. Hants.*

Date of Birth .... *24th January 1817*

Description .... Height *5ft 5* Complexion *Fair*

Hair *Dark* Eyes *Dark*

Marks *Harp on Right Arm*

Ship in which he is entered .... *Victoria & Albert*

Date of Entry in Do. .... *1st January 1851*

Ratings in Do. .... *Quarter Master*

Date of Volunteering for Continuous and } *1st July 1853*
General Service ....

Period for which he has Volunteered .... *Six Years*

Date of Badges .... *2 Badges 1st January 1849*

Date of Certificates, or Class as Seaman Gunner..

Number of Register Ticket................ *290.728.*

Former Service stating the names of the Ships, *Rattlesnake . 8th Nov 1833 .*
Blonde . 1st Dec 1833 . 15 Nov 1837
and the dates, whether in the Royal Navy } *Apollo . 27 Mar 1838 . 25 June 1838*
Edinburgh . 3 Aug 1838 . 4 July 1840
Illustrious . 21 Oct 1840 . 9 June 1845
or the Merchant Service .... *President . 12 Sept 1845 . 6 Feby 1849*
Vict.a & Albert . 6 Mar 1849 . 31 Dec 1850

(See over)

*Continuous Service
papers for 3835 Charles
Hoggett, in ADM
139/39. Dated 1 July
1853 when he was
Quartermaster aboard
the Royal Yacht, this
page lists at the bottom
his previous ships. It also
gives his personal details
and description, includ-
ing a tattoo of a harp on
his right arm.*

June 1838. He spent two shillings a month on tobacco, 7s.4d. on soap and £1 2s.3d. on navy slops. In a few moments we have transformed Charles Hoggett from a name on a medal into a living, breathing, tobacco-using young seaman in the days of sail, born and raised within smell of the sea in the Royal Navy's heartland.

The muster opened up three directions for research. It was possible to backtrack through HMS *Apollo's* musters to find the beginning of Hoggett's service, or forward through HMS *Edinburgh's* musters to see what happened when that ship's commission ended. There was a third option: a certificate of service may have been compiled when Hoggett applied for his medal, for a pension, or for a place for a child at a Greenwich Hospital school. A quick check with ADM 29 might save a long hunt through muster rolls.

There is a semi-alphabetic index to ADM 29 (certificates of service), on open shelves in the Reference Room. There was one Charles Hoggett on the difficult manuscript list, with a reference to ADM 29/56, page 414. The Charles Hoggett on ADM 29/56 page 414 was the same Charles Hoggett who served on HMS *Edinburgh* during 1840. The service record echoed crew number 417 on HMS *Edinburgh* from 3 August 1838 to 14 July 1841, joined from HMS *Apollo*.

The single sheet displayed a complete record of the 24 years 324 days which Charles Hoggett spent in the Royal Navy, from 30 May 1831 until 22 May 1857. The certificate included dates of promotion and exact periods spent with each vessel. He entered service on HMS *Rattlesnake*, and subsequently sailed on HMS *Blonde, Apollo, Edinburgh, Illustrious, President*, and finally HMS *Victoria and Albert*, finishing his career as Quartermaster on board the last-named - the Royal Yacht.

The sheet provided another all-important piece of information: a continuous service number, 3835, was written at the top. Charles Hoggett volunteered for continuous service on 1 July 1853; a detailed record of service could now be found.

Hoggett appeared in the index to the continuous service register, ADM 139, available in the Research Enquiries Room. The reference given was ADM 139/39. His papers repeated the information already learned, but gave further particulars. His CS papers revealed that Hoggett was born at Portsea on 24 January 1817. He was 5ft 5ins tall, with a fair complexion, dark hair, dark eyes, and a harp tattooed on his right arm. He volunteered for six years' continuous service on 1 July 1853. Now it was possible to actually visualize the small, tattooed, man-o'-war's man whose medal I possessed.

Once Hoggett's ships were known it was possible to trace his voyages. This involved ordering over 30 musters. At the front of each book a log records where each muster took place, enabling the reader to calculate the route taken. Musters also record the appointment Hoggett held on each ship as he progressed through the ranks.

Musters WO 37/8295-7 chart Hoggett's first voyage aboard HMS *Rattlesnake*, September 1831-November 1833. HMS *Rattlesnake* was a 6th Rate, with a complement of 164. Charles Hoggett served as a boy first class. His place of birth was noted as Union Street, Portsea. He volunteered on 30 May 1831, aged 18. The captain's log, ADM 51/3394, records the event

with the bald statement "Enlisted one boy". The *Rattlesnake* sailed for Rio de Janeiro in September 1831 and spent two years showing the flag around South America, calling at Buenos Aires, Montevideo, Valparaiso and ports in Chile, Bolivia, Ecuador and Mexico. During the voyage Hoggett "satisfactorily performed his duty"; he was appointed ship's clerk on 11 June 1832 - from which we can infer that he was literate - and was rated ordinary seaman on 2 September 1833. He was paid off from the *Rattlesnake* on 12 November 1833, "From the service as per order".

HMS *Rattlesnake's* Complete Book, ADM 37/8297, contains a Description Book. Charles Hoggett is described as 5ft 5ins tall, with brown hair, light blue eyes, a fair complexion, and aged 19. Hoggett volunteered as a boy class I for HMS *Blonde*, a 5th Rate, on 1 December 1833 after only two weeks ashore. His second voyage followed much the same route as his first (ADM 37/8784-9). HMS *Blonde* patrolled the west coast of South America for three years, and returned to Portsmouth in October 1837. Hoggett was rated ordinary seaman on 4 March 1836, and able seaman on 1 July 1837; he was paid off at Portsmouth on 15 November. HMS *Blonde's* Complete Book (ADM 37/8790) contains another Description Book; Hoggett's particulars are unchanged from those in the *Rattlesnake's* book.

Charles Hoggett signed on for a troopship, HMS *Apollo*, on 27 March 1838. He spent 91 days as an able seaman on this vessel, all in the waters around Portsmouth (ADM 37/8667). On 3 August 1838 he joined HMS *Edinburgh*, a 3rd Rate man-o'-war with a complement of 520 men commanded by Captain W.W.Henderson CB; he was listed as able seaman, number 417. HMS *Edinburgh* was stationed in the West Indies, but sailed to the Mediterranean before being ordered to Syria in November 1840. After the medal action off Acre she returned to Portsmouth via Malta and Gibraltar. Charles Hoggett was paid off on 14 July 1841. His conduct was described as "good".

Hoggett joined HMS *Illustrious*, rated able and with the number 301, on 21 October 1841. She was a 3rd Rate built in 1803, with a complement of 540, commanded by Admiral Sir Edward Codrington. Between November 1841 and May 1845 HMS *Illustrious* cruised the Caribbean, the east coast of America and Canada (ADM 38/969-76). Charles Hoggett was promoted twice during this commission. In April 1843 he was appointed yeoman of signals; and he was made captain of the foretop on 10 February 1845 - a thoroughly competent seaman aged 28, with 12 years at sea, he was given a post of responsibility which demanded a man respected by his shipmates. He left the ship at Portsmouth in June 1845; and returned to sea on HMS *President* three months later. Hoggett signed on as an able seaman, but was promoted to captain of the main top on 1 May 1846. Musters ADM 38/1458-1463 and complete book ADM 38/8765 describe the voyage, which encompassed South America, Capetown, Mauritius, Mozambique and the Seychelles. HMS *President* crossed the Indian Ocean to

OPPOSITE *Certificate of service for Charles Hoggett, in ADM 29/56. This lists his sea service with dates and ranks.*

714 C.S. № 3.835

Charles Hoggett

4.	Rattlesnake 78	30 May 31	B.V.	11 June 32		1	—	14
8	"	12 June 32	Clerk	2 Sept 33		1	—	83
153	"	3 Sept 33	Ord	12 Nov 33	Service	—	—	71
8	Blonde	1 Dec 33	B.V.	23 Jan 35 / 3 Mch 36		1	—	54
	18	24 Jany 35						
228	"	4 Mch 36	Ord	30 June 37				
	"	1 July 37	A.B.	15 Nov 37	Off	2 " "	297
60	Apollo good	27 Mch 38	"	25 June 38	Service	" " "	91
417	Edinbro	3 Augt 38	"	14 July 41	Off	2 " "	347
301	Illustrious	21 Octr 41	"	2 April 43		1 " "	104
	" V.good	3 April 43	Yeoman Signal	9 Feby 45		1 " "	314
	"	10 Feby 45	C.F.J.	9 June 45		" " "	120
233	President	12 Sept 45	A.B.	30 April 46		" " "	231
	" V.good	1 May 46	C.M.J.	6 Feby 49	Off	2 " "	283
88	Victoria & Albert V.good	8 Mar 49	A.B.	29 Augt 50		1 " "	177
	" V.good	30 Augt 50	Q.W.	31 Decr 50	Off		
7	" V.good	1 Jany 51	"	30 Decr 53			
11	"	31 Decr 53	"	22 May 57	Date of Letter	6 " "	268

Including as S.P.O. from Caps

9. 306

and adpt Dr. 1. 314

24 — 324

W. 30 June 1857.

Sumatra and Indonesia before returning to England via Capetown in January 1849. ADM 38/8765 contains a Description Book; the usual particulars are given, with one important difference - Charles Hoggett was listed as a married man, so between his travels he had found himself a wife. His character was described as "very good".

Charles signed for his last ship, the Royal Yacht HMS *Victoria and Albert*, on 6 March 1849, where he remained until his discharge in July 1857; this notable honour proves that he was a man hand-picked for his seamanlike skills and excellent record. From August 1850 he was ship's quartermaster. Most of this period was spent in coastal waters around the South Coast, apart from a brief trip to Gibraltar, Bordeaux and Cowes during the summer of 1850 (ADM 38/2086-7, 9254-5). Musters record that Hoggett made an allotment from 1 April 1849, and also confirm that he signed for Continuous Service in July 1853.

In the Description Book for HMS *Victoria and Albert* in ADM 38/9255 Hoggett had suddenly and inexplicably grown to 5ft 9ins, with red hair, blue eyes and a florid complexion; he was recorded as born in January 1814, and as having no marks or scars. His character was described as "excellent". A previous Description Book for the Royal Yacht, in muster ADM 38/9254, gave completely different details: then he was apparently 5ft 7ins, of dark complexion, with blue eyes and black hair, married, and living in Portsea. He was shown working as a rigger in Portsmouth dockyard from September 1849 to February 1850.

Having established Hoggett's sea service, it was time to explore other possible avenues presented along the way. Charles Hoggett passed the examination for a Greenwich Hospital pension on 9 July 1857, recorded in ADM 6/318; the ledger notes name, length of service, and entitlement to a life out-pension. Portsmouth 2nd District monthly pension returns are in WO 22/90; Charles Hoggett was listed in August 1857 under Section III, "Pensioners newly admitted to Out-Pension". His rate of pension was £23 4s.0d., effective from 23 April 1857. The records cease in February 1862 and Hoggett was not mentioned again, so presumably he did not die or move out of the area before then.

Hoggett arranged an allotment from HMS *Victoria and Albert* on 1 April 1849; allotment book ADM 27/106 records that it was made to his grandmother, Elizabeth Mather, of 26 Southampton Row, Portsea. At this point it was considered that little further information about Hoggett was likely to be uncovered at Kew. However, HMS *Edinburgh's* log books for November 1840 might describe the bombardment of Acre where Hoggett earned his medal.

The captain's log for 3 November 1840 (ADM 51/3154) is very informative. Captain Henderson describes how the *Edinburgh* took station off the South Battery at 1.00pm, in line of battle with the rest of the fleet. At 2.17p.m. a fort opened fire on HMS *Castor*, and *Princess Charlotte*, *Thunderer*, *Powerful* and *Bellerophon* replied. At 2.25p.m. a shell exploded on one of HMS *Edinburgh's* quarterdeck cannonades, killing four seamen and injuring several others, including the master and two officers. Five minutes later *Edinburgh* commenced firing on the forts, which "were keeping up an intense fire on us". At 4p.m. a tremendous explosion came from the direction of the Citadel. Cheering was heard, and the crew of the *Edinburgh* cheered in turn. At sunset she ceased fire. The ship's log (ADM 53/498) repeats the story of the battle, adding little extra detail. Apparently when the "tremendous explosion" took place near the Citadel a great many shells exploded in the air near the ship.

The log for 4 November records that the morning was spent repairing sails and assessing damage caused by fire from the shore batteries. During the afternoon the amount of ordnance used during the battle was accounted for, right down to the number of slow fuses expended and two swords, belts and scabbards lost overboard.

So there we have it: the naval career of Charles Hoggett in quite some detail, courtesy of the records held by the Public Record Office. We know when he joined the navy, the ships he sailed upon, where he went, the positions he held, what he looked like, how much money he earned and his pension entitlements. We even know the role HMS *Edinburgh* played in the naval bombardment off Syria. Not bad, considering we started with a medal and a name; and we haven't finished yet ...

OPPOSITE *Detail from the Captain's Log of HMS* Edinburgh, *3 November 1840, in ADM 51/3154. This describes the bombardment of Acre, the action which earned Hoggett his NGSM with clasp SYRIA. The lower part of this page notes the names of those killed and wounded when an enemy shell struck one of the quarterdeck carronades.*

Acre East. Signals. 1.55 Gen.d 53 – 4.15 Gen.d prep.
432 – 4.40. M.G.B. a v n. o H.B. a H.P. J.C.P. Comp.s North.
J.V.P. Comp.s W.N.W. –

Remarks &c.a H. M. S. Edinburgh, 3.d November 1840 –

At Anchor off Acre.
Standing to the West.

A.M. 4.0. Put Launch, Shortened in cable
to 30 fms. and cleared for Action.

9.30. Weighed and made Sail, Squadron,
Turkish, and Austrian Admirals, and Ships
in Company. 10.20. Observed Steam Vessels
fire on the Town of St Jean d'Acre.
12. Squadron in company.

Distance	Latitude D.R.	obs	Longitude D.R.	Corrected	
					1 Vble B6 297 78
–11–	–11–	–11–	–11–	–11–	

Bearing and Distance.   Water Exp.d 4½ Tons
Rem.d 220 –11–

P.M. 1.50. Princess Charlotte, Powerful, Thunder and Bello-
rophon formed Line of Battle and bore up to engage Forts,
and Edinburgh and Benbow to take Station off the South Battery.
Phoenix Shelling the Forts. 2.13. Standing in for the Forts.
2.17. Fort opened fire on the Castor. Princess Charlotte
Powerful Bellerophon Thunderer opened
fire on Forts. 2.25. A shell from Forts Struck a quarter
deck Gun, burst and killed Walter Stacker, I. Oakely S.
Geo. Langton Drummer, and John Crease Private Marine.
Wounded Commander F. D. Hastings, Mr Davies, Master,
Mr Plimsoll, Asst Surgeon, Mr F. Boys, midshipman.
Jas. Turnbull, S. Joshth Moston Serjt Marines, and Jas. Rich-
ards, 2nd Class Boy. 2.30. Shortened Sail and Anchored
On att Bower from Stern in 5 fms. Veered to 3 Shackles.
Let go B.B. under foot then Commenced firing
generally on th Forts which were keeping up a fierce
fire on us. 4. Obs.d a tremendous explosion in direction
of the Citadel, heard cheering, Cheered. At Sunset Ceased
firing. Captain and Lieut Clark went inside the mole to
reconnoitre. –

At Anchor off Acre

Vessel when anchored, the foremost battery
on What the fort N.N.W. &c. And the Castors
= Marin Battery on ... to front N.B.: in 5½ fms.
under the Stern and bound under this Bower
distance from the Martock Fort. About 120 yards.

CHAPTER 8:

P.R.O. - ROYAL MARINES RECORDS

The Royal Marines have played a distinguished part in nearly every British military campaign since medals were first awarded. Their unique role as Britain's sea soldiers, fighting both aboard Royal Navy warships and in landing parties, has resulted in a wide selection of medals being won by members of the corps.

RM medal entitlements can be verified from **medal rolls** in class ADM 171 at the PRO, like naval medals (indeed, most forms of Royal Marines documentation are to be found alongside those of the Royal Navy). However, the unique role of the Royal Marines often led to individuals earning Army gallantry awards, most notably during the First World War.

Paperwork available to medal researchers at the PRO is broadly similar to Army and Royal Navy records. Personal details on the medal and the date of the campaign provide the basic information. Different medals presented to the same man make it possible to estimate dates of service, and one or all medals in a group may carry the names of ships served upon. The letters "RM" normally follow the name of the recipient, as one would expect. However, it is not unusual to see RMA or RMLI, denoting men who served with the Royal Marine Artillery or Royal Marine Light Infantry - the corps was split into these two branches between the 1850s and 1929.

Research into commissioned officers and other ranks leads down two distinctly separate paths, which are best described independently.

Officers' records

Royal Marine officers have the unique distinction of appearing in both **Army and Navy Lists**. Their details appear in the Army List from 1740, in Hart's Army List from 1840, and in the Navy List from 1797. The New Navy List gives details of Royal Marine officers from 1840. Some entries contain information dating back many years. Surviving issues of a separate annual publication entitled **List of Officers of the Marine Forces** can be seen at the Public Record Office, spanning 1757 to 1886. One set for the period 1757-1850 is in ADM 118/230- 336 (partially indexed from 1770); another, for 1760-1886, is in ADM 192/1-44.

Many types of record for Royal Marine officers are akin to those of naval officers, which is not surprising given the close affiliation between the two services. Officers' **service records** are in ADM 196; records survive from 1793, although comprehensive coverage only exists for all officers commissioned after 1837. It is possible to view service records for officers up until 1915. The documents are fully indexed in the Research Enquiries Room, and there is an alphabetical list to officers' service papers stretching right up to 1970. Service records for Royal Marine Artillery officers 1798-1855 are in ADM 196/66.

In 1822 Royal Marine officers were the subject of a **survey**, the results of which are in class ADM 6/405. The documents give name, rank, seniority, age and information about pay and allowances. If the officer was commissioned between 1755 and 1814 he may be recorded on **commissions and appointments registers** in ADM 6/406. Registers provide date of commissioning and dates when officers took up particular appointments; extra details are sometimes given. The books run in date order

The Egypt Medal, 1882, the LSGC, and the Egyptian Khedive's Star to Pte. Joseph Full of the Royal Marines. The ribbons are blue and white and solid blue, a suitably naval-looking display for a "Bootneck".

and are not indexed.

Half-pay records for Royal Marine officers are within Audit Office records AO 1/257-261, for the years 1758-1827. Other half-pay returns are in ADM 6/410-413, for the years 1789-93 and 1824-29. An address book for officers on half-pay in 1837 exists in PMG 73/2. Marine officers' **casualty returns** appear in the same registers as those for naval officers. Deaths between 1893 and 1956 not due to enemy action are in ADM 104/109-121, indexed by ADM 104/102-108 or internally. Each entry states ship or unit, rank, date, place and cause of death. The registers of Marines killed or wounded as a result of enemy action are in ADM 104/144-149, internally indexed from 1854 to 1915; thereafter, until 1929, they are indexed separately by ADM 104/140-143. The registers record ship or unit, rank, date, place and cause of death and age. Wounds are also described.

A series of **obituary books** survive from the 19th century. ADM 11/51-52 contains Marine officers' obituaries from 1833 to 1846; those for 1846-72 are in ADM 6/448.

After 1862 Marine officers had to supply copies of their **marriage certificates** in order to guarantee their widow a pension in the event of their death. A few certificates survive in ADM 13 for marriages between 1806 and 1902. All records are indexed. Pre-1866 certificates are card-indexed in the Research Enquiries Room. Indexed registers in ADM 6/323-328 outline requests for assistance to the **Compassionate Fund** made by the dependants of deceased officers, 1809-36. Most records concern orphaned children and show the relationship between the applicant and the deceased, age and address of the applicant, as well as personal information about the officer, including rank, date of death, ship, length of service and sometimes other details. Information about Marine officers' **widows' pensions** can be found in four separate classes, each relating to a different time span. The earliest, covering from 1712 to 1831, are in ADM 96/523. These are followed by records dating from 1836-70 in PMG 16, 1870-1919 in PMG 20, and finally, 1921-26 in PMG 72.

Other ranks' records

Four divisional depots recruited Royal Marines, situated at Portsmouth, Plymouth, Chatham and Woolwich, although the last only from 1805 to 1869. Throughout each marine's career his **service records** were kept and up-dated by his parent division. However, while at sea marines appeared on naval records with the rest of the ship's company.

Marines spent long periods at sea, and ships' **muster rolls** can be used to track their movements in exactly the same way as they can for seamen. These can be particularly important where service records cannot be found but the researcher has knowledge, perhaps from a medal in his possession, that the marine served on board a given ship at a given time. For more detail about ships' musters, see the previous chapter.

Another set of documents which help to chart a man's movements are **effective and subsistence lists** in ADM 96. These are similar to Army muster and pay lists. Although they give no personal details they show the whereabouts of a marine at a given time, and as they list men by division and company

they can be used as a research tool to point the way for a more focused search through other document classes.

Research into medals awarded to Royal Marine other ranks is dictated by determining into which **Marine division** he enlisted. This can often be identified from the prefix to his service number on a given medal: CH indicates a Chatham recruit, PO relates to Portsmouth and PL to Plymouth. (W is very rarely found, if ever, since the Woolwich depot ceased to accept recruits in 1869, before this practice apparently began.) Each marine continued to be administered from his original depot division throughout his service, although after leaving the depot his subsequent career was spent intermingled with men from all four divisions.

If the original division cannot be identified research is more difficult. It is then necessary to wade through records for all four depots to find relevant documents. However, once traced within the paperwork for a particular division, any other material relating to the man will be with records for the same division, so only one long search is required.

There are wide variations in the material which has survived from the four individual divisions. Paperwork originating from each is very similar, closely resembling documentation for Royal Navy ratings and Army other ranks. However, surviving holdings of certain types of record differ between the four depots. The earliest surviving attestation papers are for Chatham Division, dating from 1790, while the most recent records available are papers relating to men discharged from Portsmouth Division up until 1923. Royal Marine Artillery attestations are in three different batches, together spanning 1860-1925. The three types are each arranged alphabetically in ADM 157/2848-3269.

Attestation records are the best place to look when starting research. Records for all divisions stretch from the mid-18th to late 19th century, apart from Woolwich Division. They are kept separately in ADM 157. The papers are in order of enlistment or discharge date, but there are two nominal indexes available to simplify the search for an individual's documents. A card index in the Research Enquiry Room lists all existing attestations from the 19th century, and a complete index to all Royal Marine attestations held at the PRO is in ADM 313/1-26.

Attestation documents give an abbreviated history of service, including postings and ships; medal entitlements are usually noted. A personal description is also recorded, together with details such as place of birth and previous trade; next-of-kin are often named. **Description books** were compiled for marines in a similar fashion to those for soldiers and sailors. Numerous different types of register are loosely termed "description books", as the format varied over the passage of time and between parent divisions. Those that survive are in class ADM 158. Coverage differs from one division to another. Description books are stored by division and then semi-alphabetically by date of attestation.

The earliest books are for Royal Marine Artillery recruits dating from 1705. Generally divisional registers begin from the late 18th century and continue until the 1880s. Deal Depot description books take over where the divisional books end and run from 1881 to 1940. The books briefly describe each recruit, and give place of birth, trade and age on enlistment. Although they do not contain a service history they show promotions, and often include date of death or discharge.

Records of service for marines began officially in 1884, when recruits were first given official numbers (although in practice a system of numbering had been introduced years before). These are in ADM 159. To locate the **service record** for a given marine it is necessary to know his service number. Medals stamped with the service number provide an obvious short cut; the unique number can be found by reference to class ADM 313/27-109, a register of those records which still exist, alphabetical by division and date of enlistment.

Service records are the best source of information about RM other ranks available at the PRO. They give a full service history and abundant personal details. The military record includes dates and names of ships, notes about conduct, promotions, demotions and confirmation of medals earned. They also record a brief physical description, place and date of birth, occupation and religion. Service records for Portsmouth and Chatham Divisions stretch from the 1840s to just after the turn of the century. RMA and Plymouth Division records begin in the 1850s and finish at approximately the same time. Records for Woolwich men can be found with those for the division they transferred to. Records begin before the introduction of the numbering system in 1884, because the new system adopted the unofficial system already in place and records were made retrospective.

Service records are subject to a 75-year closure rule. Where it is desired to find out about a man who enlisted within the past 75 years, application should be made to: The Royal Marines Drafting and Record Office, HMS *Centurion*, Grange Road, Gosport, Hants PO13 9XA. Sadly, in many cases the easiest men to research are those who died in service. Marine casualties are well documented at the Public Record Office, although usually amalgamated with those for the Royal Navy.

Marine casualties are arranged by several different criteria. Deaths not caused through enemy action, 1893-1956, are in ADM 104/109-121. Prior to 1951 records are indexed by ADM 104/102-108, afterwards they are internally indexed. Deaths caused by enemy action 1900-41 are listed in alphabetical order in ADM 104/122-126. Likewise, 1939-48 deaths, due to enemy activity or not, are alphabetically listed in ADM 104/127-139. Research material concerning Second World War casualties is supplemented by *A Register of Royal Marines' War Deaths 1939-45*, produced by the Royal Marines Museum, giving additional information about each man, where known. Full information about the last resting place of marines killed during the Great War is in ADM 242/7-10. This burial roll is alphabetical and gives name, rank, number, date and place of birth, next-of-kin, ship and the exact location of the grave.

An indexed series records casualties in action 1854-1929 in ADM 104/144-149, including the First World War. Indexes to the 1915-29 registers are in ADM 104/140-43; these include details of wounded men. Earlier fatalities are recorded in ADM 141/1-9 and ADM 154/1-9, listing deaths from any cause with next-of-kin details, date of death and ship. This series begins in 1802 and finishes in 1878.

Retired marines were entitled to apply for a Greenwich Hospital Pension. **Certificates of service** were compiled by the Pay Office to support their claims, and marine certificates are with those for seamen in ADM 73/1-35. The series is alphabetical and spans 1790-1865. The certificates are identical to those described for seamen in Chapter 7, giving a full record of service taken from pay records, including time at sea and on land, rank, promotions, and an assessment of conduct at the conclusion of each posting.

Each division kept **discharge books** to record men leaving the service. Names are listed semi-alphabetically by date of discharge, with a few sparse details. They also state the man's intended place of residence. PRO holdings vary from division to division. A full run survives for Plymouth Division 1761-1919, while only twenty-odd years at the turn of the 19th century still exist for Portsmouth men.

The wide variety of documents in ADM 73 concerning **Greenwich Hospital in-pensioners** have already been outlined in the previous chapter; all the records list marine in-pensioners along with former seamen. Marine **out-pensioners** 1814-46 are recorded alphabetically in ADM 22/254-443. War Office payment returns in WO 22 give identical details to those listed in the last chapter.

ADM 142 indexes **wills** completed by seamen and marines; the wills themselves are in class ADM 48, spanning 1786-1882. As one would expect, they give an insight into family relationships.

Each marine division kept a **register of births, marriages and deaths**, of particular interest to researchers seeking a more rounded picture of their man. Again, there are wide variations between the surviving holdings for each division. The most complete are those for Chatham, running from 1830 to 1913, while only marriage returns for 1869-81 survive from Portsmouth registers. Even where registers do survive there can be great variations in how well they were maintained. Marines are normally listed by company, with separate pages for sergeants, corporals and privates. There are spaces for wife's full name, date and place of marriage, children's names, dates and places of birth. Some are meticulously completed, others are not. The registers are also annotated with date of discharge or death of the marine. Reason for discharge is stated, and whether or not to pension. Children's deaths are often shown.

Many men were recruited on a "hostilities only" basis for the First World War. The attestations for **short service marines** are sorted by service number in ADM 157/3270-3625, indexed in ADM 313. Their service records survive in many cases in ADM 159, indexed in ADM 313.

War diaries were maintained for Royal Marine units during the First and Second World Wars and many survive. They follow the same format as those compiled by Army formations, outlined in Chapter 15, although small RM units were often attached to larger groupings and it can be difficult to identify correct records without a lot of prior research or knowledge. Royal Marine war diaries rarely name individuals, apart from

Record of Service for Joseph Full between June 1862 and July 1883, in ADM 157/331; his three medals are noted at upper left.

RECORD OF SERVICE.

356 Joseph Full, Private.

Company	Promotions, Reduction, Casualties, &c.	Rank	Period of Service in each Rank. From	To	Amount of Service Years	Days	
35		Private	12 June 62	20 July 83	21	39	
		Service towards Limited Engagement.			21	39	
		— ,, — G.C. Pay & Pension			21	39	

In possession of 5 G.C. Badges
5th from 12 June 1883.
Medals Long Service & Good Conduct
Egyptian & Khedive's Star.

Noemtion

		Afloat					
		Prs Royal	18 Feby 64	6 June 65	1	109	V.G.
		Indus	27 Feby 66	30 Sept 68	2	216	V.G.
		Fox	15 May 73	31 Decr 74	1	231	V.G.
		— ,, —	1 Jany 75	18 Oct 76	1	291	Exempty
		Juins	6 Sept 77	26 Feby 80	2	174	Exempty
		Cambridge	1 Oct 80	17 June 81	—	260	Exempty
		Tamar	18 June 81	2 Oct 82	1	107	Exempty
		Dk of Well.	3 Oct 82	9 Novr 82	—	38	Yrienly
		Tamar	10 Novr 82	15 June 83	—	218	Exempty
				Afloat	12	184	1644 1460
				Ashore	8	220	
					21	39	4044 365

		Ashore.					
			12 June 62	17 Feby 64	1	251	V.G.
			7 June 65	26 Feby 66	—	265	V.G.
			1 Oct 68	14 May 73	4	226	V.G.
			19 Oct 76	5 Sept 77	—	322	Exempty
			27 Feby 80	30 Sept 80	—	216	Exempty
			16 June 83	20 July 83	—	35	Exempty
					8	220	1315 1095

Further particulars of Pte.Full in ADM 157/331,
including confirmation of his medals (lower left) and
his bout of sickness in the East Indies (lower right).

officers and those singled out for some special reason. However, where it is known that an event occurred on a certain date the diary may well record details. First World War diaries can be ordered from ADM 116 and ADM 137, indexed by individual unit. Those for the Second World War and some later campaigns are in ADM 202 and DEFE 2.

The documents listed above are the principal sources available at the Public Record Office. There are others, but a book of this scope is not the place to list them all. More determined researchers will doubtless find them and pursue those considered worthwhile.

Research Notes

Joseph Full

The medals awarded to Joseph Full tell some brief details about his service. The Long Service and Good Conduct Medal indicates that he spent a considerable time in the Royal Marines and served on board HMS *Fox*. It has a narrow suspender and impressed naming, which means that it was presented between 1877 and 1901. The Egypt medal is dated 1882 and impressed to "J Full Pte RM HMS *Tamar*", giving us a specific date and a second ship.

There is an index to Royal Marine attestation papers in the Research Enquiries Room at Kew, and Full is listed with the reference ADM 157/331. This document box was ordered. His papers were quite detailed, providing a full record of service.

Joseph Full was born on 12 June 1843 at Buckfastleigh, Devon. He was a labourer, 5ft 6ins tall, with a fresh complexion, brown hair and dark hazel eyes, with no other distinguishing marks, and was Church of England by religion. He enlisted for 12 years at 11.35am on his 19th birthday, 12 June 1862, at East Stonehouse, Devon. He was paid a £1 bounty with a free issue of kit. Prior to enlistment he had joined the South Devon Militia on 22 April 1861; he was released from militia service on 11 June 1862, provided that he enlisted in the regular forces.

Full was posted to 63 Company in the Plymouth Division, and transferred to 35 Company on 15 May 1872. Knowledge of his division opened the door to other documentation, but his attestation papers were very informative. A certificate of service was with the papers, recording periods spent on shore and afloat, including the ships which he served upon. His conduct was also assessed. This is summarized as follows:

Ashore Plymouth   ... 12/06/1862-17/02/1864... Very Good
Afloat HMS *Princess Royal* ... 18/02/64-06/06/65 ...   VG
Ashore Plymouth ... 07/06/65-26/02/66 ... VG
Afloat HMS *Indus* ... 27/02/66-30/09/68 ... VG

PROCEEDINGS ON DISCHARGE. 129

PROCEEDINGS OF A BOARD, held at *R. M. Barracks Plymouth*
date *20th July 1883*

to verify and record the Services, Conduct, Character, and cause of Discharge of } *35 C⁰ Joseph Full Pte* Royal Marines.

President.

Colonel Jones C.B. &c.

Members.

Captain Nepean.   *Capt Byans.*

THE BOARD having examined and compared the Divisional Records, and such other Documents as appeared to them to be necessary, report that after making every deduction required by Regulation, the Service up to this day, which he is entitled to reckon towards Pension, amounts to *21* years, *39* days, towards Good Conduct Pay to *21* years *39* days, and towards completion of limited engagement to *21* years, *39* days, as shown by the detailed statement on the 3rd page; and further that his DISCHARGE is proposed in consequence of

[Here state whether—completion of period, at own request, or as unfit for further service. Or any other cause. If by purchase, state the amount, and by whom the money has been received.]

having Completed 21 years Service

With regard to his CHARACTER and CONDUCT, the Board have to report that upon reference to the Parchment Certificate and Defaulter's Book, it appears that *his Character is* *Exemplary*

[Insert opposite—the man's Character, the number of Good Conduct Badges in his possession, and all Medals, Badges of Merit, or gallant conduct in the Field, conferred upon him; and if in possession of a School Certificate, record it and state the class.]

In possession of 5 G.C. Badges. 5th from 12th June 1883. In possession of Long Service & Good Conduct Medal also Egyptian Medal & Khedives Star.

State if entered or not in Divisional Defaulter's Book, and how often.

No entry

Also if tried or not by Court Martial or the Civil Power, and how often.

No.

[If this man received Wounds, &c., in action, or other Injuries in or by the Service, although not invalided on account thereof, state here the nature of the wound, or injuries, and when and where he received the same, and whether in possession of a Hurt Certificate.]

No.

35 C⁰ Joseph Full Pte on being asked up to what date he has been paid, he answered, that his Account is balanced up to *20th July 1883*; and being further asked whether he has any claim on the Service for Arrears of PAY, ALLOWANCES, or CLOTHING, answered that *he has none,*

and in confirmation thereof, affixes his signature hereto.

Jas. Full ___ Signature of Soldier.

Additional Certificate in the case of a soldier who takes his discharge at his own request.

I declare that I do of my own free will request to be discharged from Her Majesty's Service.

Jas. Full ___ Signature of Soldier.

THE Board have ascertained that his Ledger Account is correctly balanced, and signed by the Officer Commanding his Company, and they declare that they have impartially inquired into, and faithfully reported upon, all the matters brought before them, in accordance with Regulation.

Howard S. Jones. Col. 2nd Com⁰ President.

RWH Nepean Capt R.M.L.I }

T. Byan Capt RMLI } Members.

H.F. Hilton Blancale

Colonel Commandant
Plymouth Division.

I have carefully examined the Proceedings of this Board in all its details and I find them in every respect correct.

LEFT *Joseph Full's discharge papers; his unit is noted as 35th Co. Royal Marines, his character is given as exemplary, and his medals and five Good Conduct badges are again confirmed.*

OVERLEAF *Description Book entry for Joseph Full, in ADM 158/226. This is a good example of the care which has to be exercised when researching individuals through manuscript documents (even leaving aside the fact that they are often only barely legible). On the left hand page "our" Joseph Full, from Buckfastleigh parish, Ashburton, Devon, appears as the third name up from the bottom; he is noted as having brown hair and dark hazel eyes. Altogether this page includes no less than five men with the surname Full from the Ashburton area - and six names above "our" Joseph's entry is yet another Joseph Full, from Woodland parish, Ashburton. He is described as having dark brown hair and light hazel eyes, and is distinguished by a small wart in front of his left ear lobe and several small scars to the forehead.*

Old Establishment.	New Establishment.	Date of Attestation. Day & Month.	Year.	Name.		Age.	Size. Feet.	Inches.	Where Born. Parish.	Town.	County.
Rt.	39	26 July	1838	Charles 4/125	Judge	20	5	7	Sturminster Newton	Sturminster	Dorset
" 59	58	27 Feb.	1847	Daniel 21/61	Fussell	18	5	6¼	Hilsley	Wottonunderedge	Gloucester
" 63	44	19 Mar.	"	William	Judge 1 Mark 19 Mar. 1852	20	5	7½	Sturminster Newton	Sturminster Newton	Dorset
"	55	18/21 April, Service extended 30 Aug. 1864	1852	Richard	Full	20 6/12	5	7½	Woodland	Ashburton	Devon
"	—	11/14 "	"	Henry	Full	19	5	4½	Do	Do	Do
"	59	27/28 May, Service extended 2 Dec. 1863	"	Thomas	Full	22 10/12	5	7½	Do	Do	Do
√	57/37	27/28 ", Service extended 2 Dec. 1863	"	Henry	Full	19 2/12	5	7	Do	Do	Do
"	—	7/8 Feb.	1854	William	Fursman	19	5	6¾	Staverton	Totnes	Do
	15	2/3 June, 5 May 1866 Service extended	"	John 11/132	Fursey	19	5	6¼	Hatherleigh	Hatherleigh	Do
"	59	31 Oct. / 2 Nov.	"	John 25/25	Furze	20	5	6¼	Witheridge	Chumleigh	Devon
"	67	26/27 Jan.	1855	John	Furze	19 2/12	5	5¾	Philleigh	Tregony	Cornwall
"	79	23/24 Nov.	1857	Edmund 14/14	Furze	21	5	7¾	Oldsworthy	Oldsworthy	Devon
"	87	18/19 Decr.	"	George 11/240 19/133	Furze	18½	5	6¾	Kilkhampton	Stratton	Cornwall
"	11	29/30 Oct.	1858	Joseph	Full	19 5/12	5	9¼	Woodland	Ashburton	Devon
"	39	16/18 Apl.	1859	Benjamin 12/147	Fullagar	21	5	6¼	Stoke Newington	London	Middlesex
√	57/3	9 May, 7 Apl. 1868 Service extended	"	John 17/192	Fuke	18	5	4¼	South Molton	South Molton	Devon
√	56/37	11 May, 7 April 1868 Service extended	"	John 12/186	Furson	18	5	4	Bideford	Bideford	Devon
	23	19/21 Nov., 7 Dec. 1869 Service extended	1861	Henry	Judge	18	5	7½	Childockford	Sherborne	Dorset
"	35	6/7 Jany.	1862	Thomas 20/156	Fursman	18½	5	6	Staverton	Totnes	Devon
"	68/35	11/12 June, 23 June 1870 Service extended	"	Joseph	Full	19	5	6½	Buckfastleigh	Ashburton	Devon
"	19	24 Feby. / 2 March	1863	Samuel 25/78	Furzer @ Samuel Radford	18	5	6	Crewkerne	Crewkerne	Somerset
		27/29 Augt.	1861	Edward	Furzer	18	5	6½	Haselbury	Crewkerne	Somerset

Annotations: Richard Full — Parchment; Henry Full (57/37) — Parchment; John Fursey — 31 Aug. 1860. Release from South Devon Militia with attestation; John Furze (67) — Volunteer from Royal Cornwall Rangers, released with attestation; Benjamin Fullagar — Volunteer from King's Own Lt. Infy.; John Fuke — Parchment; John Furson — Parchment; Thomas Fursman (35) — Release from South Devon Militia with attestation; Joseph Full (68/35) — Parchment; Samuel Furzer — 24 April 1863 confessed he belonged … a day for …

Colour of			By whom Enlisted.	Where Enlisted.	Trade.	Former Service.	Observations.	When set off the Rolls.		Reason.
Hair.	Eyes.	Complexion.						Day & Month.	Year.	U
Fair	Hazel	Brown	Captain Edwards	Yeovil	Mason	Scar on left thigh from a Burn		13 Augt	1859	D. "Length of Service"
Br	Hazel	Fresh	Cpl. Trahar	Stroud	Dyer	Recruit Party under charge of Colt Fielding Gloucester	1st Class	27 Feby 63 25 Feby	1868	DD Plymouth Hospl
	Blue		Cpl. Jarring	Sturminster	Labourer	Recruit Party under charge of Capt Nelson Dorchester		19 Mar 61 30 April	1853	D. "Phthisis" in Plymouth Hospital
Br	Grey		Corpl Jefferies	Broadhempston	Farm Laborer	Capt Curry Totness		19 June	1873	D Completed 21 Years Service
Br	Grey	Fair	Do	Do	Do	Do	Do	22 April	1852	rejected Under the Standard Height of 5ft 7½in
Br			Sergt Milton	Woodland	Laborer	Do	Do	6 Mar	1866	DD Plymouth Hospital
Br			Do	Do	Do	Do	Do	22 Jany	1874	D Completed 21 Years Service
Br		Fresh	Pte Tacey	Staverton	Miller	Capt Gray Totnes		11 Feb	1854	rejected enlargement of features, about the left knee
Black	Hazel	Dark	Sfl James Margell H? Quart		Laborer	. . .	Protestant	3 March	1868	D. Ch. Criostitis.
Dark Brown	Grey	Fresh	Pte Wm Brailey	South Molton	Do	Capt Hocker Exeter	Protestant	13 Decr	1866	D. The period of Service for which he was attested having Expired —
Brown	Hazel	Fresh	Sfl Geo Gozencroft	Bodmin	Miner	Capt Forbes Bodmin	Do	29 Augt	1855	D. "Phthisis"
Brown	Grey	Yellow	Sergt Major Mayell	Head Quarters	Labourer	. . .	Do	6 Feb	1862	D. Phthisis
	Hazel	Fair	Do	Do	Do		Wesleyan Do	29 April	1863	D with disgrace as a worthless & incorrigible character
Dark	Hazel	Fresh	Do	Do	Farm Laborer		Protestant	19 Nov.	1859	D. Epilepsey
Br	Hazel	Fair	Sergt Chas Berry	Curragh Camp	Laborer	Capt Fellows London	Do	12 Octr	1863	Transferred to Woolwich Division
Brown	Hazel	Fresh	Sergt Heal	Barnstaple	Fryer	Revd David Barnstaple	Wesleyan	4 March	1881	D Completed 21 Years Service
Br	Grey	Fair	Sergt Jas Baker	Bideford	Gardener	Do	Do	17 Feby	1874	D. Jaundice.
Br	Grey	Fair	Sergt J.O. Deuty	Yeovil	Labourer	Capt Little Yeovil	Protestant	9 Sept	1875	DD Accidentally Drowned by the sinking of the Whaleboat at Cruwys
	Grey	Fresh	Sergt Major Mayell	East Stonehouse	Do	. . .	Wesleyan	20 July	1864	DD Battn Japan (at Yokohama)
Brown	Dark Hazel		" Jones	Do	Do	. . .	Protestant	20 July	1883	D Completed 21 Years
Brown	Blue		"	Do	Do		Do	20 Sept	1867	D Paid £20

South Devon Militia was placed under a Stoppage of 1d
Enrolled 29 July 1882. Released 5th May 1883.

| Brown | Grey | Fair | Corpl Wm Curry | Crewkerne | Marble Sawyer | Capt Little Taunton | — | 30 Augt | 186? | |

Ashore ... 01/10/68-14/05/73 ... VG
Afloat HMS *Fox* ... 15/05/73-18/10/76 ... VG & Exemplary
Ashore Plymouth ... 19/10/76-05/09/77 ... Exemplary
Afloat HMS *Sirius* ... 06/09/77-26/02/80 ... Exemplary
Ashore Plymouth ... 27/02/80-30/09/80 ... Exemplary
Afloat HMS *Cambridge* ... 01/10/80-17/06/81
Afloat HMS *Tamar* ... 18/06/81-02/10/82
SS *Nevada*
Afloat HMS *Duke of Wellington* transport ... 03/10/82
    09/11/82
Afloat HMS *Tamar* ... 10/11/82-15/06/83 ... Exemplary
Ashore Plymouth ... 16/06/83-20/07/83 ... Exemplary

The certificate of service notes that Joseph Full was recommended for a gratuity on five occasions. The overall assessment of his conduct and character at discharge was exemplary. A further record of service lists the number of years and days Full spent with each ship or establishment, as well as confirming the dates of each posting. Joseph Full served for a total of 21 years 39 days, of which 8 years 220 days was spent ashore and 12 years 184 days afloat.

A separate sheet records promotions, medals and decorations, good conduct badges, service forfeited, wounds, times invalided, and a description. Personal particulars shown are identical to those on enlistment. The sheet confirms that Full was awarded the Long Service and Good Conduct Medal in June 1875 and the Egypt Medal and Khedive's Star on 19 May 1883. The Egyptian grant was paid on 6 May 1883. Joseph Full earned five Good Conduct Badges at regular intervals, on 11 June 1865, 11 June 1870, 12 June 1874, 11 June 1878 and 12 June 1883. He was never entered into the defaulters' book. The sheet also records that he could swim. The only occasion he was invalided was on 17 June 1865 in the East Indies, when he suffered from phthsisis and dysentery. He was never wounded.

Royal Marine discharge books are in ADM 184, and Joseph Full's discharge is listed in ADM 184/41. The entry in the book repeats information already found from attestation papers, namely rank, length of service, date of discharge and discharge address. A further physical description is found with his discharge papers; at the age of 40 years and one month, Full was described as 5ft 8ins tall, with a fresh complexion, grey eyes, brown hair, with no marks or scars. His discharge address was 46 High Street, Stonehouse. Four different copies of defaulters' books are with the papers. There are no entries, only various comments about good conduct badges and dates of embarkation and transfer.

Private Full earned his Egypt medals while on board HMS *Tamar*, but unfortunately no musters for the 1882 period are held by the Public Record Office.

Plymouth Division marriage and birth register, ADM 184/43, might have provided new information not given with the documents already seen, but unfortunately his name does not appear in the register. Description Book ADM 158/226 repeats the description from his enlistment papers, with age, place of birth, date of enlistment and facts already established. There was no trace of an attestation in WO 96 for the South Devon Militia.

Muster returns for Full's first ship, HMS *Princess Royal*, were ordered (ADM 38/6892 and 6893, complete book ADM 38/8779). He joined the ship on 18 February 1864, as number 46 on the RM list. She sailed in April 1864 to Simon's Bay, Capetown. From June to August HMS *Princess Royal* crossed the Indian Ocean to Trincomalee, Sri Lanka, and then up the east coast of India to Madras in the Bay of Bengal. She returned south via Trincomalee and then along the west coast of India to Bombay.

Full was discharged to HMS *Penguin* on 18 January 1865; checks with the muster show him listed with the supernumaries. On 15 February 1865 he transferred to the *Orestes* for passage to England. Full's discharge from HMS *Princess Royal* was explained by the description book contained in ADM 38/8779: he was invalided to *Penguin* for passage to England, probably with phthsisis and dysentery as recorded with his attestation papers. His character was given as "very good". Some details of his description had miraculously changed since enlistment: he might have grown from 5ft 6ins to 5ft 8ins, but apparently his eyes had altered from dark hazel to grey, his hair had lightened from black to brown, and his complexion was now fair, not fresh. (He still originated from Buckfastleigh... .) He was described as single, vaccinated for smallpox, and a woolcomber by trade.

ADM 38/6479-6484 are the musters covering the time Full served on HMS *Indus*, a gunnery ship on home service; the entire period was spent at Hamoaze. Full joined her on 27 February 1866 from HQ Plymouth, and was listed as Private No.405 on the muster. Nothing of consequence was discovered from this roll, and Full was discharged back to HQ Plymouth on 30 September 1868.

No musters or logs survive for the periods Private Full subsequently spent at sea, so his later voyages remain a mystery. We know that he was off the Egyptian coast aboard HMS *Tamar* during 1882, but no further details are forthcoming. (This was the campaign in which British forces supported the Khedive of Egypt against a revolt led by Arabi Pasha, a naval bombardment of Alexandria being followed by Gen.Sir Garnet Wolseley's victory at Tel el Kebir.)

There appeared little more to be found at the PRO, and it was time to look further afield for more information about Joseph Full.

CHAPTER 9:

P.R.O. - ROYAL AIR FORCE RECORDS

Medals earned by aircrew of the flying services are very interesting to research. Surviving documentation is completely different to that for the other two services, and often provides extremely detailed accounts of combat in the air. Unlike warfare by land or sea, the air war involved individuals or small groups; any contact with the enemy was reported in minute detail, offering great opportunities for research. Flying personnel are frequently listed in the documentation by name, and it is possible to build up a dossier of the events in which an individual airman participated. Perhaps because of this, medals awarded to aircrew fetch a premium price, particularly those associated with memorable actions such as the Battle of Britain or the Dambusters raid.

Unfortunately, only a small percentage of the total personnel of the flying services actually took to the air. From the earliest days of aerial combat a small army of riggers, mechanics and other assorted groundcrew were required to keep each aircraft in action. Comprehensive records survive for the men in the air, but the vital if unglamorous services of groundcrew were often left unsung. Do not be surprised if groups of medals awarded to ground staff fail to yield results.

The Royal Flying Corps (RFC) was formed on 13 May 1912, and the Royal Naval Air Service (RNAS) became a separate entity during the summer of 1914. The two amalgamated into a single service, to be called the Royal Air Force, on 1 April 1918.

There was huge public interest in the new air services during the early part of the century. A generation of small boys became adept at squinting into the sky to recognize different types of aircraft. Flying aces became the modern knights on horseback - the rare examples of identifiable warriors amid the generalised carnage of two World Wars. Many became household names, their actions documented in newspapers and books or filmed on newsreel. Countless books have been and continue to be published telling in detail the stories of pilots, squadrons, aerial campaigns, types of aircraft, airfields and any number of associated subjects. These enable RAF medal researchers to look at all aspects of the man and his service.

The PRO holds a wide selection of RAF operational records, and another major collection is held in the archives of the RAF Museum at Hendon (covered in Chapter 12); these are the two principal sources for research into medals to the air services.

The 1939-45 Star, Aircrew Europe Star, and War Medal 1939-45 to F/Sgt. Thomas Davis.

Great War medals can be found impressed with the initials RFC, RNAS or RAF. Many groups contain both stars or gallantry decorations to the RFC or RNAS and later awards marked RAF, demonstrating the development of the air service. Medals awarded to men who transferred in from other units were often impressed with details of the original unit. Entitlement to RFC/RAF Great War campaign medals can be confirmed by medal index cards in WO 329 (see Chapter 15). RNAS medal records are listed with those for the Royal Navy in ADM 171. They were listed with HMS *Pembroke* until February 1915 and thereafter appear under HMS *President*.

Gallantry awards and citations, where published, appear in the *London Gazette*, held in class ZJ 1 at the PRO; some recommendations for awards appear in class AIR 1. Incomplete records of foreign decorations are in AIR 1/1169, and MIDs in AIR 1/2318. Indexes for the DSO, MC and DCM are now available at the PRO. First World War DSOs and MCs are in WO 389 on microfilm, by *London Gazette* date order. The record often includes details of the action leading to the award. Great War MCs are indexed in WO 389/9-24.

A new selection of gallantry medals was created during the First World War to recognize members of the air services: the Distinguished Flying Cross, Air Force Cross, Distinguished Flying Medal and Air Force Medal. In 1942 the Conspicuous Gallantry Medal was extended to cover RAF personnel as well as those from the Royal Navy. The Victoria Cross remained the

Lancaster bomber crews of No.9 Squadron, Royal Air Force, assemble their flying kit in preparation for a mission. (Courtesy Pam Spencely)

supreme decoration for valour. Royal Air Force personnel were sometimes awarded medals associated with the other two services.

The comparative youth of the flying service presents obvious difficulties to the researcher. **Personnel records** for men discharged after 1 April 1918 are still kept by the RAF and excerpts can only be supplied at the request of next-of-kin; thus few medal collectors can gain access to an official service history. Family medal researchers may be able to obtain details from the RAF on payment of a fee. If the present owner of a group of medals can trace the man's next-of-kin and they prove agreeable, the MOD will probably release details to the researcher on receipt of a covering letter of authorization. Records of men serving with the RAF after April 1918, including RFC and RNAS personnel, are maintained for officers by PG 5a(2) Section, RAF Personnel and Training Command, RAF Innsworth, Gloucester, GL3 1EZ; P Man 2b(l) Section administers records concerning RAF other ranks.

Even without access to personnel records, a great deal can be discovered from unit papers kept at the Public Record Office. It is often possible to unearth details of every mission flown by aircrew. If the medal recipient was ground staff there is sometimes a chance of finding some information from squadron orders or station records, if they survive from the appropriate time period.

The career of an RAF officer can be pursued through the **Air Force List** in the normal way; a complete run is held on shelves at Kew. The details given are similar to those in the

Army and Navy Lists, brief, but sufficient to build up a history of places, squadrons, dates of promotion and transfer. Until 1918 RFC officers appeared in the Army List and RNAS officers were included in the Navy List.

Document class AIR 1 forms the basis of research into all First World War medals to flying personnel. The class is composed of records drawn together by the Air Historical Branch of the Air Ministry and later deposited at Kew. Papers originate from a host of sources, and it is assembled in no discernible order. That said, the varied documents in AIR 1 are an excellent source of information. There is a card index to AIR 1 in the Research Enquiries Room, which gives a thorough description of information contained within each group of documents. (Note, however, that this index includes paperwork discarded prior to the arrival of documents at Kew.) There is also a comprehensive "idiot's guide" to AIR 1 at the front of the class list, which helps to focus efforts on paperwork likely to yield results. When ordering material from AIR 1 the original Army Historical Branch reference number must be given with the PRO piece number, making a four-part document reference number.

A complete **muster list of RAF other ranks** was drawn up in April 1918 at the amalgamation of the RFC and RNAS. From the service number impressed on a medal it is possible to locate a few details about the man, from the returns in AIR 1/819/204/4/1316 and AIR 10/232-237. Men from the RFC kept their original numbers, while 200000 was added to the original number of those from the RNAS.

A number of lists and returns compiled by various criteria survive. They include a list of RFC men posted to the British Expeditionary Force up to November 1918, and records of

RNAS officer postings from January 1916 to September 1918. These are just two examples of the many types of roll to be found in AIR 1. There are also collections of squadron orders (often giving names), casualty returns, recommendations for awards and promotion boards.

Surviving **squadron records** vary from unit to unit, but material available can be quickly identified from the class list. Squadron records are comparable to battalion war diaries, except that there is much more likelihood of finding individuals mentioned. Importantly for medal researchers, squadron records regularly record gallantry medals awarded to members of the unit and sometimes note citations.

Communiqués are another good source of information. The weekly reports include the name and squadron of individuals who took part in noteworthy events. Many copies of RAF and RNAS communiqués are held at the PRO, and communiqués for the RAF, RFC and RNAS are at the RAF Museum. In addition, pilots were required to report any contact with the enemy and returns submitted are held in AIR 1.

Documents at the PRO for the **Second World War** are better organised than Great War records. They are broken down into several different classes, each containing material on a similar theme. However, while a variety of documents detail the actions of aircrew, few refer to ground staff.

Document classes AIR 24-AIR 29 outline the activities of each echelon of RAF command, as follows:

AIR 24 ... Commands
AIR 25 ... Groups
AIR 26 ... Wings
AIR 27 ... Squadrons
AIR 28 ... Stations
AIR 29 ... Miscellaneous units

AIR 27-29 are of most interest to medal researchers. The others supply an overview of events, but squadron and station records follow the day-to-day happenings of the combat units, mentioning names and outlining operations in great detail.

All station records include a **monthly summary of events** on Form 540; completed at squadron level, this gives immense detail about each action carried out, including dates, times, type of duty and target. The Summary of Events column records the main facts about the mission, including casualties, weather encountered, estimated degree of success, and a list of the aircraft employed - which usually identifies individual pilots.

Monthly squadron records are accompanied by Form 541, which varies in content, but should give date, aircraft type and serial number, crew list for each aircraft, type of duty, times of departure and landing, and details of sortie or flight. The latter column records what befell each individual aircraft during the course of the mission, including engine problems, flak encountered, time of attack, attack altitude, markers seen, impact of bombing, aerial combat and anything else of relevance.

With a little luck it is fairly easy to compile a complete record of an aircrewman's war. It is a humbling experience to see what an individual endured to earn the medals under research. Through reading daily mission reports it is possible to visualize the nightly claustrophobic horror faced by bomber

LAC Thomas Davis, wearing a cap with the white "peak" section marking a cadet, during his flight training in Canada. High quality copies cannot be expected from old snapshots or wartime newsprint, but any portrait image is worth having. (Courtesy Stephen Escreet)

crews, and the loneliness and exhaustion withstood by fighter pilots as the long years of air fighting ground on. No other type of medal offers the opportunity to gain such an insight into the exploits of the recipient.

The best hope of finding mention of groundcrew lies with **station documentation**, if it survives. Logs detail guard duty postings, misdemeanours, absences, promotions and a host of other daily happenings. If it is known that an individual was based at a particular place and station orders still exist, they can be well worth checking. Appendices sometimes survive with station logs in AIR 28, providing supplementary information about personnel on the base, listing social activities, postings, honours, punishments and so on, reflecting the day-to-day life of the station. Other ranks and officers are listed, making appendices a useful research tool.

Squadron and station records frequently mention gallantry decorations awarded to unit personnel. Otherwise, verification of RAF gallantry entitlements is achieved through the **London Gazette**. Some recommendations for decorations are in AIR 2. There are no medal rolls for Second World War campaign stars at the Public Record Office.

Many airmen became **prisoners of war**, and several classes of PRO papers contain information about men in this category. Some provide interesting background reading on the subject,

while others give details of individuals. AIR 14 holds numerous documents of interest to those researching medals awarded to POWs. Pieces 469-71 contain accounts of how certain airmen came to be captured in German-occupied Europe, and piece 1233 also holds relevant files. AIR 20/2336 is probably the best starting point for research into POWs; this is an alphabetical record of all German-held RAF POWs in 1944-45, listing the camp where the man was held.

Medals awarded to **casualties from both World Wars** are frequently the most easily researched. Records of airmen killed are at Myddleton Place (see Chapter 13). The Great War index merely gives name and date of death; the Second World War index notes number, unit and rank, although it does not record men who died within the United Kingdom.

The RAF Museum at Hendon (see Chapter 12) keeps card records of First World War casualties from the RFC and RNAS. These provide extra information, such as type of aircraft flown and cause of death. The index is sketchy for the early days of the conflict, and not 100% reliable, but it is a good source nevertheless. The records are predominantly concerned with fliers killed over the Western Front.

After establishing date of death, squadron and station records at the PRO can be viewed to see if an account of the incident survives. Second World War squadron and station records will nearly always mention the event. It should be possible to discover the mission the aircraft was engaged upon and how it came to grief.

The crew of Lancaster ED656, V-Victor of No.9 Squadron, pose at RAF Bardney during the summer of 1943; P/O. "Paddy" Robinson is second from left, and F/Sgt. Davis (detail opposite) is in the centre. (Courtesy Dr. Andrew Hobley)

Some further material is open to Second World War casualty researchers. Surviving members of bomber crews brought down by enemy action submitted reports about the incident, now in AIR 14/3466-3473. Similar reports in AIR 14/3213-3227 were submitted by aircrew who witnessed the loss of other aircraft or who knew something about aircraft which failed to return. The records are not complete, but the class list can be quickly scanned to see coverage of squadrons and time periods.

Aircrew involved in aerial combat submitted reports describing the incident. These detailed the circumstances, damage sustained, rounds fired, enemy aircraft claimed as shot down, and so on. The coverage is incomplete and it is necessary to check the AIR 50 class list for squadrons and dates. These **combat reports** are very detailed, and any found involving the man under research make interesting reading.

RAF aircrew kept **log books** recording time spent in the air and outlining missions undertaken. A small collection of log books can be seen in AIR 4, although only a representative sample. A larger collection can be seen at the RAF Museum.

Two important indexes are maintained by private individuals and offer researchers an opportunity to consult records gleaned from a variety of sources:

Miss Eunice Wilson keeps an **index of RAF personnel** from the Second World War period. The index includes any airman's name which comes to her attention, from whatever source. Miss Wilson is swift to point out it is not a complete register, but may well provide hitherto unknown material. To check the index, send a self-addressed envelope and two first class stamps to Miss E.Wilson, 143 Harbord Street, London SW6 6PN. The more information supplied, the more chance there is of success; give name, rank, squadron, dates of service, date of death if applicable, and as many other details as possible.

David Barnes, of 21 Bury New Road, Ramsbottom, Lancashire BL0 0BT, keeps **records of airmen from the First World War**. For a small fee, generally under £5.00, he can consult a large index. He also maintains records of service for RNAS officers, extracted from a variety of official sources. Mr Barnes has compiled a biographical Roll of Honour for RNAS casualties of all ranks. Other indexes held by Mr Barnes include listings of Military Medals awarded to RFC, RAF and Australian RAF personnel, a list of airmen interned in Holland, First World War air POWs, and an index to Silver War Badges awarded to Royal Flying Corps personnel. He is also able to trace casualties from the RAF/RFC and RNAS. Mr Barnes is in the process of alphabetising the RAF Other Ranks Muster Roll

from April 1918, currently arranged by service number. The roll gives dates of enlistment and trade employed upon. Mr Barnes operates a scale of charges, starting at £2.00 for checking an entry in *Soldiers Died ...* , up to £5.00 for the Record of Service of an RNAS officer.

Further sources, including the RAF Museum at Hendon, will be explored in later chapters.

Research Notes

Flight Sergeant Thomas Davis

The medals awarded to Flight Sergeant Davis could not be researched at the PRO without some preliminary enquiries. Before any steps could be taken it was imperative to find out the squadron to which he was attached. The condolence slip accompanying the medals provided a starting point, and a phone call to the Commonwealth War Graves Commission opened the door to further research. According to their records, Thomas Rhodes Davis flew as a bomber navigator with No.9 Squadron RAF, and died on 23 November 1943.

Operation record books for No.9 Squadron can be seen on microfilm at Kew in AIR 27/127. Thomas Davis first appeared in the ORB on 29 May 1943, when the squadron - based at RAF Bardney, west of Washingborough in Lincolnshire - bombed Wuppertal. Flight Sergeant N.J.Robinson was the pilot, and the crew was made up of Sgts.R.Taylor, R.J.Pitman, W.E.Jones, L.E.Mitchell, J.Casey and T.R.Davis. They flew in Lancaster serial number W4133, departing at 2229hrs; they attacked their primary target at 0134hrs, and "good fires spread over a large area"; they landed back at Bardney at 0405 hours.

Davis continued to fly with F/Sgt. (later P/O.) Robinson and his crew. He took part in 25 raids between the end of May and his eventual death, listed below:

29/5/43 ... Wuppertal
11/6/43 ... Dusseldorf
12/6/43 ... Bochum
24/6/43 ... Elberfeld
28/6/43 ... Cologne
3/7/43 ... Cologne
9/7/43 ... Gelsenkirchen
12/7/43 ... Turin
24/7/43 ... Hamburg
29/7/43 ... Hamburg
15/8/43 ... Milan
17/8/43 ... Peenemunde
22/8/43 ... Leverkusen
27/8/43 ... Nurnberg
31/8/43 ... Berlin
3/9/43 ... Berlin
22/9/43 ... Hanover
23/9/43 ... Mannheim
8/10/43... Hanover
18/10/43... Hanover
20/10/43... Leipzig
3/11/43 ... Dusseldorf
10/11/43... Modane
18/11/43... Berlin

Place	Date	Time	Summary of Events SECRET.	References to Appendices
BARDNEY, LINCOLN.	22.11.43		**Attack on Berlin by Night.**	
			Twelve of the thirteen No. 9 SQUADRON crews detailed, reported having	
			attacked the primary in 10/10ths cloud, which prevented observation of	
			results, but the glow of fires was reflected and one large explosion seen.	
			One aircraft abandoned the mission due to engine failure.	
			Attack on Berlin by Night.	
	23.11.43		Nine of the thirteen No. 9 SQUADRON crews detailed, reported having	
			attacked the target with the aid of Path-finding marking, which was well	
			concentrated. Glow of fires was seen for a considerable distance on the	
			homeward journey. One aircraft (P/O. Robinson) crashed at E.T.R. 10 miles	
			N.E. of BASE, all except two members of the crew being killed. Another	
			aircraft also crashed locally but there were no casualities. Two aircraft	
			returned early on account of engine failure.	
	24.11.43		No operations ordered.	
			Cancellation of Operations.	
	25.11.43		Ten aircraft of No. 9 SQUADRON were detailed for operations, which were	
			cancelled at 22.32 hours owing to adverse weather conditions en route.	
			Attack on Berlin by Night.	
	26.11.43		Nine of the twelve No. 9 SQUADRON crews detailed, bombed the primary in	
BARDNEY			clear weather, good fires were seen well concentrated. Seven of these	
			aircraft landed away owing to weather conditions at BASE. One aircraft	
			attacked KOBLENZ as engines were affected by severe icing. Two aircraft	
			were cancelled.	

Detail from RAF Bardney's monthly summary of events, in AIR 28/50, showing the entry for the night of 23 November 1943 mentioning the crash in which F/Sgt.Davis was killed with all but two of P/O.Robinson's crew.

One of the most notable of these missions was that flown against the German V-weapons research establishment at Peenemunde on 17 August 1943. The ORB described the raid: "A new, but important target, was chosen for a large scale attack at night". It goes on to say that "The target was found by all our aircraft and well taken care of. Many buildings were seen on fire, and the whole area was a mass of flames". Avro Lancaster ED656, with Davis navigating, was in the air from 2127 to 0403 hours; the primary target was attacked at 0045hrs from 7,000 feet. The stick of bombs fell about 100 yards to port of the green target indicator, and large fires were observed.

The last mission flown by Thomas Davis was a raid on Berlin on 23 November 1943. He flew with his usual crew on Lancaster ED656, with the addition of Pilot Officer C.G.Hinton. They took off at 1708hrs, but never returned. The aircraft crash-landed at 2345hrs during the return flight, approximately ten miles north-east of Bardney. All of the crew were killed apart from two gunners, Sgt.Casey and F/Sgt.

Mitchell, who were both taken to RAF Hospital Rauceby. No explanation for the crash was given.

RAF Station Bardney records are in AIR 28/50. The daily log for 23 November 1943 mentions the crash. The record summarizes an "attack on Berlin by night"; nine crews attacked the target with the aid of Pathfinders. Target marking was apparently well concentrated, and the glow from fires could be seen from a considerable distance by crews making their way home. The log goes on to say: "One aircraft (P/O Robinson) crashed at ETR, 10 miles NE of base, all except two members of crew being killed." Unfortunately no appendices for RAF Bardney survive before 1944 in AIR 28.

The reason Lancaster ED656 failed to make it back to Bardney remained unknown. Class AIR 14/3466-3473 is made up of K reports written by crew survivors of aircraft shot down; a brief search revealed no trace of any records for No.9 Squadron during November 1943. Crew from another aircraft might have seen an incident involving Davis's bomber. AIR 14/3213-3227 contains reports by other crews of combats which they witnessed; but a search of these returns also proved fruitless. A final conclusion had to be postponed until a visit to the RAF Museum at Hendon could be arranged. Aircraft history cards held there would most likely provide an answer.

AIR 50/179 reports on aerial combat between No.9 Squadron crews and enemy aircraft. Davis might have been engaged

	TYPE & NUMBER		DUTY	UP	DOWN	REMARKS
23/11/43 (Contd)	LANCASTER. ED. 656.	P/O. N.J. ROBINSON. P/O. C.G. HINTON. SGT. R.G. TAYLOR. F/SGT. T.R. DAVIS. P/SG T. B.J. PITMAN. SGT. W.E. JONES. F/SGT. L.E. MITCHELL. SGT. J. CASEY.	Bombing – BERLIN.	1708.		This aircraft crashed on return at approx. 2345 hrs. 10 miles N.E. of base. Sgt. Casey and F/Sgt. Mitchell taken to R.A.F. Hospital, Rauceby. Remainder of crew killed.
	LANCASTER. DV. 293.	P/O. R.A. BAYLDON. SGT. R.S. COTE. P/O. R. OTTER. SGT. J.K. WIDHOP. SGT. E. EGAN. SGT. R.J. BARON. SGT. A. RICHARDSON.	Bombing – BERLIN.	1700.	2005.	Returned early. No target attacked. Engines overheating. Difficulty in climbing. Bomb load jettisoned.
26/11/43.	LANCASTER. EE. 188.	F/O. W.M. REID. SGT. S.W. RICHARDS. P/O. R.D.H. PARKER. SGT. D.G. MOIR. SGT. B. HAYHILL. SGT. C.J. GLEDELL. SGT. G. BROWN.	Bombing – BERLIN.	1721.	0056.	Primary attacked. 2125 hrs. 21,500 ft. Manu. red T/I's a few green T/I's and some scattered Wanganui flares seen before bombing. A few fires seen burning. P.F.F. concentration T.I's good but Wanganuis scattered.
	LANCASTER. DV. 334.	P/O. H.E. WARWICK. SGT. THOMAS. F/SGT. T. BUTTERFIELD. F/SGT. J. GRAHAM. F/SGT. G.T.M. GAINES. P/O. E.N. ARMSTRONG. F/SGT. N.E. OWEN.	Bombing – BERLIN.	1728.	0003.	Primary attacked. 2126 hrs. 21,000 ft. Green T.I's cascaded 2123 hrs. Few incendiaries dropped short, but good concentration of fires in centre of T.A. Route markers seen.

Detail from No.9 Squadron's monthly operations record, in AIR 27/117, recording the loss of Lancaster ED656 and listing Davis among those killed.

in combat with enemy night fighters on missions prior to 23 November 1943, so the records were checked, but unfortunately Davis and his crew did not feature.

The Station Operation Log Book in AIR 14/2520 provides reports on operational events at RAF Bardney, giving a minute-by-minute account as events unfolded. Many entries are in code or abbreviated. The log for 23/11/43 is summarized as follows:

1020 ... 1, 3, 5 + 6 Gps nominated for bombing mission.
1025 ... 9 Sqn offer 13 a/c.
1100 ... Proposed route 1 as the previous night. Second route suggested.
1130 ... Bomb loads and fuel allocated.
1150 ... Route 1 confirmed.
Zero hour 2000hrs - to be confirmed after mid-day met. conference.

FPC ... 1300 hrs
Squadron callsign ... NTS
1857 ... R-Roger (P/O Ling) returned early; port inner engine failed.
2005 ... Y-Yankee (P/O Bayldon) returned early; overheating and gaining no height.
2347 ... All a/c landed safely with the exception of V-Victor (P/O Robinson - two of the crew, F/Sgt Mitchell and Sgt Casey, safe), which crashed Map Reference 48/765963; and N-November who crashed at Minting, all crew safe.

At this point PRO research into F/Sgt.Davis was concluded; without further material to go on, enquiries would be purely speculative. Other sources appeared to offer a better chance of progress.

CHAPTER 10: PRINTED SOURCES

Previous chapters have outlined information available at the premier source of military archive material in the United Kingdom. Further research establishments will be explored in later chapters. This chapter will outline the printed sources. Although it is preferable to visit military archives in person, a great deal of useful information can be extracted from well-researched reference books.

Apart from their reference value, contemporary books add colour to the story of the medal recipient. Eyewitness accounts bring events to life. Without knowledge of the action and excitement of a campaign we are left with a dry litany of dates and places. Some unremarkable clasps resulted from fearsome skirmishes in arduous terrain and climatic conditions. Bringing long-forgotten adventures to the surface is one of the joys of medal research.

Regular medal researchers should consider assembling a personal reference library. This is not as easy as it sounds. Military reference works are expensive and many are long out of print. Although there has been a recent trend towards reprinting some sought-after volumes, they remain expensive. For those with limited funds - which means most of us - it can be frustrating to spend money on books instead of medals. The best answer is to balance spending between the two, until a useful basic set of reference books has been gathered; thereafter, more elusive volumes can be added as and when they surface.

Many medal collectors derive as much pleasure from their bookshelves as they do from their medal cabinets. Several book dealers specialise in military reference books, and some medal dealers market books as a sideline. Many supply lists on a regular basis and are happy to receive details of books wanted by collectors.

Books intended as research tools rarely make exciting bedtime reading; invariably they list names and entitlements, enabling collectors to verify awards swiftly and accurately. Bear in mind that an expensive volume, purchased to follow a single line of enquiry, may then lie dormant on the bookshelves - while it could have been seen at a reference library and the required information extracted at no cost. The moral is, think before you buy. Do you *really* need to own a certain book? Regular medal researchers will gain more benefit from buying reference books than those with only an occasional interest.

There is no foolproof method of building a reference collection. Relevant books have to be bought when they appear on the market, funds permitting. Rare items are snapped up, so move quickly when a desired book is seen. However, a few essential books are readily available and can be bought at the outset.

Books for medal researchers cover a wide spectrum. Some specialist books produced specifically for the collecting fraternity can be invaluable to researchers. Other books on a variety of military themes may find a place in the researcher's library, depending on his collecting interests. Useful books for medal research fall into several categories:

Medal books

Every collector should own at least one book describing all medals and clasps, noting numbers awarded, rarity, units involved, and a brief description of each medal. It is difficult to research any medal without possessing some basic knowledge. A general medal reference book also helps the beginner recognize different types of medal and make an assessment of their value.

Several good titles are currently available. The best reference to British campaign medals is *British Battles and Medals* by Joslin, Litherland and Simkin. The book is beautifully produced and features every campaign medal awarded to British personnel since 1588, with details about units and ships present, numbers awarded and a historical report on each action or campaign. If one book had to be selected to be the medal collectors' bible, this would be it.

The annual *Medal News Yearbook*, produced by the publishers of the monthly collectors' magazine *Medal News*, provides similar information. It also covers orders, decorations, life saving awards, long service medals and coronation/jubilee medals. Although the yearbook is less detailed than *British Battles and Medals* it is less expensive, lists a wider range of awards, and contains a useful price guide.

British Gallantry Awards by Abbott and Tamplin is the definitive work on the subject of gallantry medals. Each medal is portrayed in great detail, and the authors explain the significance and history attached to every award, giving examples.

Among the dozens of other books written about medals some focus on a single type of award, such as books about the Meritorious Service Medal by Ian McInnes; others expand upon a theme, like Alec Purves' *Medals, Decorations and Orders of the Great War 1914-18*. All are worthwhile for those with an interest in the subject featured.

Campaign histories

Most collectors specialise to some degree, and their specialisation dictates purchases for their bookshelf. Books describing campaigns in which they are interested should always feature. These are more likely to portray what ordinary soldiers and seamen endured than a specialised book aimed at the medal market. Knowledge of why the campaign took place, the way it was conducted and how events unfurled are an important part of research. Understanding puts history into perspective and explains why battles were fought. Campaign histories rarely mention individuals apart from high-ranking officers or those concerned with noteworthy events, but can be very enlightening.

The First World War has attracted more authors than any other conflict. Books were produced while the war was still being fought, and new titles continue to appear. Meanwhile, it is rare to see books about the Boxer Rebellion, the Ashanti campaign, or a multitude of other small colonial wars. Medal researchers who are enthusiastic about small wars find it hard to put together a reference collection. The reason is obvious - that particular war has failed to ignite the interest of the public at large. Without a reawakening of public awareness, long-ago wars rarely command the attention of publishers. Medal researchers who are intrigued by small campaigns face an uphill struggle to track down material. There is nothing new on the market, so they have to try and locate surviving copies of books written at the time.

Yet some of these limited campaigns still capture the imagination of military enthusiasts. The Zulu War is a prime example; perhaps largely due to the huge popularity of the memorable 1960s feature film *Zulu*, the particularly bloody battles fought in South Africa in 1879 still exercise a gruesome fascination. So while contemporary books about this conflict are extremely difficult to track down, a rebirth of interest has encouraged a new generation of authors over the past two decades, and highly detailed accounts are available.

Unit histories

Unit histories fall into two categories: the first usually describes the history of a regiment from its inception up to the time of writing, and the second narrates the story of the unit through a single campaign. Both are excellent sources of information. "Broad brush" unit histories make good reading and act as a quick reference to the unit's part in particular campaigns. The most prestigious battles are covered in great detail, although some lesser skirmishes may only rate the odd line, and individuals are rarely mentioned. Histories of a unit's role in a single campaign are the most useful for medal research. Many were written immediately after the events, while incidents remained fresh in the minds of the author and/or his eyewitness sources.

Unit histories have appeared after every war, but most were written after the two World Wars, covering all sizes of unit from division down to battalion. Many list gallantry awards and casualties. Obviously, it is the histories written about small units which represent the best research sources. There is more chance of finding a sought-after name in the text, and daily events can be examined in detail. They are especially helpful with casualty research, making it possible to investigate the unit's activities on the date of death. There is also good potential for discovering the deed which resulted in a gallantry medal being awarded when no citation can be found elsewhere.

Brigade and divisional histories focus on the bigger picture. A divisional history may represent the best record available, as only a small percentage of battalions published the story of their exploits. Divisional histories frequently appear on the market at reasonable prices, but regimental and battalion histories are hard to come by and very expensive. Most can be seen at regimental museums or national military museums. *A Bibliography of Regimental Histories of the British Army* by Arthur S.White is a helpful guide to published unit histories; it lists every regiment, outlining the periods and campaigns covered.

Medal and casualty rolls

Published medal rolls are principally intended for collectors. The material has generally been extracted from original rolls, and entries have sometimes been expanded with additional information from other sources. Medal and casualty rolls have not been published for every campaign, although a few more appear each year. It should be noted they are not infallible, and when visiting the PRO or India Office Library it is advisable to check details given against appropriate medal rolls. Some rolls are lavish productions, based upon years of research; at the other end of the spectrum are shorter versions concerned with small scale campaigns or recipients of a single clasp.

Gallantry medal rolls can also be purchased. These are useful, well-researched references which can save time and effort in checking entitlements. Citations are frequently included. The Victoria Cross is the best documented, but a number of volumes list recipients of lesser awards. Several examples are listed in the Bibliography, many of which include biographical details and photographs. The published medal roll is an essential purchase for a medal researcher primarily interested in the campaign featured. It acts as a check list and allows the collector to make informed judgments when purchasing medals.

Casualty rolls have been published for a large number of wars and often contain biographical information. The amount of text devoted to each entry varies, largely dependent upon the numbers killed. Apart from research potential, they are important to medal collectors for the stark reason that the death of any serviceman tends to enhance the price of his medals.

Some of the best known casualty rolls and memorial books were produced during and after the First World War. Every conceivable body wanted to honour its fallen, and rolls of honour were produced by schools, towns, companies and the like. Public school memorial books are very good sources of information about officers. Some memorial books simply list names, while others include biographies and photographs. One of the best known is the five-volume *De Ruvigny's Roll*, which contains short biographies of many officers and men killed in 1916-19, with numerous photographs. *The Bond of Sacrifice* offers similar information about officers who died in 1914- 15. *Our Heroes* features casualties with an Irish connection from Mons to the Somme. These are but three examples.

Every soldier who died during the conflict is listed in a monumental work entitled *Soldiers Died in the Great War*, republished in recent years by J.B.Hayward. This is divided into 80 parts, each comprising a list of names for a certain regiment or corps. Casualties appear alphabetically by battalion within the volume for their parent regiment. Each entry shows surname, forenames, place of birth, place of enlistment - with place of residence in brackets if different - number, rank, date of death, theatre of war, former regiment and number if applicable, and also gallantry awards. Individual parts can be purchased separately, and any researcher interested in Great War medals awarded to particular regiments would be well advised to buy the appropriate volumes.

Alternatively, *Soldiers Died ...* is now also available on CD Rom; searches can be carried out by surname, date of death or any other criteria published in the original volumes. This makes the information much more accessible.

A separate book lists *Officers Died in the Great War 1914-1919*. Surprisingly, this gives less personal information than *Soldiers Died ...* ; names are listed alphabetically by regiment, with rank and date of death. Gallantry awards are shown, and some attachments to other units are noted. A figure adjacent to the surname indicates the battalion, if known. Occasional notes give extra information, such as "drowned" or "died in enemy hands". *Officers Died ...* includes RFC and RAF casualties.

The Roll of Honour: Royal Flying Corps and Royal Air Force for the Great War 1914-18, compiled by H.J.Williamson, lists commissioned fatalities in alphabetical order, with rank and initials. Date of death is usually given and squadron details are included where known. The second part of the book contains an extract from the Commonwealth War Graves Commission Arras Memorial Register, often recording extra information. The last part of the book lists other ranks, with number, rank and year of death. Details have been taken from the *St Katherine's Register*.

The titles mentioned above represent only a fraction of the rolls available; more are listed in the Bibliography.

First World War books

Thousands of books have been written about the 1914-18 War. Any could be informative to a medal researcher, depending on the role of the medal recipient. However, a few volumes could be regarded as indispensable, providing useful starting material for every group of medals researched.

The Times Diary and Index of the War 1914-18, originally published in 1922 and reprinted in 1985, provides a day-by-day account of the war. The book is particularly valuable when researching casualties, identifying military activity on the day in question. It is sometimes possible to find descriptions of naval actions difficult to establish elsewhere.

A Record of the Battles and Engagements of the British Armies in France and Flanders, 1914-18, by Brigadier E.A.James OBE, TD, accurately records units present at every battle on the Western Front, down to brigade level. Brigadier James produced another important title, *British Regiments 1914-18*, which records the wartime activities of every battalion. A typical entry shows date and place of formation, movements around the UK, date sent to theatre of war, brigade assignment, amalgamations, reassignments and eventual disbandment.

Probably the most researched medals for the First World War were awarded to participants in the Battle of the Somme. *British Battalions on the Somme* by Ray Westlake outlines the role of each battalion involved, and is essential for anyone interested in medals associated with Somme veterans. *The First Day of the Somme* by Martin Middlebrook is similarly useful to those researching medals to men who became casualties on 1 July 1916; it gives a blow-by-blow account of events on that bloodiest day in the British Army's long history.

For naval researchers, *British Vessels Lost at Sea 1914-18* is an important reference, containing details of both naval and merchant marine losses. The amount of information varies from entry to entry, but normally shows date lost and approximate location. *A Dictionary of Disasters at Sea during the Age of Steam 1824-1962* in two volumes, by Charles Hocking, is another excellent reference work for naval casualty researchers.

In recent years a number of well-researched and very detailed books have been written about the RFC and RAF. Since so many fewer men were involved in the air war, authors can focus on individuals to a greater degree than in books about the Army or Royal Navy. *A Contemptible Little Flying Corps* by I.McInnes and J.V.Webb is a roll of officers and men serving in the pre-war RFC; 1,400 names are listed, together with much biographical information. Medal entitlements are shown where known. Each day of the air war is documented in *The Sky Their Battlefield* by T.Henshaw. The author examines every known example of aerial combat, and there is an index containing 11,000 names. *Above the Trenches* records Great War fighter aces and flying units from 1915-1920; 800 individual biographies and a comprehensive list of claims document the heroes of the air.

The books listed form only the starting point; the researcher's particular interests will obviously dictate other selections for his bookshelves.

Army, Navy and Air Force Lists

Army, Navy and Air Force Lists provide the starting point when researching any officers' medals over the last two centuries. Hart's Army List is even more attractive, giving details of campaign service. Original copies rarely appear, and fetch high prices when they do. Some useful editions of Hart's Army List have been reprinted by the Naval and Military Press, and although they are not cheap they are at least available. Fortunately they can be consulted at the Public Record Office and various other military archives, museums, libraries and record offices.

General reference works

Military books are not the only published works which featuring people who were awarded medals. Army officers were traditionally drawn from the gentry and to a lesser extent the aristocracy, and (at least up to the end of the Great War) many held titles. When researching officers *Debrett's Peerage* is worth checking. Likewise, *Who Was Who?* or contemporary volumes of *Who's Who?* offer potential for biographical details.

Each collector will have personal views about essential general reference books and his interests will dictate which specialised volumes are indispensible. Experience points to books worth adding to a personal library. Each medal researched can lead into different areas, and the best printed reference to an individual might have no military connections whatsoever. The subject may have become a leading light in industry or a profession, thereby featuring in a trade directory, local history, or any number of other books. Where you look depends upon what leads you discover during the course of research.

There are also some "general" military works which provide excellent background reading, although containing no information specifically about medals. *Nelson's Navy: The Ships, Men and Organisation 1793-1815* by Brian Lavery is an excellent example; this lavish work is an all-encompassing guide to life at sea around the start of the 19th century, and should be required reading for any person keen on researching naval medals from that era. Likewise *The Sailing Navy List* by David Lyon can be consulted by naval medal researchers to find out about the ships upon which their man sailed. It includes details of all Royal Navy vessels from 1688 to 1860.

Regimental magazines

Regimental and formation magazines are an excellent source of material about individuals. They grew in popularity towards the end of the 19th century, and most regiments produced a version to document events. Many continue to the present day, although they may have undergone several changes as regiments merged and remerged. Some ceased publication for periods during the two World Wars, but a few stayed in production.

Regimental journals note the day-to-day trivia of regimental life. Football matches, tug-of-war competitions, educational qualifications, promotions, amateur dramatic productions and concert parties, shooting competitions, and a host of other happenings are featured. Recent awards are difficult to research, and regimental magazines offer one of the best sources of information available. Unlike service records, only released by the MOD many years later, magazine articles featuring individuals can be viewed right up to the present day. Magazines can be seen at regimental museums and are also available at the National Army Museum. They also provide good photographic coverage of men concerned in military and sporting events.

* * *

The most valuable books available to medal researchers are also the most expensive. Original copies of old books have become rare and therefore costly. Out-of-print books reprinted in modern editions are equally expensive due to their inevitably small print runs for a specialist market. However, by being selective and making use of library services a large outlay can be avoided. Some sought-after volumes appear at car boot sales or collectors' fairs, so patience and a good eye can pay dividends.

A bibliography listing books offering potential for medal research appears at the end of this book. It is not exhaustive, merely a guide to the type of titles available. Most of the books on the list have been printed or reprinted in the last few years and are available direct from publishers, or appear frequently on book dealers' lists. Hundreds of excellent works were published prior to this and are much harder to track down.

Specialised researchers will be aware of them and they will become known to those new to the hobby. Finding a personal copy is not so easy.

Research Notes

Charles Hoggett
No search was made, apart from a brief look at *British Battles and Medals* by Joslin, Litherland and Simpkin. The entry describes how Admiral Stopford commanded an allied fleet sent to throw the invading Viceroy of Egypt, Mehemit Ali, out of Syria. The fleet bombarded and captured Acre on 3 November 1840.

Edward Heymer
Edward Heymer took part in the charge of the 16th Lancers at the battle of Aliwal, described in several books. *The Military Memoirs of Lieut-General Sir Joseph Thackwell GCB, KH, Colonel 16th Lancers*, by Colonel H.C.Wylly, were published in 1908. Brigadier Cureton, the officer commanding the cavalry brigade at Aliwal, wrote to Thackwell on 31 January 1846: "... the cavalry behaved extremely well, the 16th Lancers and 3rd Light Cavalry suffered severely, but fully achieved their object ... I do not think the Sikhs will be much inclined to face the British in the open again." Thackwell himself described the battle of Sobraon, where Heymer also fought, although the 16th Lancers played little part in the proceedings.

Edward Heymer had been at the battle of Maharajpoor three years before. Thackwell described how the 16th Lancers advanced at 6a.m. in the right column. Two men and 22 horses from the regiment were killed, and six men wounded. The battle was fought out by infantry, and Thackwell expressed dismay that the cavalry were not deployed.

The best account of the battle of Aliwal was found in a semi-fictional book, *All For a Shilling a Day* by Donald F.Featherstone, which attributes words and deeds to men present on the day. The description of the battle is extremely thrilling and paints a harrowing picture of a cavalry charge. Major General Sir Harry Smith's despatch from Aliwal to the Adjutant General of the Army is reproduced. He wrote: "I directed a squadron of the 16th Lancers under Major Smyth and Captain Pearson to charge a body to the right of the village, which they did in the most gallant and determined style - bearing everything before them, as a squadron under Captain Bere had previously done, going right through a square in the most intrepid manner with the deadly lance."

Sir Harry - himself a hero of the Peninsular War and Waterloo - went on to say that "no troops in any battle on record ever behaved more nobly; British and native, no distinction; cavalry, all vying with HM's 16th Lancers, and striving to head in the repeated charges the enemy fought with much resolution: they maintained frequent rencontres with our cavalry hand to hand. In one charge upon infantry of HM's 16th Lancers, they threw away their muskets and came on with their swords and targets (shields) against the lance."

James Lunt devoted a chapter to Aliwal in his regimental history, *The Scarlet Lancers*. He also explained some quaint regimental customs. Apparently a gong inscribed with regimental battle honours hung from a tripod of lances outside the Regimental Quarterguard; the pennons were kept starched to commemorate the lance pennons found stiff with blood after Aliwal.

Henry Harvey

The Army List was the most essential source of information about Henry Harvey's Army career; it was possible to follow his service through successive volumes. Hart's Army List even described the part he played in the Afghanistan campaign, for which he was awarded the medal. Army List details were as follows:

Commissioned Ensign	...	05/06/1858
To 1/25th	...	8/10/1858
1858-59	...	Gibraltar
Promoted Lieutenant	...	1/04/1860
1860	...	2/25th
1861	...	Aldershot
1862	...	Shorncliffe
1863	...	Edinburgh
1864-68	...	Ceylon
1869	...	Shahjehanpore, Bengal
1870-72	...	Bareilly, Bengal
Promoted Captain	...	15/03/1873 - 1/25th
1873	...	Kinsale
1875	...	Buttevant
1876-78	...	Fyzabad, Bengal
1879	...	Peshawur
1880	...	Afghanistan (Khyber Line Force)
1881	...	Half-pay and promoted Major 1/07/1881
1882-87	...	Bengal
1888	...	not listed
1890	...	Retired List. Promoted Lt.Col.1/07/1888. Retired on same date.

Harvey is listed on the retired list until July 1916.

The most authoritative book written about the Second Afghan War was by Sydney H.Shadbolt; *The Afghan Campaigns of 1878-1880* was published in London in 1882 in two volumes, one of which provided biographical details of every officer engaged in the war while the other described the conduct of the campaign. Major Harvey's service was summarized as follows: "Major H.J.Harvey served with the battalion in the first campaign, taking part in the Bazar Valley Expedition. Commanded a mixed force in a very exposed position in the Khyber, at Landi Khana."

The 1/25th suffered a cholera epidemic at Faizabad during autumn 1878; it therefore appeared unlikely that the battalion would take part in the war. After requesting active service they were ordered to the front on 18 October 1878. On 21 October they were ordered to Jhelun in service order, and arrived three days later. From 1 to 19 November the battalion marched to Haji Shah and joined the 1st Brigade, 2nd Division, part of the Peshawar Valley Field Force. The battalion crossed the Indus on 4 December and advanced to Jamrud. Four companies took

part in the Bazar Valley Expedition during January 1879. One man was killed and two wounded on 26 January, when tribesmen opened fire on piquets. The following day 300 men searched Chinar Hill and killed eight of the enemy.

On 29 January a force was detached from the battalion to destroy the towers at Halwai. The mission was successful, for the loss of one man wounded. The battalion was sent to Landi Kotal to perform escort duties until the first campaign ended. These duties were sometimes extremely arduous. Henry Harvey was not present for the second Afghan campaign.

The Afghan Wars 1839-42 and 1878-80 by Archibald Forbes, London, 1892, also gives an account of the part played by the 1/25th in the war. The Peshawar Valley Field Force, including Harvey's battalion, totalled 10,000 men and 30 guns.

The regimental history, *All the Blue Bonnets, the History of the King's Own Scottish Borderers* by Robert Woollcombe, contains a detailed chapter about events in Afghanistan. Woollcombe amplified the accounts given by Shadbolt and Forbes; he was able to draw upon the memoirs of Lt.Charles Woollcombe, who recalled forced marches in burning heat, freezing nights, and the ever-present threat of cholera. The Bazar Valley Expedition involved four companies from the 1/25th, with cavalry, 28 elephants and two Royal Horse Artillery guns. The expedition built *sangars* on high ground to dominate the passes while the main force advanced. They demolished defensive towers constructed within fortified villages. The enemy fought a rearguard action, sniping at encampments by night and ambushing any isolated men or small parties. In other words, this was an absolutely typical example of campaigning against the tough and crafty tribesmen of the North-West Frontier. The regimental diary recorded the object of the expedition as to punish the Zakka tribe, who remained intractable; another object was to explore unknown territory between the Bara Valley and Tirah, while impressing the inhabitants with the long reach of the British Empire.

The wartime diary of Harvey's daughter Winifred was published in 1995 under the title *The Battle of Newlands*, describing the German occupation of the Harvey family home in Guernsey during the Second World War. A biographical note mentions Colonel and Mrs Harvey, stating that he had served in the Indian Army and retired at the age of 47; he bought a property in Guernsey in the Village de Putron before he married a woman 14 years younger than himself. In 1906 he bought Newlands. The Harveys were what was known in those days as an "Army family"; his son, also Henry, followed him into the Army, and his brother attained general rank.

Joseph Full

No search was made. As a private, Full was unlikely to be mentioned in any books, and never took part in any military engagement.

David Boyce

No trace of David Boyce was found in any printed material. However, the role of his battalion, the 9th Royal Irish Fusiliers, is very well documented. No battalion history was ever published, but the *History of the Ulster Division* by Cyril Falls relates the story of all 36th Division units during the Great War. *Orange, Green and Khaki* by Tom Johnstone contains similar information.

Both books describe the battle of Langemarck, Third Ypres, where Boyce was wounded on 16 August 1917. Troops advanced through clinging mud towards impregnable concrete gun emplacements which proved virtually untouched by the Allied artillery barrage. Many were massacred by enemy artillery in assembly trenches before going over the top; those who survived were mown down in swathes by enemy machine guns. The thinned ranks could not pass by strongpoints as planned, and were forced instead to take each one in turn. Amazingly, survivors from the 9th RIF, on the extreme right of the divisional front, took an enemy position at Hill 35, sweeping the Germans back from prepared positions. For long hours the battalion clung to the gains made until eventually forced to withdraw by enemy fire. A total of 1,278 wounded other ranks from the division passed through the dressing station between 16 and 18 August; my grandfather David Boyce was one of them.

The Royal Irish Fusiliers by Henry Harris goes into some detail about the battle of Langemarck. Harris describes No Man's Land as a badly cratered quagmire. Fifty casualties were suffered from artillery fire before the attack was launched. The battalion advanced behind the barrage, only to be met by enemy artillery and machine gun fire from pillboxes. The fire from a strongpoint at Hill 35 stopped the advance until it was taken by a rush of men. By then the battalion had fallen behind the protecting barrage and was at the mercy of every German machine gun. Attempts to dig in on Hill 35 failed; the CO was mortally wounded, and too few men were left to defend the position. Survivors retired yard by yard under heavy fire, incurring further casualties, until back at their original trenches. During the assault ten officers and 36 men were killed, with 335 wounded and 85 reported missing.

From my grandfather's account, he was probably one of the missing. He talked of lying in No Man's Land awaiting stretcher bearers and fearing discovery by a German patrol. Given the conditions in which the battle was fought, the determined resistance of the enemy and the weariness and disorientation of survivors, it is a wonder he was ever brought in.

George Reeve

Between his enlistment in 1902 and the outbreak of the Great War, Reeve was regularly mentioned in the regimental magazine *Faugh a Ballagh* for sports and shooting achievements.

Reeve featured several times in *The First Battalion, The Faugh-a-Ballaghs in the Great War* by Brigadier A.R.Burrowes. He was wounded on 18 January 1916, and the regimental history reveals that German snipers were extremely active on that day; a Lt.Kirby was badly wounded, and the battalion war diary later revealed that Reeve was slightly wounded in the same incident.

George Reeve was wounded again on 12 October 1916. The Borrowes history explains that an attack took place to establish a position for an assault on Le Transloy. Lieutenant Reeve's battalion left the trenches at 1405hrs, but followed a creeping barrage too closely and suffered casualties. The ensuing delay allowed the Germans to man machine guns at a strongpoint untouched by artillery. Repeated attacks were repulsed at heavy cost, until the attack was abandoned. Six officers were killed and only five officers and 209 other ranks were left unwounded.

The history details Reeve's MC action on 3 May 1917. The battalion left their trenches at 0415hrs and came under heavy fire from the Rouex Chemical Works. They became mixed up with men from other battalions, taking heavy casualties from machine gun fire. "Second Lieutenant G.Reeve, although wounded, reorganized these troops, and dug in on a line west of the Chemical Works as far north as the railway line, and held this position throughout the day. He was recalled at 2210, and withdrew, bringing his wounded with him." His whereabouts had been unknown until 1400hrs, when he and his men were found by a reconnaisance patrol sent out from the battalion line.

The battalion history tells the day-to-day story of life in and out of the line. From other research it is possible to work out Reeve's movements on a daily basis. Such a record almost makes other research superfluous.

A chance reading of *Shot at Dawn* by Julian Putkowski and Julian Sykes threw up another mention of George Reeve. Private G.Hanna, 1st Royal Irish Fusiliers, was sentenced to death on 5 November 1917 after absenting himself just five hours after joining the battalion. Lieutenant George Reeve was selected to command the firing party. The death sentence was carried out on 6 November under Reeve's command.

A variety of other books refer to battles the battalion was involved in, portraying the horrors Reeve experienced at the front. He went through everything from Mons in 1914 to the start of 1918, apart from short periods of convalescence, so he fought in nearly every battalion action during the war. It is truly remarkable that he survived as long as he did.

Thomas Davis

No book research into Thomas Davis was carried out. He is likely to be listed in various RAF and Humberside Memorial Rolls, and numerous books provide background reading about the role of RAF Bomber Command during the Second World War. A history of No.9 Squadron has not been traced to date.

CHAPTER 11: NEWSPAPERS AND MAGAZINES

Contemporary newspapers and periodicals are an excellent source of material for medal researchers. They sometimes provide the compelling nuggets of information which add spice and character to a dry litany of places and dates. This should not be surprising. After all, lively stories are the lifeblood of a news editor, so where better to look for interesting tales about "our man" than between the pages of a newspaper? Who is to say that he did not make headlines at some point in his life, for whatever reason?

While it may be rather fanciful to hope for an extravagant story featuring the man under research, there is always the chance of finding an occasional paragraph mentioning his activities. Few people travel through life without their name appearing in print at one time or another. Away from the banner headlines of the national press, weekly provincial papers have churned out the seemingly mundane trivia of everyday life for well over a century. This "trivia" leaps off the page when it concerns the man we are interested in, suddenly turning his shadowy two-dimensional figure into a living, breathing man of his time.

Old newspapers also include an abundance of articles about medal campaigns. These provide a contemporary insight into the conduct of the war and indicate what sort of life the soldier endured. General reports may even shed light on individual actions at which our man is known to have been present. It is possible to find mention of incidents concerning his unit or ship which were hitherto unknown.

Background research into large scale campaigns, like the Boer War, is largely dictated by clasps awarded with the medal. It can be worth reading papers from around the dates when an action took place to discover more about the occurrences of the day. Bear in mind that reports usually appeared in the press long after the action took place; however, given the documented dates of a medal action, it is a simple matter to retrieve daily reports from correspondents about the progress of fighting.

Campaigns since the Crimean War have been well reported. Sir William Howard Russell was the first true war correspondent, as we would understand the term today. His despatches from the Crimea were published in *The Times*, and were forthright, accurate and dispassionate - telling the British public of the hardships suffered by ill-equipped, undernourished British soldiers during the severe winter of 1854-55. Russell established a tradition for factual war reporting, laying the groundwork for following generations.

However, articles about people rather than large events are of much greater significance to medal researchers. Service personnel of all ranks are no different from anyone else - they do things, good and bad, which are highlighted in the press (particularly their home town press). If anything, military figures are more newsworthy than the average civilian; people love to read about their heroic deeds - and they also like to read about uniformed men involved in scandal. Between these two extremes lie reports about all the daily happenings of life.

Notable military personalities usually figured regularly in national paper reports, and received substantial coverage in their local provincial press. When researching medals awarded to a high-ranking officer it should not be difficult to find reference to his activities. Discovering mentions of junior ranks is not so easy, but do not let this put you off. Even the most lowly soldier can feature in a local paper report for all manner of reasons. The difficulty is in not knowing where to start looking.

It is important to be realistic about the likelihood of a particular soldier being named in print. Given the huge numbers of newspapers published, it is necessary to define research parameters from the outset. To be successful it is vital to establish as many known facts about the man as possible, and to arrive at the newspaper library armed with lines of enquiry. Newspapers are not a primary source of research into individuals, and it is unrealistic to begin searching without something concrete to go on. So what is likely to have been reported?

The answer is obvious: news. Therefore, consider anything known about the soldier that could be newsworthy. Various military happenings make news. The more obvious ones are acts of gallantry, courts martial or appearances in civilian courts, sporting events, promotions, medal presentations, and of course death and wounds. The medals act as the key to locating material. Any gallantry medals forming part of the group probably came to the attention of the press, even during the First World War when thousands of men were decorated. The campaign medals and clasps identify dates and places where the soldier was present. Research carried out at the PRO probably identified postings between campaigns and may have highlighted other dates and places to scrutinise. Life-saving and sports medals are often dated, making it easier to discover whether the relevant events were reported in the newspapers.

An impression of the exploit of Col.Bell VC, Royal Welch Fusiliers, published in the Illustrated London News *of 2 June 1860.*

If anything noteworthy is known about the soldier's subsequent civilian career then this too may present possibilities. It is worth checking local papers for births, marriages and deaths; such columns are generally mundane, but occasionally reveal details of the man. Obituaries of senior officers in the broadsheet papers can be an excellent starting point for research.

Three local papers are likely to publish items about any given individual. These are the newspaper serving his place of origin; papers published close to where he was stationed; and papers published in the region of any significant incident. Having established happenings which may be newsworthy and where these events might be reported, it is time to start looking.

The **British Newspaper Library**, situated opposite Colindale Underground station in Colindale Avenue, London NW9, is the major newspaper archive in the United Kingdom. Original copies of national and provincial newspapers are stored there, within the confines of a large, rather drab building. A visit to the library is a pleasant experience, however. There is no charge for the service, and the old newspapers take the researcher back to different eras through evocative advertisements and quaint reports from bygone times. The library is open Monday to Saturday from 10am to 4.45pm; parking space is limited, but it is possible to leave a vehicle in side roads within easy walking distance.

The main collection dates back to 1801, although there are some earlier provincial issues. Most papers published prior to this date are held at the **British Library**, Great Russell Street, WC1. Magazines, journals and foreign publications are also available at Colindale.

Visitors are issued with a reader's pass, valid for one year, after providing proof of identity. After selecting a vacant desk they are free to explore the massive holdings at their disposal. A catalogue lists newspapers held, alphabetically by place of publication. The index shows newspaper titles and outlines date coverage available. A separate card index lists papers and magazines alphabetically by title.

When likely papers are identified they can be ordered by completing simple carbon-duplicated slips. The specified papers are delivered to the researcher's desk in large bound volumes, each containing a span of original papers to cover the specified date. With provincial papers the binder normally covers a year, and up to four may be ordered at any one time. Initial orders take up to an hour, but by immediately re-ordering on receipt of the first batch it is possible to establish a rolling delivery to make the best use of time. Some newspapers are on microfilm, and film readers are available in a separate room.

Copies are obtained by completing a duplicated form and placing a marker at the relevant page; the form can be added to throughout the day. There are a range of charges for photocopying, but a full page copy represents about the best value. It is possible to order enhanced copies and photographic copies, although these are considerably more expensive. At the time of writing photocopies range from £0.40p to £2.00, depending on the size of the newspaper. Enhanced copies cost from £9.50 to £17.50, and photographs from £21.15 up to £28.78. Readers have the choice of taking their own copies

from microfilm or paying slightly more for copying by library staff.

The huge holdings of the newspaper archive serve to underline that aimless blanket searches are very time-consuming and rarely rewarding. When researching a "standard" medal group, with no knowledge of any specific details and where the recipient survived the conflict, there is little chance of a useful result. Prior to the Boer War it is rare to find any news items about other ranks. The only exceptions are individuals recognized for gallant deeds or very extraordinary feats; sometimes casualties feature. Early weekly regional papers consisted largely of advertisements and merely amplified national news stories. Most soldiers originated from the lower reaches of society, meaning that their actions were of no consequence to the majority of newspaper readers.

Suddenly, however, when manpower requirements escalated during the Boer War, military tentacles reached further than ever before into mainstream society. As a consequence soldiers became more newsworthy. Families with men in South Africa wanted to read about what was happening to them. Some provincial papers adopted their local regiment and printed regular bulletins about their endeavours. This is when newspapers become interesting to medal researchers. Soldiers' names were sprinkled throughout reports, which mentioned actions they fought in, casualties or fever victims, and sometimes more interesting material about a particular soldier or group of soldiers.

A vastly greater expansion of the military occured during the First World War by the recruitment of millions of volunteers and, from 1916, conscripts from civil society. Regional papers were full of news about local men; towns and country areas were immensely proud of "their" battalions, and those at home eagerly awaited the slightest news about them. In many cases a full page or more was devoted to the activities of the unit.

The coverage was massive and very varied. Soldiers wrote to newspapers recounting their experiences; families requested news of missing relatives from their comrades at the front; obituaries appeared, sometimes detailing the circumstances of the soldier's death and giving other interesting background information. Acts of gallantry were proudly reported, along with items about men taken prisoner, promotions, wounded men, and miraculous discoveries of men thought dead. War poems composed by local soldiers appeared alongside requests for food parcels. To scan the pages of a local paper published during the Great War is an excellent way of grasping the mood of the time.

Officers who won fame - several of them posthumously - in the Zulu and Second Afghan Wars, depicted in The Graphic *of 1 March 1879. They include not only famous Isandlwana casualties such as Cols.Pulleine and Durnford, and the Rorke's Drift VCs Lts.Chard and Bromhead; but also Maj.Gen.Maude, commanding 2nd Division, Peshawar Field Force, in which Henry Harvey of the 25th Foot served.*

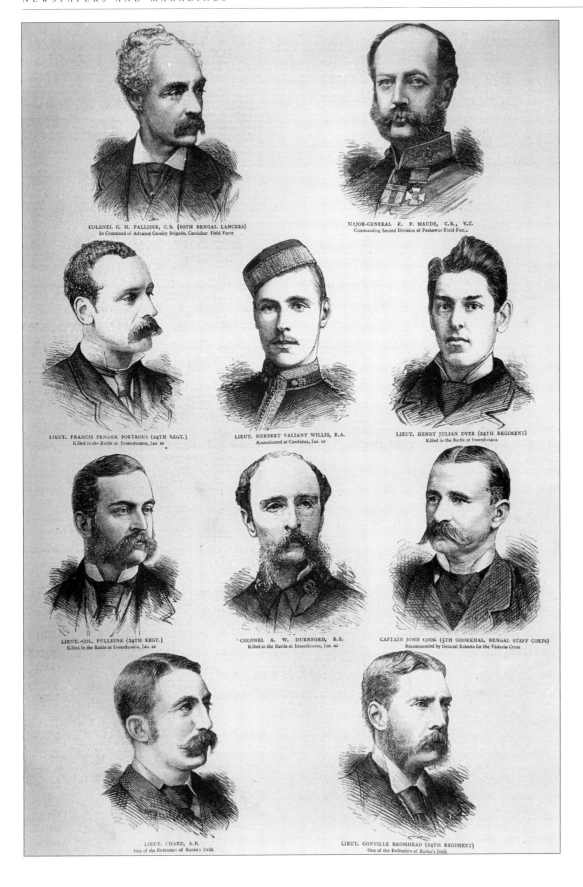

COLONEL C. H. PALLISER, C.B. (10TH BENGAL LANCERS)
In Command of Advance Cavalry Brigade, Candahar Field Force

MAJOR-GENERAL F. F. MAUDE, C.B., V.C.
Commanding Second Division of Peshawur Field Force

LIEUT. FRANCIS PENDER PORTEOUS (24TH REGT.)
Killed in the Battle at Insandusana, Jan. 22

LIEUT. HERBERT VALIANT WILLIS, R.A.
Assassinated at Candahar, Jan. 12

LIEUT. HENRY JULIAN DYER (24TH REGIMENT)
Killed in the Battle at Insandusana

LIEUT.-COL. PULLEINE (24TH REGT.)
Killed in the Battle at Insandusana, Jan. 22

COLONEL A. W. DURNFORD, R.E.
Killed in the Battle at Insandusana, Jan. 22

CAPTAIN JOHN COOK (5TH GOORKHAS, BENGAL STAFF CORPS)
Recommended by General Roberts for the Victoria Cross

LIEUT. CHARD, R.E.
One of the Defenders of Rorke's Drift

LIEUT. GONVILLE BROMHEAD (24TH REGIMENT)
One of the Defenders of Rorke's Drift

This trend of reporting has continued to the present. The style is less jingoistic now, reflecting changing attitudes, but the essential mood is the same when British soldiers are involved in any conflict. (My own local paper gives widespread attention to local soldiers posted to Bosnia, regularly reporting on their progress.)

Newspapers are an excellent source of photographs, particularly for soldiers from the Great War period. Men of all ranks were pictured regularly, often in connection with gallantry awards and casualties. Group photos of men leaving for the front, others of wounded men convalescing, and small portrait pictures of correspondents were also common. It is always satisfying to obtain a photograph of the man awarded the medals in your collection, and newspapers - despite their spotty reproduction of low resolution "screened" photos on coarse newsprint -

When researching the press coverage of a particular action remember that illustrations might be published several months after the event. These portraits of Zulu War casualties and heroes appeared in The Graphic *of 3 May 1879, more than three months later.*

often provide the best hope of this.

When researching casualty groups the best starting point is at the end: the most notable feature of many soldiers' lives was, tragically, the manner of their death. After establishing a date and place of death from sources mentioned in previous chapters, look at likely local papers for an obituary. If there is one, it may mention other newsworthy deeds which can be researched in their turn. Likewise with a gallantry group, articles concerning the bravery award may mention other acts to search for.

For collectors engaged in research of particular battalions or regiments the first step is to identify the newspaper providing the most information about the unit. For instance, the author's research into medals awarded to the Royal Irish Fusiliers for the Great War has identified the *Armagh Guardian* as providing the most extensive coverage; other newspapers contain items about the regiment, but the most concentrated reporting is found in this paper. Be prepared to patient, however: when researching a particular name it takes approximately one day to work through copies of the paper from 1914 to 1918.

LIEUT. F. H. MACDOWELL, R.E.
Killed at Isandlwhana, Jan. 22, 1879

LIEUT. H. H. HARWARD, 80TH REGIMENT
The Only Surviving Officer of Intombe

MR. W. A. DUNNE, COMMISSARIAT DEPARTMENT
One of the Defenders of Rorke's Drift

LIEUT. G. F. J. HODSON, 24TH REGIMENT
Killed at Isandlwhana, Jan. 22, 1879

LIEUT. J. P. DALY, 24TH REGIMENT
Killed at Isandlwhana, Jan. 22, 1879

Provincial papers are an excellent means of identifying soldiers wounded in action. Even when it is known that an individual was wounded it can be extremely difficult to track down details. Local papers usually listed all local casualties, whether killed, wounded or shell-shocked, on a weekly basis. Careful examination of war diaries at the PRO may indicate likely occasions when a soldier might have become a casualty. Citations for gallantry awards are sometimes printed in full; promotions are noted; and there are often excellent eyewitness accounts of actions in which the local unit was involved. The *Armagh Guardian* is far from unique; papers from all over the country mention individual soldiers, even if only a brief paragraph about their death, offering condolences to a local family. Other serving members of the family and fatalities are often noted.

It is always worth telephoning the library before a visit, to check whether they hold the run of papers sought; apart from gaps in copies held, many newspapers have ceased publication at various dates, some to reappear under another name or after amalgamation.

Researchers outside London should check with a local County Record Office before travelling, to see if they stock the required publications. Major libraries can also be helpful in this respect. Alternatively, staff at Colindale can carry out research by post, although there is a significant delay owing to the number of requests received.

The library at Colindale also holds **magazines**, which can yield good results for the researcher. Periodicals such as *The Illustrated London News* and county magazines frequently covered military items. As with newspapers, the more knowledge one already has, the more productive research is likely to be.

Regimental magazines, by and large, do not fit the criteria of the newspaper library collection. However, some forces' newspapers are held at the library, particularly those published around the end of the Second World War. Copies of *Union Jack* from around 1943 to 1946 are listed, in varying editions, each dedicated to a particular theatre of war. Certain individual units produced in-house papers and a few examples survive from a variety of units, such as *Cock o' the North* produced by the 1st Battalion, Gordon Highlanders in 1946-47; *The Lincoln Imp*, organ of the 4th Battalion, Lincolnshire Regiment in 1945-46; or *The Minden Post* produced for the KOYLI in 1948-51 - there are several others. Presumably in the immediate aftermath of war men found themselves with time on their hands and put it to good use. It goes without saying that if you are researching medals to one of these units from the period, such elusive pulications can be an excellent source.

The library holds a run of *The Regiment*, a journal about soldiers and the Army containing many personal details, dating from 1896 to 1917. There are also copies of the *Royal Engineers Journal* running from 1896 to 1904. More recent service magazines such as *Soldier* are also present.

Trade journals are worth checking for the First World War, given that the majority of participants were civilians in uniform rather than professional soldiers. News concerning them was of interest to their erstwhile colleagues, and was likely to appear in magazines associated with their profession.

Newspapers offer unique opportunities to embellish the story of a given soldier, particularly those serving in the present century - who often prove surprisingly frustrating to research by conventional means. It is pleasing to add some human colour to their service record by discovering interesting items from an unusual source.

Research Notes

Charles Hoggett

The only newspaper mention found to date was in the deaths column of the *Portsmouth Times and County Journal* on Saturday 7 February 1903. It reads: "HOGGETT - On the 1st inst, at the Green Posts, London Road, Charles Hoggett, aged 85."

Edward Heymer

No mention was found, although this is hardly surprising given his brief life after discharge from the Army.

Henry Harvey

An obituary notice was found in the *Guernsey Star:*

"The death occurred at noon Monday of Lieut.-Colonel Henry James Harvey, late King's Own Scottish Borderers, at his residence, 'Newlands', Prince Albert Road, at the age of 80 years. Colonel Harvey had been ill for some weeks. With him passes away a member of an old Guernsey family who have done much for their island. The Colonel left the Service in the eighties and came here, serving on the Town Douzaine, Poor Law Board and as Constable of St Peter Port. He was treasurer of the local branch of the CMS for over 20 yrs and at one time churchwarden of Holy Trinity Church. He leaves a widow and three children to mourn his loss: Captain HJ Harvey, KOSB, who is at Peshawar, India, and the Misses W and E Harvey, and also a brother, Major-General JR Harvey, Mount Durand, and three sisters."

A full report also followed the funeral, in the *Guernsey Evening Press* of Saturday 9 July 1921. The article describes the funeral at the Town Church, and how he was laid to rest at Foulon Cemetery. It also records the hymns and mourners.

Henry Harvey's widow Beatrice died on 4 April 1930 and her death and funeral were also fully reported in the *Guernsey Evening Press*.

Joseph Full

The only pieces found relate to his death. The *Plymouth Evening Herald* contained an obituary notice placed by Full's family for three days, from 14 to 16 May 1935: "FULL - In loving memory of our dear father, Joseph, died 13th May, aged 90, at 53 Lisson Grove. Sadly missed by his sons, daughters, sons-in-law, daughters-in-law, also his grandchildren. Re-united." On 18 May the same paper printed a brief entry in the "Thankyou" column: "FULL - The relatives of the late Mr Joseph Full wish to THANK all friends for kind expressions of sympathy; also for beautiful floral tributes sent in their recent sad bereavement."

These brief notices show a different side to Joseph Full the Royal Marine. He may never have advanced in rank during his

In the Council Chamber.

A Cogan-Whiting Combination.

The Wounded and Halfpenny Fares

We are told that "adversity brings strange bedfellows." Similarly the exigencies of debate bring strange alliances. There were some curious combinations during the course of Monday's meeting of the Town Council. Imagine, if you can, any affinity between Councillor Cogan and Alderman Whiting. Their opinions and policies are as a rule as opposite as the poles, and evidently the doctor realised the incongruity of the situation, for he exclaimed, "I don't know that I have ever agreed with him before." And we think he was about right. Time was, and not so very long ago, when Ald. Whiting and Councillor Cogan were at daggers drawn, the one accusing the other of being a Tory obstructionist, barring the path of progress, or words to that effect.

What was the bond which bound such antagonistic elements together? Strangely enough it was the proposition of Councillor Phipps to lop a year off the school age during the war, to enable the manufacturers to get more labour. The Education Committee had refused to do it, and Councillor Phipps was desirous that they should think it over. There was a decided cleft over the question, which split the Council into three parties. There was Councillor Phipps, and those who thought with him, who argued that there was no harm in obtaining additional labour by employing boys over 13 where their parents wished it. The safeguards promised were that they must be physically fit, the employment must be suitable, they are to spend two evenings a week at a night school, and the concession was to be for the period of the war only.

Opposed to this were those whom we regard as idealists, like Alderman Hill and Alderman Campion, business men like Councillor D. P. Taylor—who got very angry with Alderman Whiting—Alderman James and Councillor Wareing, who believed the last year of school life, that between 13 and 14, vital to the child. The third division was the Socialist party, who saw in the scheme a desire for cheap labour and a reduction of wages generally, and were not slow of accusing the manufacturers of desiring "child slavery." In the end, however, Councillor Phipps was successful, and the Education Committee is to have another opportunity of considering the question. One of the strongest points made for the reduction was that of Alderman Whiting, that during the last year the children as a rule only repeated the lessons of the previous year.

Far Cotton members were up in arms over the curtailment of their tramway facilities, but the Council supported the Committee in this, though on the question of half-penny fares for wounded soldiers the boot was, we were pleased to see, on the other foot. The Ex-Mayor spoiled the market, so to speak, for Councillor Drage, who, having prepared an amendment on the subject, had the mortification of being forestalled. Councillor Parker moved the reference back in the hope that

H. MOSS & SONS.
30, GOLD STREET.

Practical Picture Frame Makers,
Artists' Colourmen, Fretwood Merchants.

Large assortment of British Made Toys.

the facilities would be retained, and Councillor Drage, who seconded, declared amid laughter that he had been beaten by a short head. Councillor Drage had, we believe, only intended to move in the interest of the wounded soldiers, and in this we are with him, for the average soldier, fit and well, is quite as capable of paying full fare, or walking, as the case may be, as a civilian. With the wounded it is different. They ride to ease their aching limbs, and some concession ought to be made to them. Councillor Parker's amendment was accepted, however, and the Tram Committee will have the opportunity of reconsidering the question. In view of the fact that the Chairman, Councillor T. D. Lewis, admitted that the case of the wounded had been overlooked in coming to a decision, there is good ground for supposing that they will receive sympathetic treatment.

Life Saved by a Tin Box

Photo "Independent."
Pte. R. Gates, 1st Northamptons, holding the tin box which saved his life, and Pte. G. Gibbs, who was badly wounded at Aubers Ridge.

The other day the above two wounded heroes of the Northamptons called at the "Independent" Office to thank us for the gifts we have been able to send out to the Regiment through the generosity of our readers. One of them was Pte. R. Gates, "A" Co., 1st Northamptons, whose miraculous escape from certain death was described in our columns last year by Corpl. Freir, and illustrated with a sketch done in the trenches. His good luck followed him up to October 13th, when he was gassed, sustained a bullet wound in his left arm, and is also suffering from rheumatism. He triumphantly produced the souvenir which saved his life, as well as the bullet which was stopped by the tin

box he was carrying in his pocket. "When I was hit," he said, "it seemed like a blow from a sledge hammer. I staggered back and then began to count my limbs so to speak. On unbuttoning my tunic a bullet dropped out. It had shot off two buttons and gone through a tin of peppermint lozenges in my side pocket. But for this tin I should not be here to tell the tale." Pte. Gates was in the battle of Aubers Ridge, and was lying on the field for fifteen hours. "The way the Northamptons went into that action was," he said, "simply splendid. Immediately poor Major Cautley gave the order 'Over the parapet boys' we advanced just as though we were on a ceremonial parade. I shall never forget the wonderful bravery of the officers, particularly Capt. Blomfield Dickson. He was one of the most heroic officers who went into the action, and was killed hanging on the barbed wire." Pte. Gates added, "We all said the 'Independent' was our best friend out there, and the tins of pine-apple you sent us were the talk of the Regiment."

Pte. G. Gibbs, who is a native of March, has been in the thick of the fighting, and has been twice wounded, the last time being at Aubers Ridge when he had a lump taken out of his right shoulder by shrapnel. He, too, was full of thanks for the comforts sent out through the "Independent" fund, in fact, if only our subscribers could personally meet these gallant boys and realise for themselves how grateful they are for these gifts they would feel amply rewarded for any sacrifices they have made for their sakes.

Promoted on the Field.

And Recommended for the D.C.M.

Sec.-Lieut. G. Reeve.

A splendid record of service is possessed by Sec.-Lieut. George Reeve, who has just been given a commission in France, in his own regiment, the Royal Irish Fusiliers. He has served in the regiment for just over 13 years, since he 16 in fact, and earned rapid promotion. He was flag sergeant and instructor of signallers when war broke out, but was subsequently promoted Regimental Sergt.-Major. In addition to being given a commission he has also been recommended for the D.C.M.

Sec.-Lieut. George Reeve is the eldest son of Mr. and Mrs. George Reeve, of King Street. His father served for 13 years in the Militia, and three of his brothers are also serving, Pte. Sam Reeve with the 7th Northamptons in France, Corpl. Harry Reeve with the 8th Northamptons, and Pte. Sidney Reeve with the 3rd Northamptons, a family record to be proud of.

Patriotic Employees.

The employees of the firm of Messrs. J. T. Meadows and Son, have set a wonderful example of patriotism. Of the 45 employed on the outbreak of war 30 joined the colours. Five have since been killed, and 17 or 18 wounded, several more than once. Mr. J. T. Meadows is himself an old soldier, having served in the Northamptons.

At low right, this page of the Northampton Independent *of 11 December 1915 gives details of George Reeve's field commission and recommendation for the DCM - a first rate example of the value of combing local press reports. (By permission of the British Library).*

service with the Victorian "Bootnecks"; but he was a happy family man who left behind him children and grandchildren when he finally died in the enormously changed world of the mid-1930s.

David Boyce

My grandfather never trod the path of fame; he was an honourable and decent man, but making news was not his style. He worked, cared for his family, went to war when duty called - and eventually died, almost unnoticed outside his immediate circle. So at first glance the research potential offered by the Newspaper Library seemed pretty limited. Yet Colindale provided the single most sought-after piece of information about David Boyce, which I was unable to discover from any other source.

More than anything else, I wanted to find out where and when my grandfather was wounded; and the edition of the *Armagh Guardian* published on 7 September 1917 contained the answer. The paper printed a long list of casualties from the recent action involving the 9th Royal Irish Fusiliers, and 22888 L/Cpl.D.Boyce appeared on the list. The recent action was the battle of Langemarck on 16 August 1917, and this knowledge opened the door to further research. The *Armagh Guardian* also revealed that David's brothers were wounded on several occasions during the war.

George Reeve

The heroism displayed by George Reeve during the Great War ensured that he would feature in numerous newspaper articles. Indeed, so much was written about him that only a summary can appear here. Reeve made news at his place of origin, the place where his regiment was based, and the place where events took place.

The most detailed reports were found in the *Northampton Independent*, published where Reeve grew up. The first article, headlined "Promoted on the Field - And Recommended for the DCM", appeared on 11 December 1915 together with a portrait photo: "A splendid record of service is possessed by Sec.-Lieut. George Reeve, who has just been given a commission in France, in his own regiment, the Royal Irish Fusiliers. He has served in the regiment for just over thirteen years, since he was 16 in fact, and earned rapid promotion. He was flag sergeant and instructor of signallers when war broke out, but was subsequently promoted Regimental Sergeant Major. In addition to being given a commission he has also been recommended for the DCM.

"Sec.-Lieut.George Reeve is the eldest son of Mr and Mrs George Reeve, of King Street. His father served for 13 years in the Militia, and three of his brothers are also serving, Pte Sam Reeve with the 7th Northamptons in France, Corpl Harry Reeve with the 8th Northamptons and Pte Sidney Reeve with the 3rd Northamptons, a family record to be proud of."

An even longer report with another photograph was featured in the *Independent* on 6 January 1917. The headline this time was "Local Officer's Thrilling Experiences". Part of the previous article was repeated, with the following additions: "He went to France with the original Expeditionary Force in mid-August 1914, and fought at Mons and all through the retreat nearly to Paris. He took part in the battle of the Marne, and then fought in the battles of the Aisne and the Oise and the many minor engagements which culminated in the fearful battle of Ypres.

"Early in 1915 he was promoted Co.-Sergt.-Major and awarded the Military Medal for bravery at the second battle of Ypres. The following July when on patrol duty near Hill 60 he came into contact with an enemy patrol and was wounded in the head with a hand grenade. In November 1915 he was promoted Lieutenant on the field and kept in his old battalion, the Royal Irish; and his splendid services caused him to be singled out for mention in Sir John French's New Year despatches.

"In February last while raiding enemy trenches near Beaumont Hamel, Lieut.Reeve was wounded in the leg, and on leaving hospital he was granted a month's leave at home. He returned to the Somme, and during the October operations he was again wounded in the leg and sustained severe shell shock while gallantly leading a company to the attack on enemy positions. He has now thoroughly recovered, and expects soon to return to his battalion at the front.

"Before the war Lieut.Reeve was a well known army athlete, representing his battalion in all branches of sport. Three of his brothers have joined the forces, and one of these, in the 7th Northamptons, has been missing since August 17th."

(The repeated emphasis on Reeve's being commissioned into his old battalion is significant. Commissioned rankers were normally transferred, since it had long been the conventional wisdom that discipline might suffer if they found themselves commanding men who had once been their comrades in the ranks. That Reeve returned to the 1st RIF was a clear tribute to the leadership qualities he had demonstrated as a warrant officer.)

Meanwhile, events involving Reeve had not passed unnoticed by the *Armagh Guardian*, published at the home of the regiment. His Military Medal was announced on 17 November 1915. Second Lieutenant Reeve was listed among the 1st Battalion wounded on 28 January 1916. On 25 May 1917 he appeared again on the wounded list, under the heading "1st Battalion in Action Again - Heavy Casualty List". Reeve's Military Cross was announced in the *Armagh Guardian* on 27 July 1917, complete with the full citation.

George Reeve's tragic death was widely reported. Three Northampton papers carried the story, as well as several in Colchester, where the accident occurred. A short article also appeared in *The Times*. The subsequent inquest received widespread coverage in Northampton and Essex (strangely, there was no mention in the *Armagh Guardian*). The most informative report in Northampton papers was printed in the *Northampton Independent* of 26 October 1918 under the headline "Killed in Motor Accident - Gallant Officer's Death": "The funeral took place with military honours at Northampton, on Monday, of Lieut George Reeve MC MM, Royal Irish Fusiliers, who having survived the dangers of strenuous campaigning from Mons to the Somme, was run down and killed by a motor car at Colchester recently, his skull being fractured". The article lists his military achieve-

Somme Heroes of the Northamptons

Taken at a training centre in England, the above photo shows a number of Northampton men who survived the awful battle of the Somme, and have returned to this country. Among those in the group can be recognised Pte. C. Cox, Pte. W. Brown, Lc.-Corpl. A. Smith, Corpl. Elliott, Pte. H. Woodhams, Lc.-Corpl. L. Harper, Corpl. C. Wykes, Lc.-Corpl. W. E. Lawcock, and Pte. H. E. Hudson, and every service battalion of the Northamptonshire Regiment in France is represented.

In the Council Chamber.

New Year's Gifts for Teachers.

There was magic in the air on New Year's night if one may judge by the felicity of the Town Council meeting on Monday. With perhaps a solitary exception, every member seemed busy turning over a new leaf on which was plainly writ "Brevity is the soul of wit." Never has the Council Chamber been the scene of such blissful unanimity; all were of one mind, and the business ran along as smoothly as well oiled machinery. Apparently the general public anticipated the harmony which prevailed, for the seats of the scornful were unoccupied.

Everyone got a pat on the back, except Alderman Whiting, who made the mistake of preaching to the converted for the full time allowed—ten minutes. Northampton's citizens were the first to receive complimentary reference. We are becoming more studious, according to Coun. Robinson, who told us that 368,813 issues were made from the Free Library during the year, a record, and an increase of 23,000 over last year. We are living in strenuous times, but still we find time to read, and an increasing number have leisure to study educational literature.

Not only are we growing more studious, but Coun. Taylor revealed the pleasing fact that we are becoming more thrifty, for we are saving £3,000 a week under the War Savings scheme. This sum is paid in every week by the 100 associations formed in the town some of which have as many as 1,000 members. "And this £3,000 will be £4,000 in five years time," proudly announced Coun. Taylor. "Do we understand that £3,000 is coming in every week?" asked Coun. Catt in astonishment, to the amusement of his colleagues, and he seemed hardly to believe it when the answer came in the affirmative from several quarters.

Well as Northampton has done, however, the elementary school teachers did better, for all except headmasters got a rise of £10 a year. Quite a nice New Year's gift, though the ratepayers will not receive the news quite as joyfully, as it means £4,000 a year, or threepence on the rates. Not a voice was raised against the increase, and probably the teachers wish they had emulated "Oliver Twist" and asked for more. It was over this rise that Ald. Whiting ruffled the serenity of the proceedings by flogging a dead horse for ten minutes, much to the disgust of the Mayor, whose efforts to prevent what he considered digressions were in vain. Coun. Taylor made the most startling announcement

of the discussion when he declared that although the average salary paid to Northampton teachers is lower than the average of fifty selected areas, the aggregate is higher. This is a serious state of affairs, for it shows that despite the number of teachers who have joined the Army, our schools are still over-staffed. When can we expect our Education Committee to put its house in order and close superfluous schools? Surely there never was such a time as the present for such action, when numbers of temporary teachers are engaged. This would certainly be more valuable to the public than the promised scheme to "still further develop the awards for members of the teaching profession."

The only other item of note was Coun. Drage's speech calling attention to the large amount of money lost to the town through the fares of all passengers on the trams not being collected. Anyone who uses the cars regularly knows what a number of fares are missed on every car, and it is quite time that some effort was made to remedy the loss.

Local Officer's Thrilling Experiences.

Lieut. G. Reeve.
(Photo, Greenway).

A thrilling record of war service is possessed by Lieut. G. Reeve, 1st Royal Irish Fusiliers, who is spending a few weeks leave with his parents at 15, King Street, Northampton. When war broke out he had been in the Army 12 years, and was a Sergeant Instructor of Signalling. He went to France with the original Expeditionary Force in mid-August, 1914, and fought at Mons and all through the retreat nearly to Paris. He took part in the battle of the Marne, and then fought in the battles of the Aisne and the Oise and the many minor engagements which culminated in the fearful battle of Ypres. Early in 1915 he was promoted Co.-Sergt.-Major and awarded the Military Medal for bravery at the second battle of Ypres. The following July when on patrol duty near Hill 60 he came into contact with an enemy patrol and was wounded in the head with a hand grenade. In November, 1915, he was promoted Lieutenant on the field and kept in his old battalion, the Royal Irish; and his splendid services caused him to be singled out for mention in Sir John French's New Year despatches.

In February last while raiding enemy trenches near Beaumont Hamel, Lieut. Reeve was wounded in the leg, and on leaving hospital he was granted a month's leave at home. He returned to the Somme, and during the October operations he was again wounded in the leg and sustained severe shell shock while gallantly leading a company to the attack on enemy positions. He has now thoroughly recovered, and expects soon to return to his battalion at the front.

Before the war Lieut. Reeve was a well-known army athlete, representing his battalion in all branches of sport. Three of his brothers have joined the forces, and one of these, in the 7th Northamptons, has been missing since August 17th.

Killed in Motor Accident.

Gallant Officer's Death.

The funeral took place with military honours at Northampton, on Monday, of Lieut. George Reeve, M.C., M.M., Royal Irish Fusiliers, who, having survived the dangers of strenuous campaigning from Mons to the Somme, was run down and killed by a motor car at Colchester, recently, his skull being fractured. Lieutenant Reeve was a sergeant-instructor of signalling on the outbreak of war, and fought in the battles of Mons, the Marne, the Aisne, the Oise, and Ypres. At the second battle of Ypres he was wounded in the head and awarded the Military Cross. In November, 1915, he was given a commission in his own regiment, and was mentioned in Sir John French's despatches. He was wounded in the leg whilst raiding trenches, and was again wounded and also shell shocked at the battle of the Somme.

On returning home he received the Military Cross from the King, and was given a hearty welcome by the Northampton Castle Ward Conservative Association. He was a fine all-round athlete, and won many prizes for his regiment.

Deep sympathy will be tendered to Mr. and Mrs. Reeve, who have lost three sons in the war—the other being Pte. Samuel Reeve, 7th Northants, killed at Loos, and Pte. Sydney Reeve, killed last May. A fourth and last son, Sergt. H. Reeve, Northants' Regt., is attached to the Royal West Surrey Regiment as instructor.

Lieut. G. Reeve.
(Photo, Greenway)

ments, and then continues: "... On returning home he received the Military Cross from the King, and was given a hearty welcome by the Northampton Castle Ward Conservative Association. He was a fine all round athlete and won many prizes for his regiment." The report finishes with the grim note that of George's three brothers, Samuel and Sydney had also been killed.

Long reports of the inquest into Reeve's death appeared in the *Essex County Telegraph* and the *Colchester Gazette*. The *Telegraph* gave an almost word-for-word account of the evidence given by witnesses.

Thomas Davis
No mention has been found to date, although many RAF raids were well reported.

ABOVE *George Reeve's accidental death is covered in the* Northampton Independent *of 26 October 1918; the report finishes with the information that two of his three brothers had also been lost. (By permission of the British Library).*

LEFT *"Local Officer's Thrilling Experiences" - the* Northampton Independent *of 6 January 1917 continued to follow George Reeve's impressive combat career. (By permission of the British Library).*

CHAPTER 12: MUSEUMS

Museums generally maintain a document archive associated with their range of exhibits, and this is the part of the building most frequented by medal researchers. Archives can range from a few relevant books at a small museum up to the vast holdings of national institutions.

The United Kingdom is particularly well served by museums. The most well-known are in London and other major cities, but hundreds of smaller museums exist throughout the country to present exhibits associated with local people, trades and events. Any of them can assist with medal research if a connection is found between their speciality and the medal recipient. Although few museums concentrate on military themes, many hold some material concerning men and units originating from their vicinity.

That said, the museums which immediately spring to mind when considering sources of information about military personnel are the Imperial War Museum, National Army Museum, Royal Naval Museum, Royal Marines Museum, National Maritime Museum, Royal Air Force Museum, and museums associated with regiments, corps and military activities.

Modern museums often have attractive thematic exhibits, using a full range of high-tech wizardry to achieve an eye-catching effect. The style of displays featured today would probably surprise those who have not visited a military museum for some years. This development is not only true of large museums, but is often found in those limited by a smaller budget. However, while the "front of house" is often laid out to entertain as well as to inform, the archive departments rarely benefit from modern technology.

These are usually understaffed and underfunded; but the archivists are usually helpful and well-informed, with a genuine interest in their subject. Material at the researcher's disposal is normally card-indexed and easily retrievable without the aid of computers. Archive material held at museums is usually split into three categories: books, documents and photographs, "documents" including microfiche and microfilm records. Some establishments also hold visual and audio records, maps, diagrams and other research aids. Museums do not as a rule hold personnel records, although there are one or two exceptions.

Any researcher is extremely fortunate to find archive material directly connected with the individual he is hunting down, but he may find the next best thing. Reading a diary kept by a member of his battalion is akin to reading one written by the man himself - they are likely to have experienced similar events. Likewise, an eyewitness account of a battle gives an insight into what it felt like for the medal recipient "to be there".

Some museums hold large collections of photographs and prints connected with their subject. As with documents, there is little chance of finding photographic coverage of the man who wore the medals, but it is reasonable to expect some images of his unit or of other troops during the campaigns he took part in.

The Imperial War Museum

The Imperial War Museum's high dome and grand facade, fronted by two huge 15in naval guns, form a vivid contrast with the shabby surrounding streets. The museum is situated in Geraldine Mary Harmsworth Park at the junction of Lambeth Road and St George's Road, London SE1, not far from Waterloo railway station. It can be reached easily by car or public transport. Three Underground stations - Elephant and Castle, Borough, and Lambeth North - are within short walking distance. (However, those arriving at Elephant and Castle are confronted by a labyrinth of poorly signposted subways which have to be crossed to reach St George's Road; my advice is to use one of the other stations.)

The Imperial War Museum is concerned with exhibits from campaigns by British and Commonwealth forces since 1914, with a heavy emphasis on the two World Wars. The archive reflects the museum's position as the foremost trustee of material for the period. The Departments of Documents and Printed Books are co-located high in the building beneath the dome. Readers can access material by prior appointment, arranged over the phone on 0171 416 5000; this appointment system ensures against overcrowding in the Reading Room. It also enables staff to note the researcher's interests and to place material at his disposal on arrival, saving time all round. The co-location of the document and book departments means visitors have access to both at the same time. They are run from separate desks in the same room by different staff, but the system works efficiently.

The document collection is card-indexed in the department office, which is not open to the public; however, staff place all relevant cards on the researcher's desk to await his arrival. Each card contains a precis of a single document or batch of documents. The researcher can scan the cards and order documents on duplicated order slips; the material usually arrives within 20 minutes. The collection is wide ranging, including personal diaries, letters, manuscript papers and memoirs donated to the museum. Some documents are very useful for medal researchers, mentioning individuals of all ranks by name and outlining events in vivid detail.

Staff from the Department of Printed Books try to place relevant volumes at the researcher's disposal when he arrives at his allocated desk. It is a pleasant feeling to realise that some thought has gone into your work before you set foot in the building. The most commonly sought-after books, including unit histories from both World Wars, are available in the Reading Room. Reading desks are surrounded by floor-to-ceiling bookshelves, and more are located on the balcony. There is a card index to all the books in the archive, arranged by subject and author. A computer adjacent to the card index allows faster, more comprehensive searches. Books can be ordered in a similar way to items within the document department, by completing a self-carbonating slip; the book is made available within a few minutes. Virtually every book likely to interest 20th century medal researchers is available under the same roof; no ordinary reference library could hope to offer such coverage.

The National Army Museum
The National Army Museum is in Royal Hospital Road, London SW3, adjacent to the Royal Hospital, Chelsea. Parking is extremely limited and the museum is best reached by public transport. Sloane Square is the nearest Underground station, ten minutes walk away. The museum does not hold personnel records, but the archive contains books, letters, diaries, photographs, engravings, prints, pamphlets and magazines. The Reading Room is on the second floor, approached via the stairs or a nearby lift. Readers must have a valid reader's ticket; application forms, stating the conditions of entry, can be obtained from the museum. It is advisable to inform archivists before a visit, to ensure that there will be space in the Reading Room; the telephone number is 0171 730 0717. Archivists can usually arrange for relevant material to be made available for the visitor.

Two large colour-coded card indexes are the key to retrieving documents from the collection. Up to eight orders can be placed every hour, using duplicated forms; items ordered are usually delivered within the hour. The first card index refers to printed material such as books and letters, arranged by author, regiment, subject, campaign and biography. Each section is cross-referenced to the others. The other index relates to illustrative material such as prints, paintings and photographs. This index is split into sections arranged by artist, publisher, person pictured, regiment, uniforms, subjects, campaigns, badges and medals. Some cards give a negative number, enabling the reader to view the illustration on a microfiche viewer in the Reading Room. The microfiche cards are arranged by numerical order in folders above the fiche readers.

Another important index for medal researchers, called the Hodson Index, is housed at the NAM. Compiled by Major Vernon Hodson, it provides information about officers of the East India Company, Indian Army and Bengal Army. Some records are far-reaching and include anecdotal information.

Army Lists are on open shelves in the Reading Room, along with current regimental magazines. A range of military reference works are on shelves next to the card indexes. Copies of the *London Gazette* are situated above each index.

The archive contains an extremely useful index to deceased soldiers. Their papers no longer survive, and this is one of the few sources available. A set of alphabetical index books refer to entries in large volumes titled *Record of Deceased Soldier's Effects*. The alphabetical index begins in March 1901, but the first volume contains entries back to at least 1899. Each volume records name, regiment, number, place of birth, trade, next-of-kin and to whom payment authorized. The next-of-kin column often contains several entries when a will apportions belongings to several relatives; the relationship of each to the deceased is given.

The archive system at the museum works very well, aided by the helpful and knowledgeable staff in the Reading Room.

The National Maritime Museum
The National Maritime Museum is set in pleasant surroundings at Greenwich Park, opposite the Royal Naval College in Romney Road, London SE10. There are no parking facilities at the museum and road parking is hard to find, costly, and only available for limited periods. The museum is midway between Greenwich and Maze Hill railway stations, and can also be reached by the Docklands Light Railway to Island Gardens Station and then via the Greenwich foot tunnel. The telephone number is 0181 858 4422.

A reader's ticket is issued on proof of identity, and the researcher is then unleashed upon the holdings. Staff assist new visitors, directing them towards relevant material. The reference library stocks books about an assortment of maritime subjects, connected with both naval and merchant service. A wide variety of documents are also housed in the building.

There are many useful books for medal researchers at the National Maritime Museum, including published naval medal rolls. Official Navy Lists and Steel's Navy List are available on open shelves. Copies of various naval biography volumes are also available, including O'Byrne's *Naval Biographical Dictionary*. The museum copy of *The Commissioned Officers of the Royal Navy 1660-1815* is particularly interesting; the services of each officer have been amplified by Pitcairn-Jones, listing some of the ships sailed upon, with dates.

The NMM is an excellent source of information about naval vessels upon which medal recipients served. A history of each Royal Navy ship can be seen on microfiche, detailing dimensions, tonnage, guns, where made and launched, service, successive captains, major actions and eventual fate of the ship. A separate microfiche series lists illustrations available through the museum's picture library. The museum holds illustrative coverage of a large number of ships in various circumstances, so it may be a theme worth exploring. Prints cost £6.50, plus a £5.00 handling charge.

The Royal Air Force Museum
The Royal Air Force Museum occupies a large site in Grahame Park Way, Hendon, London NW9. A small Reading Room is provided on the first floor of the museum building. Research facilities are open to the public every Thursday, so it is important to make an appointment some weeks in advance; the telephone number is 0181 205 2266. Ample parking is available on site and the museum can be reached easily by public transport; Colindale Underground station is five minutes walk away.

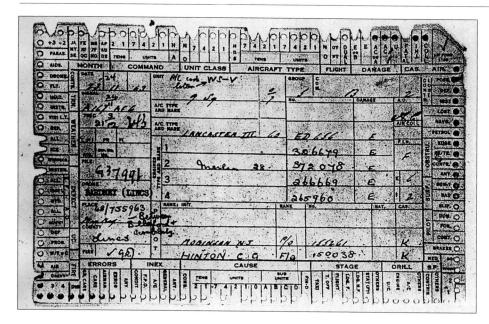

Front and back of aircraft accident card for Lancaster ED656; in the space for remarks the probable cause of the crash is given as "altimeter freezing". If true, this suggests that when almost home after nearly seven hours' night flying on this mission to Berlin the pilot was misled by a false altitude reading and simply flew into the ground - the fact that two gunners survived hints at a shallow angle of impact. (RAF Museum)

Security staff are provided with a list of visitors and issue passes at the main entrance.

Once inside the Reading Room, a resident archivist is allocated to assist researchers. The system works extremely well and material is placed before researchers in a very short space of time. It is a unique experience to be placed in the hands of someone with intimate knowledge of museum holdings, instead of wasting time discovering what is available.

Although the museum does not keep personnel records, there are some very useful indexes in the Reading Room. Those researching medals awarded to RAF casualties are likely to find some of the records particularly interesting. The indexes in the small reading area are well organized. Different topics are arranged in alphabetical and numerical order, and some provide obvious potential for medal researchers. There is an alphabetical list of men for whom the museum holds original archive material, such as a flying log book or personal diary. This is supplemented by an index of squadrons and units, recording original documents connected with their personnel held by the museum. Both Reading Room indexes are incomplete, but museum staff check their definitive listing for paperwork relevant to the person under research.

Before and during the First World War there was no recognized military flight training school; potential pilots obtained Aviator's Certificates through the Royal Aero Club. Records of pilots who achieved this are now held by the RAF Museum; these show personal details including name, rank, date of birth, profession, and home address - and most importantly for medal researchers, a portrait photo normally accompanies the documentation. The museum can supply copies.

Details of casualties between 1914 and 1925 are on a series of RFC and RAF record cards. The index is not complete for the earliest years and later cards are more thorough, but it is a useful reference for those researching casualties.

Gallantry medal researchers can view the Bulletin index, an incomplete alphabetical index to personnel awarded decorations

for bravery and good service. Each card refers to the Air Ministry Bulletin in which the event appears, often with citation. This is a short cut to discovering information contained in the original *London Gazette* entry.

There is some duplication at Hendon of material held at the Public Record Office. RFC and RAF Communiqués, some RNAS Operations Reports, and Combat Reports from the Second World War can be seen at the museum. However, PRO unit records are more extensive and any researcher would be advised to begin this line of enquiry at Kew.

The museum keeps an index of all aircraft which were shot down or crashed during the Second World War, arranged on microfiche in date order. Each record is composed of two parts. The first gives various details of the aircraft, date, target and where the plane crashed, if known. Some cards are also annotated to show cause of damage, such as "hit by flak" or "shot down by enemy fighter". The second part of the card indicates the fate of the crew. The eventual prisoner of war camp of a captured flier is indicated, or the place of burial of those who died in action. Sometimes there are notes explaining that a body was moved to a Commonwealth War Cemetery.

Accident record cards are available on microfilm in the Reading Room. They are similar to those covering planes brought down by enemy action, but arranged differently; the content also differs. To find an accident record card the researcher must know the type of aircraft flown and the date the event occurred. The index is alphabetical by make of aircraft, and then in date order.

Each card is in the form of an investigation into how the accident happened. The first part gives details of where it took place, numbers of casualties, whether or not the aircraft caught fire, and pilot's name. A number of possible causes are marked around the edge of the card, which was clipped like an old-fashioned railway ticket to indicate factors thought likely to have contributed. The second part of the card contains comments about what caused the crash. Sometimes it remains

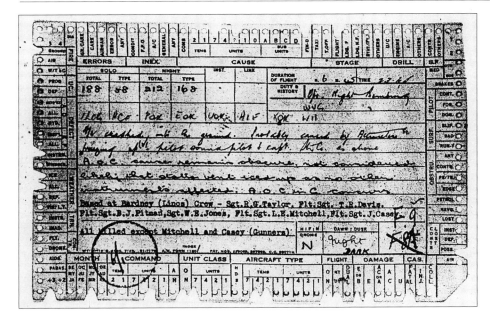

blank, but there may be several different notes added as the card passed up the chain of command. Accident Record Cards and Brought Down by Enemy Action Cards make interesting reading for casualty medal researchers.

The RAF Museum holds microfilm copies of Aircaft Records dating from approximately 1930. After identifying the aircraft normally crewed by the medal recipient from squadron records at the PRO, it is possible to check the damage sustained during missions flown when he was on board, increasing your knowledge of the experiences he went through. Most cards (Air Ministry Form 78) are completed very thoroughly, but this was not the case with some theatres of war.

A vast collection of around 250,000 photographs are stored in albums in the Reading Room, with a comprehensive index. Many of the photos feature RAF personnel, but few can be identified. It may be possible to confirm that our man is one of a group pictured, but to go beyond that is extremely difficult. Copies of photos in the collection can be supplied at prices ranging from £3.50 for a small colour machine print up to £40 for a large duplicate colour transparency.

Museum staff cannot carry out searches for those unable to visit in person, but they provide a list of bona fide researchers.

The Royal Naval Museum
The Royal Naval Museum is located in the heartland of British naval history, in Portsmouth Naval Dockyard close to the most prized reminder of the country's maritime might - Nelson's HMS *Victory* - as well as the unique mid-19th century warship HMS *Warrior*, and the fascinating remains and relics of Henry VIII's *Mary Rose*. The museum houses a significant manuscript collection and an extensive library, recently improved by the addition of books from the Admiralty Library at Old Scotland Yard. Collections are accessible by appointment Monday to Friday, 10am-4.30pm; the telephone number is 01705 861533.

The manuscript collection is divided into two sections. The "discrete" collection comprises documents gathered elsewhere and later transferred to the museum, while the "artificial" collection was assembled by the museum. Matthew Sheldon, Curator of Manuscripts, has produced a *Guide to the Manuscript Collections of the Royal Naval Museum* published in October 1997. This provides an excellent picture of document holdings, and a thorough index enables any researcher to pinpoint papers of interest. The Guide groups documents under headings and does not attempt to list every single item individually; however, at the museum papers are catalogued separately on computer, so readers can quickly locate them.

The collection embraces paperwork concerning naval personnel from the highest ranks down to the lowest. Some contain personal material and others are official documents. The archive includes letters, diaries, scrapbooks, certificates and a host of other items. The research notes of Captain Kenneth Douglas-Morris are of particular interest to medal researchers. They were made to assist him when he compiled his books *The Naval General Service Medal 1793-1840*, *Naval Medals 1793-1856*, *The Naval Long Service Medals* and *Naval Medals 1857-1880*.

The museum also houses a collection of ship magazines and wall newspapers 1881-1982. These vary from semi-official examples through to single typed sheets not intended for wider circulation. They are a good source of names, if any researcher can find coverage of a ship at the appropriate time.

The Royal Marines Museum
The Royal Marines Museum is on the Esplanade at Southsea, Hampshire. Formerly the officer's mess for Eastney Barracks, the museum is set in tranquil gardens near the sea front. The interior decor matches the grand exterior, with gold leaf decoration on the ceilings, huge fireplaces and broad staircases - few museums can boast such an imposing setting for their exhibits. The nearest railway stations are Portsmouth Harbour and Portsmouth and Southsea, both a short bus ride away.

The museum houses over 7,000 medals awarded to Royal Marines, including all ten Victoria Crosses presented to members of the Corps. Modern technology is used to present exhibits in an interesting and informative way. A wide-ranging archive collection can be viewed from 10am to 4.30pm each Monday to Friday. An appointment is required, which can be arranged by post or by telephoning 01705 819385. Proof of identity is required for a reader's pass.

Royal Marine service records are at the Public Record Office, but the museum keeps a large collection of documents, manuscripts, letters and diaries available for research. Documents are brought to the Reading Room where they can be viewed at leisure. The earliest records in the archive date from the 18th century, and there is some coverage of most campaigns. There is also a small tape and video collection. Photocopies can be supplied. The museum photographic collection dates from the 1860s and copies of photographs can be supplied at a range of costs.

The museum library houses numerous books of interest to RM medal researchers; these include Navy Lists dating from 1783 and Marine Officer Lists from 1755, and the earliest publication available was printed in 1643. The collection includes a wide variety of books on Royal Marines history and many associated topics. There are insufficient staff to cope with anything other than the most general enquiry received by telephone or in writing; researchers are best advised to visit in person, when staff will guide them in the best direction to fulfil their requirements.

Other military museums

There are dozens of regimental museums in the United Kingdom, usually located in towns historically associated with the featured unit. Many other museums exhibit collections relevant to several units from the local area, Regular, Territorial and Yeomanry. (A useful listing may be found in the 1999 edition of the Osprey - formerly, Windrow & Greene's - *Militaria Directory and Source Book*, available from Osprey Publishing Ltd, Elm's Court, Chapel Way, Botley, Oxford OX2 9LP, telephone 01865 727022.)

Nearly every regimental museum contains some type of archive facility, although most are now forced to exist on a shoestring by budgetary constraints. Some have been forced to close or amalgamate; those that remain are short-staffed and often run by a retired officer with part-time helpers. There is frequently a backlog of enquiries waiting to be dealt with, and it can take months to receive the information you request. Bear this in mind when seeking assistance. Most museums are prepared to carry out limited research on behalf of enquirers, in return for a modest donation to regimental funds or according to a set payment scale. It is preferable to carry out research personally, but this is not always possible when the museum is at a distance.

Regimental museums hold some unique (and often quite unsuspected) material not duplicated in national collections and archives, and their concentration on a single unit enables them to focus on events in detail. Sometimes, though not in possession of documents for a certain individual, they may hold information about him. For example, the Essex

Regiment Museum at Chelmsford maintains a card index, updated with information from any source that comes to light.

Any collector interested in researching medals from his own locality should foster good relations with regimental museum archivists. Once they become well known and trusted they might find that they are allowed to borrow rare reference volumes, or given access to archives whenever they want. An offer to help the staff out with enquiries will rarely be turned down and gives a good opportunity to become familiar with documentation in the archive. The archivists tend to know their material very well, so a brief telephone enquiry about an individual is never a waste of time - and could reap a rich dividend.

Research Notes

Charles Hoggett
Microfiche records at the National Maritime Museum provide details about the ships Hoggett sailed upon as follows:
HMS *Rattlesnake* Built 1822 at Chatham. 6th Rate. 20 x 32 pdr, 6 x 16 pdr, 2 x 9 pdr. South America 1831-33 under Capt.C.Graham.
HMS *Blonde* Built 1819 at Deptford. 5th Rate. 28 x 18 pdr, 16 x 32 pdrs, 2 x 9 pdr. South America 1834-37 under Capt F.Mason. Sold in 1895.
HMS *Apollo* Built 1805. Troopship 1828-38 under Capt.Alexander Karley. 2 x 9 pdr, 6 x 18 pdr, 80 men. Broken up September 1856.
HMS *Edinburgh* Built 1811 at Rotherhithe. 3rd rate. 28 x 32 pdr, 28 x 18 pdr, 4 x 12 pdr; 10 x 32 pdr carronades on the quarter deck and 2 x 12 pdr and 2 x 32 pdr carronades on the forecastle. Lisbon, North America, West Indies, Mexico and Mediterranean 1839-41 under Capt.William W.Henderson, including the bombardment of Acre, 3 November 1840.
HMS *Illustrious* Built 1803 at Rotherhithe. 3rd Rate. 28 x 32 pdr, 28 x 18 pdr, 2 x 18 pdr; 12 x 32 pdr carronades on the quarter deck and 2 x 18 pdr and 2 x 32 pdr carronades on the forecastle. (Further details on the microfiche were illegible.)
HMS *President* Built 1829 at Portsmouth. 4th rate. 30 x 32 pdr on the gun deck, 2 x 32 pdr, 12 x 42 pdr carronades on the upper deck; 4 x 12 pdr and 4 x 32 pdr carronades on the forecastle. Served as the flagship under James R.Dacres at the Cape of Good Hope, 1845-47.
HMS *Victoria and Albert* The first Royal Yacht of this name was built at Pembroke in 1843, driven by paddle wheels. She sailed under Lord Adolphus FitzClarence, until renamed *Osborne* in 1855. The new Royal Yacht was also built at Pembroke, in 1855, laid down as the *Windsor Castle*; 300ft long, 2,470 tons, the new steam yacht under Hon.Joseph Denman could travel at 18 knots.

Edward Heymer
The National Army Museum holds several prints and paintings depicting the charge of the 16th Lancers at Aliwal. The archive also keeps several books about Aliwal, detailed at the end of Chapter 10.

Henry Harvey
There are several photographs of officers of the King's Own Scottish Borderers at the National Army Museum; unfortunately only one is annotated with personal details, and Harvey was not present.

The NAM index refers to photograph albums at the regimental museum in Berwick-on-Tweed; there is also reference to an index of officers' service at the regimental museum. A telephone enquiry to the KOSB museum archivist unfortunately proved fruitless. There is no record of Lt.Col.Harvey, and photographs do not identify officers depicted.

Several books at the National Army Museum impart information about the 1/25th Foot during the Second Afghan War; details are given at the end of Chapter 10.

Joseph Full
No record of Joseph Full was found at the Royal Marines Museum. There was no illustrative coverage of the Egyptian campaign at the time he was present.

David Boyce
None of the major military museums or the Royal Irish Fusiliers Museum in Armagh were able to provide any further information about David Boyce. However, two items at the Imperial War Museum related to his battalion:

2nd Lt.Wood kept a diary in January-February 1916 which named a few individuals; Boyce was not mentioned. Capt. E.A.Godson MC kept seven pocket diaries during the Great War. These mentioned many individuals and recorded information about conditions, movements, battles, etc. Boyce did not feature by name.

Boyce spent many years as a postman after discharge from the forces. The National Postal Archive, Mount Pleasant, Farringdon Road, Islington, North London keeps records of postal employees. Unfortunately, personnel records have been destroyed and all that is available are records of appointment and retirement in yearly alphabetical ledgers. David Boyce was appointed as a postman at Portadown, minute number 11685, in August 1931. He retired in 1957 as a postman at Southend, registered number 48312, cross-referenced to his original 1931 entry. No records of Imperial Service Medals awarded to postal staff are kept at the archive.

George Reeve
Two documents concerning 1st Bn, Royal Irish Fusiliers were available at the Imperial War Museum:

Draft typed/handwritten notes by Brig.W.Carden Roe for an article published in the regimental magazine mention some individuals, but not George Reeve. The transcript of a diary kept by Capt.A.J.Troudell in 1916-17 was viewed but did not yield any mention of Reeve.

He was mentioned in the 1st Battalion history, *With the Faugh-a-Ballaghs in the Great War* by Burrowes, and also appeared in several regimental magazines prior to the war, available at the National Army Museum. These are dealt with elsewhere.

The Royal Irish Fusiliers Museum in Armagh was able to supply some useful information from the 1st Battalion Royal Irish Fusiliers Officers' Occurrences Book 1914-18 compiled by RQMS P.J.Clancy. Reeve's entry reads:

Recommended as NCO for gallant and distinguished conduct. LG 1/1/16
Commissioned 10/11/15 (List 20/11/15)
WIA 18/1/16
Admitted No 11 Field Amb, 18/1/16, wound right calf.
To 4 CCS 19/1
Admitted No 11 CCS 19/1/16. Wound right leg.
To No 1 Amb Train 22/1/16
Admitted No 2 British Red Cross Hosp, Rouen 23/1/16
To England per hospital ship *St Patrick* 8/2/16
Reported to 1 RIF (AGGHQ 0845 14/7/16)
Arrived No 49 Base Depot 17/7/16
Joined Bn 20/7/16
WIA 12/10/16 (AG List No 773, 14/10/16)
Admitted No 4 CCS 13/10/16 GSW left leg and shell shock
Admitted No 20 General Hosp 14/10/16
Transferred to England 19/10/16
Awarded MM LG 11/11/16
Arrived 16 Base Depot 6/4/17 (Reinforcements List Etaples 6/4/17)
Posted (AG Listed 323) Joined Bn 22/4/17
WIA and remained at duty 3/5/17
Awarded MC LG 18/7/17
Admitted No 11 FA 2/8/17 Pyorrhoea
To No 19 CCS 2/8/17
Admitted No 8 CCS 2/8/17
Remaining No 8 CCS 16/8/17
To duty ex 8 CCS 22/8/17
Rejoined Bn 30/8/17
To be Lt LG 5/11/17
Admitted 108 FA 5/2/18 Pyorrhoea
41 CCS 5/2/18
Admitted 41 CCS Pyorrhoea

The museum was also able to supply a photograph of Reeve receiving a prize at Shorncliffe immediately before the war.

Thomas Davis
The RAF Museum provided plentiful information about the fate of the Lancaster bomber in which Flight Sergeant Thomas Davis flew as navigator on 23 November 1943.

The Aircraft Card for 23-24/11/43 contained no report of the Lancaster being brought down by enemy action, which was initially puzzling. The solution was provided by the Accident Record Card for the same night. ED656 crashed into the ground for no apparent reason while returning from a night bombing mission to Berlin. The exact location of the crash site was given, and the card recorded an iced up altimeter as the probable cause. Pilot Officer N.J.Robinson was described as a sound pilot and captain. The AOC reported that the actual cause remained obscure. It was not considered likely that the "stalls vent" iced up, as no other instruments were affected. The card listed casualties, and the two surviving air gunners.

CHAPTER 13: GENEALOGICAL SOURCES

Family history sources add background to the story of the man awarded a medal, and illuminate avenues of research not previously apparent. Knowing his family and social origins rounds off research and gives the story a beginning and an end.

The main framework of a family tree can be established by reference to civil birth, marriage and death records, parish records, census returns and wills. Civil registration records and census returns are housed in an impressive new purpose-built **Family Records Centre** at Myddleton Place, Myddleton Street, London EC1 - near the Sadler's Wells Opera House and about half a mile from the Angel Underground station. Car access is difficult; most nearby streets only allow resident's parking and meters are very expensive.

It is possible to do a great deal of family research under this one roof, in pleasant surroundings, with the benefit of modern technology. The Family Records Centre is equipped with dozens of microfilm readers, several copiers and a few CD Rom Computers. Initial steps in family research are concerned with civil registration. By working backwards through birth, marriage and death certificates it is possible to build up a family record. Medal researchers are normally only interested in one person's background, rather than the entire family.

There has been a legal requirement to register all births, marriages and deaths in England and Wales since 1 July 1837. The index to these registrations is housed on the ground floor at Myddleton Place. It must be emphasised that only the *index* to civil records is held at Myddleton Place; the certificates themselves are stored at the General Register Office at Southport on Merseyside. They have to be ordered by post, using details taken from the index. Certificates are sent direct to the researcher. Costs are high, at £6.50 per certificate, but there are no shortcuts; without paying the fee the document cannot be seen.

Each index is very simple. Years are divided into quarters ending in March, June, September and December. Within each quarter names are listed alphabetically; for example, a birth on 5 May 1884 will appear listed in a June 1884 birth binder. Owing to the time allowed for registration of each event and late registrations it is worth checking the following quarter's entries if a name does not crop up where expected. Thousands of names appear in each volume. As usual, the more common names are the hardest to research. Only the barest details appear in each index, making identification extremely difficult, particularly when only approximate dates are known. The birth index gives only the full name and district of registration. Death registers are slightly more helpful, giving the age of the

deceased in records after 1865 - which helps to distinguish between persons with identical names. In marriage registers positive identification is possible if both parties' names are known; they are recorded separately, and can be cross-checked against one another.

Next to each register entry are two unique reference numbers, referring to the volume and page in the original district register. These numbers, together with the person's name and registration district, must be entered onto an application form to obtain a copy of the certificate. If several entries seem equally applicable it is possible to enter further details to help identify the correct certificate.

Birth and marriage certificates provide the most genealogical information. Birth certificates give the date and place of birth, full names, sex, full name of the father, full maiden name of the mother, occupation of the father, signature, description and residence of the informant, and registration details.

Marriage certificates show when and where married, full names of both parties, ages, marital status, rank or profession of each party, residence at time of marriage, full names and profession of both fathers. Any of these items of information may prove surprising, particularly interesting, or - as in most cases - completely dull. The trouble is, you don't know until you look.

Death certificates provide less information: when and where death took place, full name, sex, age (not to be relied upon), occupation, cause of death, signature, description and residence of informant, and registration details. The death certificate is naturally most interesting if the person met an unusual or violent death, which can lead on to newspaper research or coroner's documents.

Several other registers at Myddleton Place are of great interest to medal researchers. Grouped together on shelves near the death registers, they include certain **regimental registers** of births, marriages and deaths. The earliest births recorded date back to 1761, marriages and deaths to 1796. The earliest of these originate from chaplain's returns. A separate binder lists regiments in order of precedence, outlining exactly which periods of their history are incorporated into the index. Records are arranged alphabetically by surname, irrespective of the year the event took place. This simplifies matters; take the surname of the medal under research, and a single check should identify any births and marriages of interest. The register shows forenames, place, year and regiment. A different form has to be completed to obtain certificates from regimental returns, but the cost is the same as that for a standard certificate.

Separate indexes itemise **births and deaths at sea** from 1837.

> *This is the last Will and Testament of me Edward Heymer of Drui Elms Grove Gravesend in the County of Kent Pensioner I direct that all my just debts and funeral and testamentary expenses be in the first place fully paid and satisfied Whereas I have now in the Post Office Savings Bank at Gravesend the sum of one hundred and thirty one pounds ten shillings and one penny now I give and bequeath to my son Edward Charles James Heymer a Private in the 16th Army Lancers now serving in the Madras Presidency in India the sum of twenty pounds sterling also my gold watch and gold chain with the appendages also my two gold rings one being a diamond ring and the other an Indian ring also my three silver medals And I direct that the said sum of twenty pounds shall be paid to my said son out of the said sum in the said Savings Bank or otherwise out of my general estate I give and bequeath to my father Edward Heymer of number 18 Half Moon Street Bishopsgate London my suit of black clothes And as to all the residue of my estate real and Personal money money in the Post Office Savings Bank at Gravesend and the interest thereof household furniture beds bedding plate linen glass china and other effects whatsoever and wheresoever I give devise and bequeath the same to my dear wife Hester Heymer her heirs executors administrators and assigns for her and their own absolute use and benefit And I appoint Mr Thomas Jackson the Town Missionary of Gravesend Executor of this my Will And revoking all other Wills by me at any time heretofore made declare this and this only to be my last Will and testament In witness whereof I the said Edward Heymer have hereunto set my hand this eleventh day of July in the year of our Lord one thousand eight hundred and sixty six — Edward Heymer — Signed and declared by the above named Edward Heymer as and for his last Will and testament in the presence of us present at the same time who at his request in his presence and in the presence of each other have hereunto subscribed our names as Witnesses — H. W. Davison Sol.t 77 Basinghall St London — Thomas Jackson Town Missionary 68 Wrotham Road Gravesend.*
>
> *Proved at London 4th January 1867 by the oath of Thomas Jackson the sole Executor to whom Admon was granted. 2*

The register records happenings on any naval or merchant vessel registered in the United Kingdom. The Air Register Book records **births and deaths in the air** since 1949 occurring on UK registered aircraft. Other volumes list events concerning British nationals overseas, registered by the local British Consul or High Commission. These date from 1849.

Some other registers may yield information of great interest. Firstly, there is a complete alphabetical index to **Army deaths in the First World War**; checking names against this register is far quicker than trawling through medal index cards at the PRO, or the 80 volumes of *Soldiers Died ... .*

Second World War death records for service personnel are extremely comprehensive, with registers of Naval Officers, Naval Ratings, Army Officers, Army Other Ranks, and a single index to all ranks in the RAF. Two volumes also cover **Boer War** casualties. Other campaign fatalities appear in standard service death returns.

Apart from holding civil registration indexes for England

Edward Heymer's will, in which he bequeaths to his son Edward, serving as a private with his old regiment in India, his "three silver medals" (tenth line of text).

and Wales, Myddleton Place has a computer link facility to the **Scottish Record Office**. Scottish civil registration began in 1855. Early certificates contain far more genealogical information than their English equivalents, and it is also generally possible to view the details on the certificates rather than just a list of names in an index. Scottish records are at New Register House, Princes Street, Edinburgh. The Scottish office also holds similar military, maritime and consular records to Myddleton Place. Via the computer link it is possible to scan birth, marriage and death registers from 1855 to date. Parish registers dating from 1553 to 1854 can also be viewed, as well as the index to the 1891 census in Scotland. This service saves southern-based researchers the considerable expense of travelling to Edinburgh, although there is a maximum limit of two hours' access to a computer and a fee of £4.00 per half hour.

In **Ireland** registration of births, marriages and deaths began in 1864, apart from Protestant marriages for which records commenced in 1845. Records for the whole of Ireland up until 1921 are held at Joyce House, 8-11 Lombard Street East, Dublin 2, as are records for the Irish Republic from 1921 onwards. Post-1921 records for Northern Ireland are at Oxford House, 49-55 Chichester Street, Belfast. Pre-1921 Northern Irish records can also be obtained from local Northern Ireland register offices, covering the area where the event took place (a list of these is available from Oxford House).

Microfilm copies of certain parts of civil registers are held in some main libraries and local record offices. If resident at a long distance from London, check to see if it is possible to view the index nearer to home.

Before 1837 baptisms, marriages and deaths were recorded in **parish registers**. Records began in 1538 and continue until the present day. Early records are of little interest to medal researchers, but men who won medals before the Crimean War were born before civil registration began. There is no central index to parish records, so it is pointless undertaking a search without some knowledge of the person's origins. Remember that large cities were divided into dozens of parishes. Details given on an attestation document may be entirely fictitious or incorrect. So, if a brief search of parish records fails to uncover the man, it may be advisable to call a halt. Many parish registers have gone adrift over the years or suffered irreparable damage. Those that survive are often extremely difficult to read, written in spidery manuscript or stained with traces of damp. Parish registers can only be seen on microfiche.

Parish records usually offer scant reward for the research time invested. Baptismal records give the child's name and date of baptism, generally accompanied by the name of his father and occasionally the mother's name as well. From time to time a particularly conscientious vicar might have added one or two other details, such as grandparent's names, date of birth or even an address. The higher the social standing of the family, the greater the likelihood of uncovering extra facts. Marriages and deaths were also recorded in parish registers, although most medal recipients are likely to have married or died after the advent of civil registration.

Taking into account the difficulties listed above, it is still rewarding to give our old soldier a starting point and see under what circumstances he entered the world. So if there is some credible information to work on, try to spend a little time hunting for his origins.

There is a genealogical short cut to parish registers. The Mormon church has compiled an awesome data base known as the **International Genealogical Index** or IGI. The IGI is held on microfiche by many libraries, record offices and other local bodies. It contains marriages and baptisms, extracted from registers worldwide. Coverage is not complete, but it is enormous. Names are listed by surname, then Christian name, then date, for each county in England and Scotland (Wales and Ireland are treated as counties). Each entry supplies the original reference from which the information was taken. If a possible match

is found, it is advisable to check that the correct details were transferred from the original document.

A **national census** was carried out every ten years from 1801, and from 1841 onwards they contain personal details of those dwelling in all parts of the country. Post-1841 the material included in census returns can prove of great assistance. Microfilm copies of each census are available at the Family Records Centre, Myddleton Place. Large libraries and county record offices usually hold census coverage of their surrounding area as well, which can save the expense of a trip to London.

Census records reveal the family background of the future soldier, sailor or airman, and indicate his family's status in the local community. Each dwelling is listed separately. The 1841 census listed names, but rounded children's ages up to the nearest five years. Relationships between the parties were not included. From 1851 onwards each entry shows age, occupation, marital status, relationship within the household and place of origin. Armed with the details taken from military and other records it is often possible to track down the man's family in the census list.

Visitors to Myddleton Place can view an index to the entire 1881 census on microfiche. The index is arranged by county. Within counties the fiche lists surnames alphabetically, giving all the details from the census forms. As with all research, uncommon names are helpful when it comes to identifying the correct family. (Unfortunately, an "unusual" surname is often common in a localised region, as can become all too apparent when scanning the index.)

Census returns make it possible to see what happened to the man after leaving the service, but this can be difficult. Service records may provide no clue about his destination on leaving the forces. If he did not return to his original area, then if you are without any other information the best way of tracing him is to locate his death certificate and hope that he resided in the area for some years preceding.

Census returns are of interest to medal researchers who seek a full picture of their man's life. They help to establish if he married, whether he had children, and what he did before and after serving with the Colours. Finding out these things may identify marriage and birth certificates which might furnish further details. Census returns also serve another useful purpose. Army and Royal Navy personnel are listed in barracks and on board ship on the night the census was taken, so the census provides a complete record of the unit strength with names, ages and places of origin for entire battalions and ship's companies.

Medal researchers may find **probate records** very useful; they are easy to obtain, and can furnish much material about the life of the recipient. Wills proven in England and Wales since 1858 are stored in London at Somerset House in the Strand, together with Letters of Administration granted in cases of intestacy. The single reference room is full of reference volumes, running chronologically from 1858 to date. The index is alphabetical within each year. If the date of death is known, finding the relevant volume is straightforward. However, there are two things to bear in mind. Firstly, many old servicemen died penniless, so no record will be found. Secondly, there is frequently a gap between the date of death and the date the will was proven - this may be ten years or more.

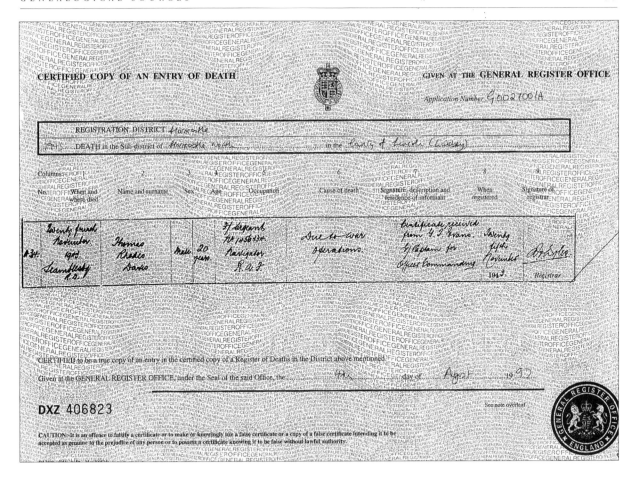

Copy of the death certificate for Thomas Davis, with cause of death shown as "due to war operations".

Where the date of death is not known, do not despair; a blanket search from 1858 to the present day is not an impossible task. It is always possible to narrow down the search field through common sense and existing information. The index is clear and well-organised - unlike many others a researcher will consult - and there is no charge for consulting the books.

The index itself is very informative, giving some significant information which is enlarged upon by the actual will. Full name, occupation, marital status, address, place of death, date of death, names of executors and relationship to the person who has died, and the value of the estate are all recorded. After completing a search slip a fee of £0.25 is payable to view the will, and this is usually produced within about a quarter of an hour. A copy can be ordered and sent on to the researcher at an additional charge of £0.25.

Wills can provide a lot of information, often running to several pages. They sometimes point to splits within families or portray the feelings of the deceased towards friends and relatives. A will also indicates the wealth of the deceased and many list notable possessions. Others are more poignant, particularly those written on forms provided to soldiers on the eve of battle during the First World War. I have seen an example where the writer put his trust in the Lord to see him through the ordeal and, failing that, entrusted his children and worldly goods to his wife. Thousands of soldiers wrote similar wills while facing almost inevitable death. They never fail to move the reader.

The ease of researching wills makes them an ideal source for those who are not particularly interested in finding out about a military man's family and civilian life, but who feel it is worth checking to see what he made of himself after leaving the forces. For those who do wish to look at all aspects of the man's life, probate records are worth examining early on in the hunt if the researcher has few other family details to go on. An alphabetical index to post-1858 wills is a recent acquisition at Myddleton Place. The microfiche is a tremendous shortcut, saving a lengthy hunt through the will books at Somerset House.

Letters of administration (Admons) are usually disappointing. They were granted to the next-of-kin in cases where the deceased failed to leave a will. Normally they take the form of a single sheet, adjudicating that his effects will be passed to a certain beneficiary.

Before 1858 probate was handled by the church. Matters were dealt with by over 300 different ecclesiastical courts, and tracking down the record of a will from this time can be a fairly complicated business. It is beyond the scope of this book to deal with pre-1858 wills in any detail. Local record offices can usually offer advice.

Irish probate records follow a similar pattern to those for

Copy of the marriage certificate for Maj.Henry Harvey and Beatrice Watson, married on 21 March 1887 at Fategarh, India. (Found in a register of Army marriages.)

England and Wales. Index books to post-1858 wills are housed within the National Archives in Dublin and the Public Record Office for Northern Ireland (PRONI) in Belfast. Unfortunately, most original wills were lost during the great fire of 1922 at Four Courts, Dublin; fortunately, transcript copies in will books were still held by district probate registries and remain intact. Sadly, will books for Dublin went up in smoke.

Since 1922 the two halves of Ireland have operated independent probate systems, with the principal registries situated in Dublin and Belfast. Records are also retained by district registries scattered around the country. These can be visited and searches carried out in exchange for a small fee. After identifying relevant entries through the annual index, copies can be obtained from surviving will books held at the National Archive in Dublin or PRONI, Belfast. The service is not cheap, as the relevant page must be photographed rather than photocopied, to prevent damage to the will book. Visiting researchers can note relevant details without applying for a copy.

Copies of some Irish wills are held at Somerset House. This particularly applies between 1858 and 1876, when Irish wills and admons are listed after the letter Z in each annual index. Anyone seeking a will for a medal recipient who died in Ireland prior to 1858 should seek advice from the Dublin National Archives or PRONI.

Scottish probate records follow a completely different pattern to those mentioned above. The important date when dealing with Scottish wills is 1824, when responsibility passed from Commissary Courts to Sheriff courts. The Scottish Record Office, HM General Register House, Princes Street, Edinburgh, holds indexes to most testamentary records proven by the various sheriff courts, and this should really be the first port of call

for anyone seeking the will of a Scottish medal recipient. The SRO records should assist the researcher to the appropriate sheriff court records and thence to the will itself. Scottish wills are particularly interesting; due to Scotland's different laws only "moveable" property - such as tools and furniture - feature in the will, which is thus likely to list virtually every item owned by the deceased, giving an excellent insight into his way of life. His medals may even be listed! The SRO may be able to assist with tracing pre-1824 Scottish wills.

Medal researchers looking at **recent awards** often find their path blocked by disclosure rules, next-of-kin rules and so on. No such restrictions apply to probate records, and a will may provide more information about service personnel from recent years than almost any other document open to inspection. Local probate records are often kept by County Record Offices and major reference libraries.

Genealogical sources are like almost any other source of information. Any of the above may lead the researcher precisely nowhere, or to a rich vein of information which makes the "man behind the medal" stand out in vivid colours. Whatever the outcome, the bare facts of his birth, marriage and death provide some background material outside his military history. They smooth off both ends of his life, and give an indication of what sort of person he was and what kind of life he led.

Research Notes

Charles Hoggett
Successive visits to Myddleton Place failed to reveal any trace of Charles Hoggett's marriage, and his birth took place before civil registration began. The IGI does not record Hoggett's baptism; and checks with Portsmouth City Museum and Record Office also proved fruitless. To date his origins are a mystery.

Hoggett left the Royal Navy in 1857 to settle with his family in Portsea. He appears in the 1881 census for Hampshire, when he lived at 54 St John Street, Portsea, with three daughters, all working as "fanners" in a stay factory. He was then aged

NAME and SURNAME	RANK and RATING	CONDITION as to Marriage	AGE Last Birthday		WHERE BORN
			Males	Females	
John Sibley	Private R.M.L.I.	Single	19		Ilchester, Somerset
Thomas Bailey	do	Married	26		Ben Haven, South Wales
Michael Trevenion	do	Single	24		Macclesfield, Cheshire
George Williams	do	do	22		Bristol, Gloucester
John Moran	do	do	25		Lanark, Scotland
William F. Pring	do	do	24		Ferozepore, E. Indies
Reuben Blackburne	Serjeant do	Married	32		Ross, Herefordshire
Thomas Roberts	Private R.M.L.I.	Single	20		Bristol, Gloucester
Joseph Full	do	Married	37		Buckfastleigh, Devon
George Salmon	do	do	41		Bath, Somerset
George Bateman	do	Single	23		Yeovelton, Somerset
Albert Miller	do	do	24		Frome, Somerset
George Sketchley	do	do	28		Birkenhead, Cheshire
Charles Cook	do	do	20		Plympton, Devon
		Total on Page 28	14		

LIST of the OFFICERS, MEN, BOYS, MARINES and of ALL OTHER PERSONS on BOARD on the NIGHT of SUNDAY, APRIL 3rd, 1881.

67 years, a widowed naval pensioner, originating from Portsea. His daughters Emily, Matilda and Alice were aged 21, 19 and 16 respectively. Emily and Alice were born in Portsea, Matilda in Gosport. Nearby, at 37 Charles Street, Portsea, lived another Charles Hoggett, aged 26, born in Portsea. He was an engine fitter, living with wife Jane and daughters Alice, 3, and Nellie, 1. It transpired that he was our Charles Hoggett's son, so the old sailor was a grandfather. There was no trace of Charles Hoggett in the 1891 census at St John Street.

Armed with information from the 1881 census, it was obvious that Charles Hoggett died after 1881 and his wife died between the birth of her last child and the 1881 census. Mary Hoggett, Charles' wife, died aged 53 on 18 July 1877, at 102 Crasswell Street, Landport, in the presence of her husband; she died from "disease of the heart and diarrhoea".

Charles Hoggett died on 1 February 1903, aged 85 years, at "The Green Post", London Road, North End, Portsmouth. The naval pensioner died of senile decay, cystitis and exhaustion. His daughter Matilda was present at the death. A will was found at Somerset House. His estate was left to his sons Charles and Harry, and daughters Emily Turner and Matilda Clarke. It does not detail individual items. The will identified a son, Harry, not recorded on the 1881 census, and confirmed the Charles Hoggett found at 37 Charles Street as a son of our Charles. Alice Hoggett, the youngest daughter in 1881, was not mentioned, so had either died between 1881 and 1903 or had possibly been disowned for some reason.

Checks with Portsmouth City Museum and Records Office retrieved some further details about the Hoggett family, which appear at the end of Chapter 14.

1881 census return for the gunnery ship HMS Cambridge; Joseph Full is the ninth name.

Edward Heymer

Heymer signed for the 16th Lancers on 15 September 1841, aged 18 years one month. He was born in Shoreditch, London. The IGI revealed that an Edward Heymer was baptised at St Leonard's Church, Shoreditch on 9 May 1824. His father was Edward Heymer senior and his mother's name was Elizabeth; no further details were given. The regimental marriage registers at Myddleton Place gave no indication of any Heymer marriage. However, regimental birth registers record two Heymer children born into the 16th Lancers around the right time. The certificates confirmed that they were children born to Edward Heymer. Harriett Heymer was born in Dublin on 17 June 1856 and baptised on 12 October 1856; Edward Heymer's name and rank were given, and his wife was recorded as Hester. Eliza Rebecca Heymer was born on 7 May 1858 in St James's, Leith, and baptised on 20 June 1858; on this occasion Heymer's wife was recorded as Esther.

Edward Heymer married Hester Whitfield, a 30-year-old widow, on 25 January 1847 at Canterbury, Kent. He was then 24 years old, living in barracks, the son of Edward Heymer, an undertaker. Hester lived in Northgate Street; her father, William Wright, was a farmer.

Edward Heymer was discharged from the 16th Lancers on 21 September 1865 to 36 Nine Elms Grove, Gravesend. There was no trace of the Heymer family at that address in the 1871 or 1881 census. Heymer was sick prior to his discharge from the Army, and there seemed a strong possibility that he might have died between 1865 and the 1871 census. Sure enough, Edward

Heymer died of phthysis on 21 December 1866 at 36 Nine Elms Grove, Gravesend, in the presence of his wife. He was recorded as a sergeant major from the 16th Lancers on pension.

So, sadly, Edward Heymer died shortly after discharge, apparently worn out by his Army service. His life story was a poignant tale - from glory on the battlefield of Aliwal to an unheroic death from disease at the age of forty-three.

Edward Heymer's will, proved on 4 January 1867, was found at Somerset House. He had £130 10s.1d. in the Post Office Savings Bank at Gravesend. He left £20 to his son, Edward Charles James Heymer, a private in the 16th Queen's Lancers serving in India; also a gold watch and gold chain with appendages, two gold rings (one diamond ring and an Indian ring) - and also "my three silver medals". Edward bequeathed a suit of black clothes to his father, Edward Heymer of 18 Halfmoon Street, Bishopsgate, London; the remainder of his property was left to his wife. This will was fascinating on two counts. Most importantly, it specifically mentioned his medals. They were obviously so important to him that he cared to make sure they went to someone who would treasure them. The will also revealed that his son Edward had followed him into the 16th Lancers, thus opening a new field for research.

It was also interesting to discover his father's address in Bishopsgate. Edward Heymer's marriage certificate stated that his father was an undertaker; now that his address was known it might be possible to find out something about him from business directories or the appropriate record office.

Henry Harvey

Civil records for Guernsey are kept at the Greffe, Royal Court House, St Peter Port. Records are also stored by the Priaulx Library and the Guernsey Archives. Births were registered from 1840 and marriages from 1919.

The Greffe traced a copy of Henry Harvey's baptismal record, identical to that found with his Army papers. There was no entry for his birth, although they did discover entries for two sisters - Mary-Anne Phillippe on 5 June 1842, and Sophia-Anne on 1 December 1844 - both born at Petite Marche, St Peter Port. The father was Jean Harvey and the mother Anne-Sophia Grut. Jean Harvey was listed as a "gentleman" or "rentier".

The Priaulx Library, St Peter Port, was able to supply a copy of the 1851 census. Young Henry J.Harvey, aged 10, lived in Queens Rd, St Peter Port, with Louisa M.Harvey (22), William J.Harvey (16), Thomas P.Harvey (13), Emily (7) and Marian P.Harvey (8). Also living at the house was Ann Fogarthy, a cook aged 27.

The 1891 Census showed Henry J.Harvey living at Midford Lodge, Kings Rd, St Peter Port, aged 50 years, a retired lieutenant colonel (infantry). His wife Beatrice E.Harvey, aged 36, born in Surrey, was also recorded at Midford Lodge, living on her own means. Two children were present: Winifred B.Harvey, aged 2, and Edith M.Harvey, 7 months. Four servants lived at the house - a cook, a housemaid and two nurses - indicating that the Harveys enjoyed a comfortable standard of living.

The Priaulx Library also furnished a copy of the parish birth record for a son, Henry John Harvey, born 26 May 1892 at Grande Marche.

There was no trace of Harvey's marriage in the general marriage register at Myddleton Place, but an entry was found in the register of Army marriages. Major Henry Harvey married Beatrice Emmeline Watson on 21 March 1887 at All Souls Church, Fatehgarh, Meerut, India. Beatrice Watson was the daughter of James Watson, a clerk in Holy Orders. They were married by Chaplain C.R.Tollemache.

According to the register of deaths for the parish of St Peter Port, Henry James Harvey died from cardiac disease at 12am on 4 July 1921 at Newlands, Prince Albert Road, St Peter Port; he was 80 years old.

Research into Henry Harvey showed the importance of referring to parish records as well as civil registration. This was exaggerated by the shortage of surviving civil records for Guernsey and made somewhat easier by the social status of the Harvey family.

The Greffe was able to supply a copy of Henry Harvey's will, proved in the Bailiwick of Guernsey on 16 July 1921. The will, made on 4 September 1915, was very informative. Harvey bequeathed a silver cup won at Hewera Elija to his son Capt.Henry John Harvey (King's Own Scottish Borderers); all his other possessions were left to his wife. Money and stock were divided between his wife and children. The will indicated that Harvey was quite a wealthy man. It would be interesting to discover how he won the silver cup of which he was so proud, but it is difficult to decipher the name of the place it was won; it reads as Hewera Elija, which means nothing at this juncture.

Beatrice Harvey's will was proved in 1930. The will is quite revealing, comprehensively listing personal possessions, including a pearl pendant, jade necklace and gold bangle, a grandfather clock in the hall, an ivory mirror, a picture of a spaniel and pheasant, a diamond ring, gold bangle, copper tray and stand, Indian mirror in carved wood, an inlaid Chippendale chair, a picture of a storm, an oak set of furniture in the library consisting of table, four inlaid chairs and oak writing table with drawers, and a picture of a Dutch cook. Beatrice Harvey's will only serves to confirm the family's comfortable status. The possessions individually listed were obviously highly prized by the family and probably requested prior to her death.

Joseph Full

Naval records recorded that Joseph Full was born in Buckfastleigh, Devon, on 12 June 1843. His birth certificate revealed that he was actually born on 22 July 1844. His father was Joseph Full, a woolcomber; his mother Mary Full, formerly Tozer, was the informant.

The 1881 census return was checked, using his 1883 discharge address. Full appeared twice, once on board ship and once at the family home in Stonehouse. Census reference RG 11/2210, Folio 124, Page 28, listed Joseph Full as a Private RM on HMS *Cambridge*, at Devonport on Sunday 3 April 1881. The entry showed Full as a married man, aged 37, born in Buckfastleigh. RG 11/2203, Folio 54, Page 15, presented Joseph Full the family man: he and his family were living at 46 High Street, East Stonehouse. Several other families lived in the

The 1881 census also recorded Joseph Full under 46 High Street, East Stonehouse, Devonport, where he is listed (sixth line) as head of the family consisting of his wife Matilda and five children. Fourteen other people of four other surnames appear also to be listed at No.46.

same building. Joseph Full lived there with his wife Matilda, 36 years. They had two daughters, Mary and Matilda, aged 10 and 2 months; and three sons, Alfred, 8, Joseph, 7, and William, 3. All the children were born in East Stonehouse. Working from the dates children were born, the marriage of Joseph and Matilda was quickly found.

Joseph, 22, and Matilda Roach, 21, were married on 13 October 1866 at Plymouth Register Office. He was shown as a lance-corporal, Royal Marines. Both gave their address as 21 Mount Street, Plymouth. Joseph's father, a woolcomber, was deceased. Matilda's father, Charles Roach, was a Greenwich pensioner. Joseph signed the register, but Matilda could only make her mark.

The family was rediscovered on the 1891 census, on RG 12/1738, Folio 53, Page 23. Joseph Full, now 46 years, was described as a Steward, Royal Navy, although he retired in 1883; it is possible that he resumed working in a civilian capacity. Also present were wife Matilda, 46, and six children. Daughter Mary, 20, was a laundress and son Joseph, 17, was a porter; William, 13, Matilda, 10, Lavinia, 5, and Eloise, 1, were at school or too young for school.

After establishing that Joseph and Matilda were alive in 1891, it was possible to track forward through death records to find out when they died. Matilda Full died on 7 May 1925 at 4 Hobart Street, Plymouth, aged 80 years. She died from "senility haemorrhage gastric"; the informant was her son, Joseph Ch. Full, who was present at the death. Joseph died on 13 May 1935 at 53 Lisson Grove (Greenbank Nursing Home), at the grand old age

of 90. The certificate stated that he was a Royal Marine pensioner; and that he died of "cerebral haemorrhage and coma" - the informant was again J.C.Full, his son, present at the death.

No trace of any will was found at Somerset House.

David Boyce
The family background of my grandfather David Boyce was never a mystery to me, but it was interesting to confirm his details from civil records. Birth and marriage certificates were obtained from family sources, leaving only a death certificate and will to search out.

David Boyce was born on 8 December 1892 at Ballynagarrick, Co.Down. His father was a weaver named Robert Boyce and his mother was Charlotte Ann Boyce, formerly Wells, both from Ballynagarrick. David Boyce married Martha Giffin (my grandmother) at St Mark's Church, Portadown, on 28 March 1921. He was working in a factory at the time, and lived in Joseph Street, Portadown. Martha Giffin was a factory worker from Georges Street, Portadown. Her father, James Giffin, was a farmer. I already knew that David's father Robert had died of enteric fever during the Boer War.

	CERTIFIED COPY OF	AN ENTRY OF BIRTH	

an Entry in an Army Register Book of Births, Baptisms and Marriages

Application Number...PSR W006928..........

Registration of Births, Deaths and Marriages (Special Provisions) Act 1957

Sixteenth Regiment of Lancers - Registry of Baptisms

Date of the Child's Birth	Place and Date of the Child's Baptism		Christian Name of the Child	Parents' Names		Rank of the Father	Name of the Chaplain or other Clergyman by whom the Ceremony was performed
	Place	Date		Christian	Surname		
1856 17 June	Dublin	1856 12 Augt	Harriett	Edward and Hester	HEYMER	Sergeant	Wm Hare Chaplain to the Forces

No. 343   I certify the above Registry to be correct
Signature of the Adjutant   Edwin Cowtan

CERTIFIED to be a true copy of *the certified copy of** an entry made in a Service Departments Register.
Given at the General Register Office, under the seal of the said Office, the   20th   day of   October   19 97 .

**If the certificate is given from the original Register the words "the certified copy of" are struck out.*

Section 3(2) of the above mentioned Act provides that "The enactments relating to the registration of births and deaths and marriages in England and Wales, Scotland and Northern Ireland (which contain provisions authorising the admission in evidence of, and of extracts from, certified copies of registers and duplicate registers transmitted to the Registrar General in accordance with those enactments."

SA 051974

CAUTION:—It is an offence to falsify a certificate or to make or knowingly use a false certificate or a copy of a false certificate intending it to be accepted as genuine to the prejudice of any person, or to possess a certificate knowing it to be false without lawful authority.

Copy of the birth certificate for Harriet Heymer, daughter of Edward and Hester, born 17 June 1856. (Found in the regimental register.)

The death certificate stated that David Boyce died on 4 July 1967 at 61 St Mary's Crescent, Swinton, West Yorkshire. He was recorded as a retired postman, aged 74 years. He died of stomach cancer. There was no trace of a will at Somerset House.

George Reeve

According to the Army List, George Reeve was born on 12 February 1884, and this was supported by newspaper articles. A widespread search revealed no George Reeve born in the Northampton area in 1884. Certificates were ordered, but none related to our man; various spellings were tried to no avail.

His death certificate presented no difficulties, although it gave no new information. He was recorded as a lieutenant, Royal Irish Fusiliers attached to the 52nd Bn, King's Royal Rifle Corps. He died on 15 October 1918 at Colchester Military Hospital from a fracture of the base of the skull, after being accidentally knocked down by a taxi cab. An inquest was held on 17 October 1918.

Initial checks on the 1891 census failed to produce any identifiable trace of the Reeve family in Northampton. Northampton County Record Office eventually traced a baptismal record for a George Reeve, details of which appear at the end of Chapter 14.

Thomas Davis

The death certificate for Thomas Davis simply recorded that Flight Sergeant Davis died at Scamblesby, aged 20, on 24 November 1943, as a result of war operations.

His birth certificate was traced from the age shown on the death certificate. Thomas Rhodes Davis was born on 26 February 1923 at Wyke House, Patrington, East Yorkshire. His father was Richard Neville Davis, a ship broker; his mother, the informant, was Violet Murray Davis, née Rhodes, of Wyke House.

CHAPTER 14: MISCELLANEOUS SOURCES

Apart from the principal archives and avenues of research dealt with in the preceding chapters, some of the bodies mentioned below may also be able to provide important and interesting material.

The **Commonwealth War Graves Commission** (CWGC) can be of great assistance when researching medals awarded to casualties since 1914. The organisation was founded by Sir Fabian Ware during the First World War, as an offshoot from the British Red Cross Society.

Galvanized into action by the chaotic situation on the Western Front, Ware sought to give every casualty a dignified place of burial, permanently marked with a simple headstone. In the early days of the war graves were indicated by a simple wooden cross, which all too often became uprooted, leaving no lasting trace. There was nothing new about this; graves from previous wars were sometimes left unmarked, or denoted by memorials of no lasting significance. Ware passionately believed that casualties deserved a better memorial, and his feelings were echoed by families at home.

Ware's ideas gained support, and the Graves Registration Commission was born in March 1915. The scale of the problem demanded a dedicated organization to keep pace with events, and the Imperial War Graves Commission was set up in May 1917. The Commission strove to record the whereabouts of the fallen until the Armistice, when work began in earnest. Battlefield conditions after four years of carnage in static positions cannot be imagined today. The transformation of shell-churned wastelands corrupted by the ungathered remains of uncountable thousands of corpses into tranquil gardens of remembrance where the dead could rest in peace is a testament to the dedication and judgement of Sir Fabian Ware and the War Graves Commission.

Their original project has evolved into a worldwide organization responsible for the upkeep of over a million Commonwealth war graves, which are visited every year by millions of veterans, relatives, and students of military history. All visitors are left with the same powerful impressions, their emotions touched by the evidence of so many lost young lives commemorated in such beautiful surroundings.

Medal researchers are regular visitors to old battlefields and their associated cemeteries. There is a certain poignancy in visiting the last resting place of a medal recipient. Often the gravestone and medals are the only tangible reminders of his existence. Visiting the grave adds a sense of realism to research and encourages the desire to keep an old soldier's story alive.

The Commission also keep registers of all Commonwealth war dead from all three services, including lists of seamen in sunken ships designated as war graves, and details of men commemorated on the Runnymede Memorial to RAF personnel whose bodies were never recovered. They receive daily enquiries about deceased servicemen and requests for the location of their graves. Today the records of the fallen are computerized, allowing a swift response to enquiries. Postal enquiries should be addressed to the Commonwealth War Graves Commission Records Section, 2 Marlow Road, Maidenhead, Berkshire SL6 7DX. The Records Section can also check details for telephone callers on 01628 34221. The information supplied by the CWGC can include unit, place and date of death, home address, next-of-kin, age and decorations. For a small fee they are able to provide a photograph of the grave, although this can take some time; an arrangement has to be made for the photograph to be taken when the cemetery is next visited on official business.

While the above arrangements remain in place, it is also possible now for subscribers to carry out CWGC searches using various criteria via an Internet website - www.cwgc.org.

The Commission has produced several publications which are very useful for medal research. An alphabetical list of casualties has been published for every cemetery and memorial administered by the CWGC. Lists for the larger cemeteries and memorials have been divided into separate parts each holding details of approximately 1,000 casualties, and these can be purchased from the CWGC priced at £8.00 each.

The computerisation of records offers important benefits to medal researchers. It is possible to obtain printouts tailored to individual requirements, a development with obvious advantages for those with an interest in one unit or formation. Records of every casualty from a given unit can now be extracted from the database, however scattered their graves. Records can be selected by ships, battalions, RAF squadrons, or whatever sub-unit is required. Family medal researchers can select by surname, and it is also possible to take details from the database broken down by home towns. The cost varies according to the number of entries extracted to fulfil the search criteria; for full details contact the Records Section at the Commission Head Office.

A set of three Michelin maps are produced by the CWGC, marked with the whereabouts of every war cemetery and memorial in the region, complete with an alphabetical index; each map is priced at £3.00. Another publication gives the whereabouts of the 374 VCs lying in CWGC cemeteries. The Victoria Cross Register, at £8.00, gives full details of each fallen VC.

Ordinary **civilian graves** are also of interest when researching a group of medals. The great majority of the men who

fought in any war survive, to be laid to rest eventually in cemeteries unconnected with their military past. The memorial
inscriptions on their gravestones can provide some information.
Unfortunately headstones become eroded by the passage of
time; some are moved, and others are broken or damaged.
Various family history societies have undertaken projects to
record details from ancient headstones before they vanish from
view. Even if a headstone cannot be found, a record of the
inscription might have been made for posterity.

Inscriptions rarely contain more than a few family particulars
and a line of biblical text, but occasionally the inscription is a little
more forthcoming. To many men time spent in the services was a
source of personal pride, especially if they took part in a notable
action. In the past, when far more people than today spent most of
their lives in a single locality, a man might be well known locally
for being a veteran of some battle or campaign (the most notable
example being the life-long prestige of most "Waterloo men").
This claim to remembrance is sometimes marked upon their headstone; such instances are rare, but they do happen. Even the most
mundane grave can be useful to researchers intent on discovering
everything about the man awarded medals. Family information
from one headstone may avert prolonged searches through civil
registers at Myddleton Place.

Soldiers who died on campaigns prior to 1914 are not
buried in Commonwealth War Graves, and the fate of their
remains was less certain. Burials often took place on the battlefield and in some haste, with the grave marked, if at all, by a
makeshift wooden cross, and stringent records were not kept.
The last resting place of soldiers from Victorian campaigns is
seldom identifiable today; but although the grave may be lost
there is usually some form of memorial tablet to commemorate
the fallen from a given campaign, sometimes listing individual
casualties. Enquiries about **pre-1914 graves** should be
addressed to the Ministry of Defence at PS4(CAS)(A), Room
1012, Empress State Building, Lillie Road, London SW6 1TR.

When researching medals awarded to casualties from campaigns in South Asia, it might be useful to contact the **British
Association for Cemeteries in South Asia**. This body holds
records of memorial inscriptions dedicated to many soldiers who
died in Asia. Enquiries should be sent to the Association
Secretary, Mr T.Wilkinson, 76½ Chartfield Avenue, London
SW15 6HQ.

By tradition, military casualties are commemorated in various
different ways. Before 1914 the death of an officer was usually
marked by a memorial of some kind. The bodies of officers
killed on campaign were often brought home for burial, while
others remained with their men who were left to rest in situ.
Whether or not an actual burial took place at home, local parish
churches and city cathedrals are excellent sources of information
on military casualties. **Inscribed memorial tablets** on interior
walls routinely give basic details of the military careers of officers
from the local gentry, and how they met their end. Successive
memorials can recount the entire military pedigree of certain
families. Occasionally stained glass windows were created to
commemorate the fallen from the parish. In some churches
memorial stones record notable local families; these usually mention military service and decorations awarded to individuals.

David Boyce, photographed in about 1910.

The collective **local war memorials** which are found today
in every British village and parish first appeared after the Great
War. The huge number of casualties among servicemen drawn
from every walk of civilian life caused shock-waves throughout
the land. Every community across the country felt the impact,
and families suffered bereavement on a scale never witnessed
before. Nearly every church contains a memorial to fallen
parishioners, listing names and regiments accompanied by a
few appropriate lines of text. There is a separate civic memorial
to the fallen in nearly every city, town, village and hamlet,
often in the well-known form of a cross surmounted by the
"sword of sacrifice". New names were added after the Second
World War to commemorate another generation of local men
who went away to serve their country in peril and did not
return. Memorial stones are also found in town halls, municipal
buildings and schools, listing name, rank and regiment.

Large commercial **companies and utilities** watched their
employees disappear to the various fronts, many of them forever.
Most felt compelled to commemorate staff who gave their lives,
and sponsored memorial tablets to be erected in prominent
positions at the place of work. Visitors to old-established companies can still see them today. British Railway companies provide a good example. The London, Brighton and South Coast
Railway Company commissioned two large memorials at
Victoria and London Bridge stations. The company management also decreed that smaller tablets should be displayed at

every level down to the smallest depot, workshop or station. If it is possible to trace the place of employment for a casualty whose medals are being researched, a check with directory enquiries may establish whether the firm still exists. If it does, a phone call to the company may uncover the location of a roll of honour.

The reader will recall from preceding chapters that the service records of post-1920 servicemen remain with the **Ministry of Defence**. None of the records can be released without the express permission of the next-of-kin. It is sometimes possible to track down next-of-kin of a medal recipient, but extremely difficult. Obviously, family medal researchers should encounter fewer problems, and may well be the next-of-kin themselves; this being the case, there is nothing to prevent an application for service details.

Army and Royal Naval records are held at the Ministry of Defence Personnel Records Section, Bourne Avenue, Hayes, Middlesex UB3 1RS. CS(R)2a Branch looks after Royal Naval Records and CS(R)2b retains Army Personnel Records. Enquiries regarding RAF officers should be addressed to Royal Air Force, Personnel Management Centre, PG 5a(2), RAF Innsworth, Gloucestershire GL3 1EZ, while those concerning RAF other ranks should be directed to P Man 2b(l) branch at the same address. Records for RAF personnel killed or invalided before 1 April 1918 are at MOD Hayes. There is a charge of £20 for searching the records; this is non-returnable, and there is no guarantee that any documentation will be found. The records cannot be photocopied. Relevant information is extracted from the papers and a typed precis is sent to the enquirer.

Local libraries often yield interesting information. Staff usually have a finger on the pulse of local research and historical societies, from which medal researchers can benefit. Invariably there is an individual or group in the area with an accumulated wealth of knowledge about military formations originating from the locality. Larger libraries frequently keep an impressive selection of military reference books. If the required volumes are not available at one branch, it is almost always possible to order them from another elsewhere in the county or even further afield; charges are nominal, and it seldom takes more than a few weeks to obtain a required book for a generous loan period. Making use of the library system saves a significant outlay, and provides the opportunity to view books and decide whether they are worth buying.

The **India Office Library**, part of the British Library, is an important source for anyone researching medals awarded to officers and men of the East India Company up to 1859 and the Indian Army 1859-1947. Records for the British Army in India post-1859 are at the PRO, apart from some out-pension documents. As this book goes to press the collection is being moved from Blackfriars Road, London SE1, to the new British Library building in Euston Road, NW1. The indexes described below may well differ when the collection is housed in the new building.

The India Office Library collection is wide-ranging and the military section is very extensive. There are medal rolls for campaigns in the sub-continent, a selection of specialised reference works including Indian Army Lists, a vast photograph and print collection, and an unrivalled assortment of manuscript documents. Medal rolls for campaigns in and around the sub-

David Boyce after returning from the Great War, with his wife Martha and daughters Evelyn and Hilda, c.1926.

continent are in document class L/MIL/5. At Blackfriars Road they were available in the Reading Room. Names and subjects of interest can be checked against a card index, divided into biographical and subject cards. Sometimes material is available for individuals whose names do not appear in the biographical index. Some categories of military document can be identified in nominal index binders. The same reference can normally be retrieved from the biographical card index.

The indexes include:

East India Company Soldier's Discharge Papers 1859-61
EIC Naval Officer Service Statements 1834
Indian Navy Officers & WOs Service Statements 1860-1945
Queen's/King's India Cadetships 1858-1939
Applications for East India Company Cadetships 1775-1860
Officer's Services for Bengal/Madras/Bombay 1860-93

Library catalogues list material available in the military collection, but the best reference is the *Guide to the Records of the India Office Military Department* compiled by Anthony Farrington, published by India Office Library and Records, London 1982. An excellent index at the rear of the book guides the researcher to all the different document classes. *A Brief Guide to Biographical Sources* by Ian A.Baxter, London 1979, is another useful reference volume to Army records of service available at the library, particularly those of other ranks.

The Ecclesiastical Records Index may interest some medal researchers. Servicemen spent long periods in India during the 19th and early 20th century; they married there, raised families there, and sometimes died there. Many entries in the Ecclesiastical Index therefore relate to soldiers. The index is split into three parts covering Bengal, Madras and Bombay. Each is arranged by first letter of surname, with separate volumes for baptisms, marriages and burials. The index is not fully alphabetical until 1910, but it is not difficult to carry out a search through relevant years. The index gives a forename together with volume and page reference. Prior to 1897 only the husband's name is indexed; wives' maiden names were not listed until 1897 in Bengal, 1899 for Madras and 1910 for Bombay. After identifying an entry the original register can be consulted on microfilm. For military personnel the rank and regiment of the father is generally shown.

Most entries in the Ecclesiastical Index are duplicated in the biographical card index, and it is far quicker to consult the main index, which is fully alphabetical. The biographical card gives the same reference and often includes the information from the baptismal, marriage or burial register.

Ecclesiastical records for Bengal span 1713-1947, Madras 1698-1947 and Bombay 1709-1947. Records from Burma are indexed with those for Bengal until 1937 and separately thereafter. Civil marriages are indexed from 1852-1911 and Roman Catholic registers run from 1835-54.

Document class L/AG/34/29 contains wills and letters of administration, which can be quite informative. Lists of possessions at the time of death can sometimes be found for soldiers who died in the service of the East India Company and Indian Army 1850-1937 in inventories forming part of Military Estate Papers in L/AG/34/40.

A large number of documents concerned with pensions survive at the India Office Library in class L/AG/23. Separate military funds were supported by subscription in Bengal and Madras until around 1862. Each was set up to provide for dependants in the event of the officer's death. The papers normally contain information about the officer, his wife and their children. L/AG/23/2 is an index listing officers and widows who received payments from the Lord Clive Military Fund up to about 1893. This was a charitable pension fund which made awards in cases of hardship.

The India Office Library is not detailed further here, because the set-up may change radically after the move to Euston Road. However, the material available will remain unchanged, and anyone interested in researching medals to men who served in the East India Company or Indian armies will find it a worthwhile place to visit.

The **Society of Genealogists Library** at 14 Charterhouse Buildings, Goswell Road, London EC1 offers good potential for researching medals. The library houses a wide selection of genealogical data, including a section to assist with research into the armed forces. The library is open 10am-6pm on Tuesdays, Fridays and Saturdays and 10am-8pm Wednesdays and Thursdays. Society membership costs £30 per annum after payment of a £7.50 joining fee. Non-members can obtain access for £3.00 per hour, £7.50 for four hours or £10 for a full

Thomas Davis' Commonwealth War Grave in St Nicholas Churchyard, Withernsea. (Courtesy Jean Nordon)

day. Charterhouse Buildings is tucked a short distance off the junction between busy Goswell Road and Clerkenwell Road; local parking is expensive and traffic is extremely congested, but Barbican Underground station is only a quarter of a mile away.

The library keeps an assortment of genealogical research sources. Some are copies of information available elsewhere while others are unique to the SOG. Holdings are divided between three different libraries. The Upper Library contains a good run of Army and Navy Lists and a fair selection of unit histories, casualty rolls and general works concerning military life. Nearby are numerous school registers; many are memorial volumes, giving biographical details of old boys killed in action. The Upper Library also has a surname card index and a number of volumes concerned with professions and occupations.

Births, marriages and deaths announced in *The Times* between 1816 and 1920 can be found on microfilm in the Lower Library, although the index runs from 1785 to 1920. A separate microfilm series contains all the entries from *Soldiers Died in the Great War*. The Middle Library is largely stocked with material related to parish registration of baptisms, marriages and deaths. The library catalogue lists parish records by county and then alphabetically by parish. Reference cards indicate the parish registers and the years they cover. There is also a monumental inscription index arranged by parish. Most records are on microfiche, but some are on shelves in bound volumes.

Copies of the Somerset House wills index, civil registration records, and a selection of census returns can also be seen on microfilm. The IGI and 1881 census index are on microfiche. There is also a microfiche index to Anglo-Indian families, which may be significant to Indian Army researchers. The full selection of card indexes compiled from different sources cannot be listed here, but virtually no aspect of family history is left untouched.

The attraction for family medal researchers is obvious, the potential for others less so, but you don't know until you look. If nothing else, it is possible to make use of standard genealogical research tools in quiet conditions with ample access to copying facilities.

County record offices exist all over the country to care for documents of local importance and promote all aspects of local research. They are greatly used by genealogists, for most act as custodians of parish registers for the surrounding area. They are normally small establishments with few staff, but helpful to anyone conducting research related to the region they cover. Military records are not a priority, but most hold records of local militia, and some material about nearby regiments or men who served with them. Record offices also have local birth, marriage and death registers, parish records, wills, census returns, newspaper indexes and many other sources. A good knowledge of what can be seen locally may save an expensive trip to London. Research at smaller record offices is also a more pleasant experience than using larger centres.

Individual researchers will have knowledge of other institutions capable of assisting with medal research. The bodies listed above are those most likely to be of use for a broad range of research. They illustrate the benefits of searching further afield than the confines of the Public Record Office.

Research Notes

Charles Hoggett
Portsmouth City Museum and Records Office found several baptismal records for the Hoggett family:
16/9/1860 Emily, daughter of Charles and Mary Ann, of Queen Street, Greenwich pensioner. Born 4/6/1859.
16/9/1860 Amelia, daughter of Charles and Mary Ann, of Queen Street, Greenwich pensioner.
4/8/1861 Matilda, daughter of Charles and Mary Ann, of Queen Street, Greenwich pensioner.
9/9/1861 Harry, son of Charles and Mary Ann, of Church Path, victualler.

Amelia Hoggett was not mentioned elsewhere, so probably died in infancy. Records revealed that Hoggett's daughter Alice died on 7 August 1882 and was buried with her mother in Mile End Cemetery. Mile End Cemetery burial records showed a Mary Hoggett, aged 53, buried 24 July 1887. Her body was brought from Crasswell Street, Landport, to Mile End, where she was buried in a "vault centre path". Alice Hoggett, 18, was buried on 16 August 1882. Her body was brought from John Street, Fratton; she was buried in a "vault of 2, SCP" (South Central Path?). It was shown half full, space for 4 or more. Mile End Cemetery no longer exists.

Withernsea War Memorial, listing T.R.Davis.
(Courtesy Jean Nordon)

Edward Heymer
There was no trace of Edward Heymer in the biographical index at the India Office Library; however, a fortunate discovery was made by chance. A card was found for a Thomas Whitfield, Private, 16th Lancers, who was buried in Meerut on 25 February 1840, aged 34. The card gave a reference to a burial record, N/1/58 f28. Knowing that Heymer married a widow named Hester Whitfield, and that it was customary for widows to remarry within the regiment, it seemed likely that Thomas Whitfield was Hester's first husband. This proved not to be the case, however. A little girl called Martha Whitfield was born on 13 October 1839 (N/1/53 f215) to Corporal John Whitfield, 16th Lancers, and his wife Hester; and was buried, aged 5, on 8 May 1845 (N/1/67 f261). This Hester Whitfield had to be Heymer's eventual wife and John her first husband - Thomas Whitfield was probably his brother.

A further card disclosed that a Hester Whitfield was born to the couple on 24 July 1844 and baptised on 21 August (N/1/66 f32). John Whitfield was by then a sergeant. Sadly, baby Hester also died - as did a heartbreakingly high number of British children in India throughout the 19th century - and was buried on 29 January 1845 (N/1/67 f112).

The Sutlej Medal roll (L/MIL/5/70) revealed Sgt.John Whitfield alive and well at Aliwal and Sobraon. Yet less than a

*The kind of ephemera some-
times found with medals,
particularly if they have
remained within the family:
a photograph of a battalion
sports team, with names,
may yield a portrait of the
medal recipient.*

year later Hester Whitfield was widowed and married to
Edward Heymer. One thing was clear: Hester Whitfield lived a
very sad life. Both children by her first husband died as infants,
her husband died and also, possibly, her brother-in-law; then
her second husband died a year after he left the Army.

The Sutlej Medal roll revealed that one lieutenant and two cor-
nets of the 16th Lancers were killed in action at Aliwal, together
with a sergeant, four corporals and 51 privates. Many others were
wounded and a number succumbed to wounds after the battle.

Document class MSS/Eur/C/471 consists of a series of letters from Major Charles Fenton, 53rd Regt, to his sister Mary.
One describes the battle of Aliwal, as follows:

"After pounding away for another hour we again advanced and
got the inspiring order: 'Prepare to Charge'. How can I give you
any idea of the British roar that then simultaneously arose from
the ranks of our noble fellows. Our Colonel raised his sword over
his head. Officers commanding companies rushed to the front
and cheered on their men and with an unbroken line on they
went, cheering in the most enthusiastic manner. The sight of our
lines' steady advance and the roar, completely discomfited the
Sikhs. They left their guns and fled precipitally before our charge,
with the exception of a few brave fellows who rushed on to us
with drawn swords and met their fate. They were gallant fellows.
The 16th Lancers then charged with other native cavalry and carried death and destruction with them. They suffered, however, a
good deal, losing two officers and about 30 or 40 men in one
square that they rode through." Fenton continues: "I have been all
over the field. Hundreds of dead lying about. The spot where the
Lancers charged was fearful. About 20 or 30 of their poor fellows
lying on the ground, hacked in the most dreadful way - some
with their heads quite severed and others' arms lopped off them,
but enough of all this... "

Some other manuscripts were scrutinised, but nothing of
great significance was unearthed.

Henry Harvey
The marriage of Henry James Harvey and Beatrice Emmeline

Watson appears in the Ecclesiastical Index at the India Office
Library. The marriage certificate was viewed on microfilm reel
N/1/199, but only duplicated details ascertained from the cer-
tificate ordered at Myddleton Place.

The Priaulx Library at St Peter Port holds indexes to Guernsey census returns and parish records for the Town Church,
where Harvey was christened. The library was able to supply
many details and the information they disclosed is included at
the end of the previous chapter.

The Priaulx Library also supplied information about an
interesting offshoot of the Harvey family. Henry's aunt, his
father's sister Margaret Ann Neve, née Harvey, was reckoned
the oldest person in the British Isles at the time of her death in
1903 aged 110, and featured in many newspaper articles. Some
of these gave details about the family. According from what was
written at the time, Henry Harvey was descended from a ship-
master who made his fortune from merchant shipping and pri-
vateering. Henry's grandfather was a colonel in the Royal
Guernsey Artillery. A magazine article from 1895 related how
the 103-year-old Margaret Neve held weekly luncheon parties
and that one of her favourite guests was Henry's three-year-old
son Henry, himself destined to be a lieutenant-colonel in the
King's Own Scottish Borderers.

The Guernsey Archive Service in St Peter Port also stores
documentation about the Harvey family, although mostly concerned with Henry's father and grandfather. One letter in the
archive, written by his sister Louisa, does give some family
background material. It was written on 16 September 1901 at
Queen's Rd, and describes family christening robes made by
Henry's mother in 1827. Louisa recalls the baby Harveys christened in them: "Harry's (Henry's) wife Beatrice had the good
robes when Winnie was born, 11th August 1888." Louisa
remembered that the family moved from 19 Saumarez St to
"Aunt's Cottage", La Petite Marche, which had been unlet for
three years. Apparently "Uncle Tom Harvey" painted three fireplaces in black marble and the dining room fireplace was
replaced by Henry's father with a real black marble one.

Apparently Henry's mother was "laid up" with John's birth on 8 December 1837 and Aunt Guille did the moving. "Mama came into the cold unfinished house at Christmas 1837 and made the best of it." The rent was £30 per year. Obviously the letter tells us nothing about Henry Harvey's military career, but it provides an interesting glimpse into the life of a loving, well-to-do family in the 19th century.

There is a Harvey family burial vault in the Brothers Cemetery, St Peter Port, dating from 1761 to 1933. Henry Harvey is commemorated on an inscription there although actually buried at Foulon Cemetery, St Peter Port. The memorial at Foulon Cemetery details Henry and his offspring. The front face is inscribed: "In loving memory of Lieut- Colonel Henry James Harvey, The King's Own Scottish Borderers, of Newlands, Guernsey. Died 4th July, 1921, aged 80. In hope of the resurrection. Also of Beatrice Emmeline his wife, died 4th April, 1930, aged 78." The rear face states: "Also of their daughter Edith Mary Collins, buried at Stithians, Cornwall. Died 12th March 1964, aged 73 years. Also of their son, Lt-Col Henry John Harvey MC. Buried at Lyminge, Kent. Died 16th September 1969, aged 77 years." Finally, the left face is engraved: "Winifred Beatrice, died 30th January 1976, aged 87 years."

The vault at the Brothers Burial Ground records several members of the Harvey clan, including Henry. His brothers were both soldiers: Thomas Peter Harvey (1837-1873) was a major in the 77th (East Middlesex) Regiment, and John Richard Harvey (1832-1922) attained the rank of major-general. Margaret Neve (1792-1903) is buried in the family vault, and so is Henry's father.

Joseph Full
Nothing was found.

David Boyce
An enquiry to the Ministry of Defence seeking service records for David Boyce revealed that his documents were among those destroyed by enemy action during the Second World War.

George Reeve
The Commonwealth War Graves Commission records Lieutenant George Reeve MC MM, aged 32, Royal Irish Fusiliers, attached to the 52nd KRRC, died on 15 October 1918. He was buried in Towcester Road Cemetery, Northampton, plot 4463, grave 17328. His parents were Mr and Mrs G.Reeve, 15 King St, Northampton. To date, no visit has been made to the cemetery.

Northampton County Record Office have been most helpful. Reeve lied about his age to enlist in 1902, making it difficult to trace his birth certificate and place of origin. However, Northampton CRO found that his baptism took place in Spratton Parish on 24 October 1886. The entry named his parents as George Reeve, a labourer, and Lydia Reeve. Further checks confirmed that George was born on 21 February 1886 in Spratton; a sister, Kate, was born in 1888.

Thomas Davis
The condolence slip accompanying medals awarded to Thomas

George Reeve photographed in sports kit before the Great War. (RIF Museum)

Rhodes Davis led to the Commonwealth War Graves Commission. The Commission recorded Davis as a Flight Sergeant, RAF Volunteer Reserve, serving with No.9 Squadron. He was a navigator, killed in action on 23 November 1943, aged 20. He was buried in grave 352, St Nicholas' Churchyard, Withernsea, North Yorkshire. Davis was the son of Capt. Richard Neville Davis and Violet Murray Davis of Streatham.

St Nicholas' Churchyard was visited. Davis' grave stood among a handful of war graves in the cemetery. Under an RAF badge the inscription reads: "1456334 Flight Sergeant Thomas Rhodes Davis - Navigator - Royal Air Force - 23rd November 1943 - Age 20." A separate inscription at the base quotes "Greater love hath no man than this. That a man lay down his life for his friends."

Davis' name appears on a memorial dedicated to men from Withernsea killed in the World Wars, which stands on Withernsea promenade. Another memorial, to the fallen of No.9 Squadron, is situated in the village of Bardney, Lincolnshire, where the squadron was based when Davis died. It takes the form of a Lancaster propeller blade set in stone.

The information obtained from the Commonwealth War Graves Commission formed the cornerstone of all research into Davis. Without it little else could have been achieved. The visit to Withernsea was also fruitful. The CWGC disclosed that Davis' parents originated from Streatham, which was slightly misleading; they actually lived in Withernsea until his death, when they moved away. The confirmation that Davis came from Withernsea led to the placing of an advertisement in the local press, which in turn led to other significant material.

CHAPTER 15: THE FIRST WORLD WAR

Great War medal research is not easy; but it can be extremely rewarding, often revealing tales of heroism, sadness, sacrifice and great poignancy. The sources outlined below are far from exhaustive. Millions of words have been written about the war - yet it is extremely difficult to find out anything about single participants. Individuals were swamped by the scale of it all. In this war, battalions developed personalities rather than individual soldiers. It is important to be realistic about achievable results, and to accept that discovering the activities of the man's unit may represent the best outcome.

All the sources outlined in previous chapters are open to Great War medal researchers, with a change of emphasis. When looking at 1914-18 medals there is usually less reliance on PRO records and more mileage in what would normally be considered secondary sources. Books and newspapers assume greater importance, offering good potential for information. Although the PRO has started to release 1914-18 soldiers' and sailors' documents, this situation will remain largely unchanged owing to the high proportion of service records destroyed during the Blitz.

So what of the medals themselves? By and large, because of the huge numbers issued, First World War medals were, until recently, relatively inexpensive. Leaving aside gallantry awards, they usually appear in what are termed "trios", of which there are two varieties, or pairs.

The 1914 Star, also called the Mons Star, was awarded to men who saw active service before 22 November 1914. A clasp carrying the dates "5th Aug - 22nd November 1914" is seen on the ribbon if the recipient was under fire between those dates. Generally speaking this is the medal of the pre-war Regular soldiers of the first BEF, which was almost wiped out by the first Christmas of the war.

Men not entitled to the 1914 Star, but present in a theatre of war between 5 August 1914 and 31 December 1915, were awarded the 1914-15 Star. The bronze star is identical to the 1914 Star, inscribed "1914-15".

Those awarded one of the two stars were automatically entitled to the British War Medal and the Victory Medal, making up a trio. Those serving in an area of conflict after 31 December 1915 only earned the War and Victory medals, known as a First World War "pair". The British War Medal is also seen singly, as presented to those servicemen not engaged in the fighting.

Members of the Territorial Force prior to 4 August 1914 were additionally entitled to the Territorial Force War Medal, subject to other specified qualifying rules. Merchant seamen who passed through war zones were awarded the Mercantile Marine Medal, sometimes together with other medals.

Bronze memorial plaques were issued to the next-of-kin of those who did not survive the war, carrying the name of the individual commemorated; rank and unit are not indicated. A commemorative scroll was issued with the plaque, giving the rank and unit of the fallen.

In recent years Great War medal prices have risen spectacularly. Groups awarded to officers command high prices, especially those including gallantry awards or to a casualty. Casualty groups to other ranks are also more expensive than those awarded to survivors. This applies to all three services. Within this general rule there are variations. For example, medals awarded to a casualty on 1 July 1916, the first day of the battle of the Somme, are more prized than those to a casualty of the first day of Loos, which are in turn more costly than those of a man killed on a normal day in the trenches. Medals to airmen, cavalry and yeomanry are more sought after than line infantry awards, although the latter rate more highly than medals awarded to corps. Medals to women often attract high prices. Pairs and trios are frequently accompanied by gallantry medals, both British and foreign in origin; others appear alongside those won in previous conflicts. A small bronze oakleaf on the ribbon of the Victory Medal indicates a Mention in Despatches.

Initial research, as always, starts at the **Public Record Office**. Verifying First World War medals to soldiers is quite straightforward, although the problem of common names is greatly magnified in a war which involved millions of men. The service number on the medals normally solves the problem, apart from a few cases where men changed number and unit several times.

Medal entitlements for Army and RFC personnel can be ascertained from microfiche medal index cards in class WO 329 at the PRO. Thousands of microfiches are arranged alphabetically in several filing cabinets. Medal index cards contain spaces for surname, first name(s)/initials, corps, rank, regimental number, entitlement to Victory Medal, British War Medal and Star, theatre of war, date of entry therein, and a space for remarks. Some cards also record entitlement to the clasp to the 1914 star. The card refers to the medal roll recording the qualification for a particular medal. The rolls can be ordered and seen at the PRO. Before this can be done, the original reference must be converted to an up-dated PRO reference for class WO 329.

Cards marked "SWB" confirm entitlement to a numbered Silver War Badge and refer to the book where entitlement is recorded. Over a million badges were issued to men discharged between 1916-1920, by reason of wounds, sickness or age.

L/Cpl. David Boyce in a posed studio portrait, 1915.

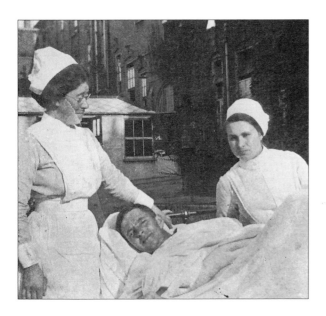

*David Boyce photographed with nursing staff at
Edmonton Military Hospital in September 1917
while recovering from the wound he received during
the battle of Langemarck.*

Unfortunately, some medal index cards were not fully completed, with spaces left blank. Even when all the boxes were completed it can be equally frustrating; sometimes the writing is indecipherable or scrawled over other entries, making both unreadable.

It is vital to discover a soldier's battalion in order to take research any further. If this is not indicated on the medal index card it can normally be established from the medal rolls. Without this knowledge it is extremely difficult to progress.

First World War naval medal records are in class ADM 171/89-93 for officers and ADM 171/94-139 for ratings. Names appear in alphabetical order and the correct register can be found from the class list, which breaks the series into alphabetical blocks. Entries provide far less detail than those for the Army. The only information given is surname, forenames, rate, number, medals earned, how issued and remarks. Some entries name the ship served upon.

"Honour sheets" in ADM 171/78-88 are very informative. These list officers and some ratings put forward for awards during the war and the results of such recommendations. Rank, seniority and ship are given, together with a description of "nature of services", reporting why they were recommended. The *London Gazette* reference is also given. There is a card index to "honour sheets" in the Research Enquiries Room. Some other gallantry recommendations for naval personnel are to be found in classes ADM 1 and ADM 116. Officers' gallantry awards are also listed in ADM 171.

Royal Flying Corps medal records are stored with those for the Army, while Royal Naval Air Service entitlements are usually with naval records in ADM 171, listed under HMS *Pembroke* up to 2 February 1915 and thereafter with HMS *President*.

Separate microfiche indexes in WO 329 record recipients of the Distinguished Conduct Medal, Military Medal and Meritorious Service Medal. All give surname, initials (sometimes forename), unit, rank and number. Each index gives the date of *London Gazette* featuring the award. The MID index is broken into three separate alphabetical batches.

New indexes for the Distinguished Service Order, Military Cross and Distinguished Conduct Medal have been made available at the PRO since February 1998. First World War DSOs and MCs feature in class WO 389 on microfilm, arranged in *London Gazette* date order. Many show details of the act for which the award was made, often with the place and date. MCs earned between 1914 and 1938 are indexed in WO 389/9- 24.

Researching "lesser" gallantry awards can be very frustrating. Although the announcement appears in the *London Gazette*, often no citation identifies the deed which earned the medal. Sometimes they were published in separate editions. Citations were rarely published for awards such as the Military Medal. There is a full index to entries in the *London Gazette* in class ZJ 1, although it is quicker to search through the appropriate

David Boyce (left, on crutches, wearing greatcoat) with nurses and a group of other wounded. They wear the bright blue hospital uniform faced white, with a white shirt and red tie.

medal index where possible. The *London Gazette* index is divided into quarterly lists, further split under each denomination of award. Once a name has been found in the index it is possible to order the correct segment of the Gazette by referring to the page number shown.

Citations were always published in the *London Gazette* for the VC, and usually published for the DSO, MC, DSC, DCM, CGM, DSM and DFM. None were published for the AFC or AFM, and only rare examples for the MM. Further details of flying awards can be found in classes AIR 1 and AIR 30. Further particulars of CGMs and DSMs may be seen in ADM 1 and 116.

Many airmen were awarded Army and Royal Navy gallantry medals prior to the inception of separate air awards in June 1918. Naval personnel serving on land frequently earned gallantry medals normally associated with the Army.

Published rolls exist for many of the awards listed above, usually including citations where known. They can normally be seen at major military museums or through the library system. Unit histories can also be used to confirm decorations, and often list foreign awards which were not published in the *London Gazette*.

Officers' records

First World War Army officers' service papers were released by the PRO during February 1998. The release includes officers who left the Army up to December 1920. Original service details were destroyed by enemy action in 1940; what remains are correspondence files, which often provide a reasonably full record of service.   Holdings vary, and the paperwork may be extremely informative or very disappointing. Everything depends on the correspondence contained in the bundle. At

least it is possible to view the original paperwork, rather than microfilmed copies.

The documents are sorted into two distinct classes. WO 339 contains papers arranged by a War Office registry number. The number allocated to an individual officer can be identified by reference to a nominal index on microfilm in WO 338. The index itself runs to 23 spools of microfilm; 21 list alphabetically officers who joined the Army between 1901 and 1922, another lists officers who joined 1870-1901, and the other records medical officers from 1871 to 1921. Each entry normally gives the War Office number, which can be used to order the required documents. If an officer continued to serve after 1921 his entry is marked "P", and his papers have not yet been released.

In other instances the entry simply records an index number consisting of the officer's initials and a number. This type of index number means that the officer's records are in a second class of documents, WO 374. WO 374 is arranged fully alphabetically. It is made up of those papers annotated as shown in the last paragraph, and officers commissioned into the Territorial Army.

After looking at service papers and checking medal index cards, the next step for research into Army and Royal Navy officers is, as ever, reference to the Army and Navy Lists. Royal Flying Corps officers were listed in the Army List until 1918 and RNAS officers appeared in the Navy List.

Officer's medals for the Great War were rarely impressed with the officer's regiment unless he was promoted from the ranks. This sometimes makes it difficult to identify the correct man from the index in the Army List. Those promoted from the ranks seldom continued to serve with their parent regiment, so be careful not to jump to misleading conclusions.

Now off crutches, a smiling David Boyce (standing, fourth from right) poses with fellow convalescents and nurses during a charabanc outing in 1918.

Information from the MIC usually prevents this type of error.

Naval and Royal Marine officers' records for the Great War period are not due to be transferred to the PRO until 2000. Their wartime role can normally be traced through successive Navy Lists, to establish dates of promotion and ships served upon. Monthly casualty returns were also published in the Navy List. The section of the *Official History of the War* covering naval operations can help to establish the part played by individual ships during the conflict. *The Times Diary and Index of the War* also details vessels involved in specific events.

If the officer should suddenly vanish from the Navy List there is a good chance that he became a casualty. Further checks can then be carried out with the Commonwealth War Graves Commission, Great War casualty registers at Myddleton Place, or *British Vessels Lost at Sea 1914-18*, originally published by Her Majesty's Stationery Office.

Records for RFC officers discharged from the forces or killed before the formation of the RAF on 1 April 1918 have been released by the PRO together with Army officers' records; RAF and RNAS officers' records have not been released. Great War aircrew officers serving with the RAF after April 1918 can be researched through the operational records in class AIR 1, as explained in Chapter 9. However, the documents in AIR 1 are of no use without knowing the officer's squadron, which is sometimes shown in the Army/Navy List. RFC officer casualties are listed in *Officers Died ...* along with their Army counterparts. Many officer casualties were listed with entries for their original regiment. The Commonwealth War Graves Commission can usually supply further details.

Other ranks' records

Personnel records for ordinary soldiers of the Great War have only recently begun to be released from the Ministry of Defence to the PRO. Around 70% of records were destroyed by enemy action during the Second World War, and those that survive are usually in a poor state of repair.

The first records transferred to PRO were the portion which escaped unscathed, known as the "unburnt" records. They represent only a tiny fraction of the men serving during the period. A programme is under way to place surviving "burnt" records on microfilm, which will take several years; the process is hampered by the fragile state of many documents. Even when the project is complete the chances are stacked against any particular set of documents being present.

Surviving service records are extremely informative. Attestation and discharge papers can be accompanied by a number of other forms, including medical history forms, conduct sheets, civil convictions, descriptive returns, casualty forms and employment sheets. Together they provide a full record of the man's life in the Army.

The "unburnt" records are in class WO 364, available in the Microfilm Viewing Room. As "burnt" records are made available they will be placed in class WO 363. The MOD are prepared to search for records not yet filmed and to provide a precis of the contents; there is a non-returnable fee of £20 for the service. This facility is open to anyone, not just proven next-of-kin.

On 1 April 1998 naval personnel records from the Great War period were released at the PRO. They follow on from those already available in ADM 188 and include men who

Place	Date	Hour	Summary of Events and Information	Remarks, reference to Appendices
	1917.			
FIELD.	1st. May.		Day Fine. Working parties were found and balance of the men were employed cutting shell slits and small shelters in the railway cutting. 2/Lieut. J. Dobson was slightly wounded but remained at duty.	
	2nd. May.		Ref. Map 51.B. N.W. & N.E. $\frac{1}{20,000}$;- Divisional Operation Order for attack next day on the RED LINE was received about 2-30 p.m.—The battalion's task being that portion of the RED LINE stretching along the edge of the lagoon S. of PLUVAIN from assembly positions in CREET trench and the embankment W. of CREET in H.24.b. Major. E.G.S. TRUELL left to take command of 12th. Manchester Regt.- handing over to Capt. R.B. NEILL. The rest of the day was spent in making preparations for the attack; a portion of officers and N.C.O's going forward to view the ground, the balance attending to issue of ammunition, rations, Lewis Guns, etc., At 10-10 p.m. the battalion moved to its assembly positions.- its strength being 18 officers and 392 Other Ranks.	
	3rd. May.		A heavy bombardment of all guns took place during the night. A heavy Machine Gun barrage commenced at ZERO, (3-45 a.m.) on German rear lines. This barrage was fixed and continued throughout the attack. At ZERO hour the 1st. Royal Warwickshire Regt. left our front line to take the BLACK and BLUE Lines, (see special Sheet, parts of squares 51b. N.W. & N.E.) At 4-15 a.m. the Battalion moved out of its assembly positions in two waves, - "A" Coy. on the Right, "B" Coy. on the Left with No. 9. Platoon of "C" Coy. as moppers up following the leading wave, with orders to move at the rate of 50 yds. in 1 minute so as to arrive at the BLUE LINE in time to leave it at 5-10 a.m. on the appearance of a smoke salvo and thence at rate of 50 yds per minute so as to reach RED Line at 5-26 a.m. in accordance with artillery programme. At about 4-25 a.m. "A" & "B" Coys. got held up on the near side of the ROEUX-GAVRELLE Road by heavy Machine Gun Fire from the CHEMICAL WORKS and a house S. of them also from the buildings N. of the CHATEAU and the CHATEAU itself. This forced "A" Coy. across "B" front and parties of the DUKE OF WELLINGTON'S Regt. and the KING'S OWN got mixed up with our men. 2/Lieut. REEVE although wounded, collected all Irish Fusiliers, re-organised them, and dug in on a line from W. of the CHATEAU to the Railway embankment where he established himself and remained until recalled by order at 10-10 p.m. He succeeded in withdrawing with few casualties bringing his wounded with him.	

A5534 Wt. W4973 M687 750,000 8/16 D. D. & L. Ltd. Forms/C.2118/13.

enlisted up until 1923, including short service recruits who signed up for five or seven years. The service records in ADM 188 give date and place of birth, date of enlistment, brief physical description, remarks on character and, most importantly, ships served upon.

Naval service records are divided into three numerical groups. Numbers 165001-178000 were allocated chronologically to new recruits January 1892-December 1893. Between January 1894 and December 1907 separate trades were each allocated a block of service numbers and the recruit's number was dependant on his chosen trade. The final group were prefixed by a letter indicating a trade group, and then numbered chronologically within each trade. For example, the service numbers of RNAS recruits from 1914-18 were prefixed F, while a stoker would have a number beginning with K.

RFC other ranks' personnel records are included among Army "unburnt" and "burnt" records already released or currently being transferred. Like Army records, the majority were destroyed during the Second World War.

Casualties

When researching First World War medals it is very important to establish whether the recipient became a casualty. This is equally true of officers and ORs from all service branches. Status as a casualty or not dictates all further research. The medal index card is often (though not always) annotated with this information, and the medal roll should certainly confirm it. Names can also be checked against the First World War

Detail from the war diary of the 1st Battalion, Royal Irish Fusiliers, in WO 95/1482. These pages include a description of the action at the Rouex Chemical Works on 3 May 1917 for which George Reeve was awarded the Military Cross.

casualty index at Myddleton Place or the relevant volume of *Soldier's Died in the Great War*, after establishing the unit from the medals.

Naval casualties are recorded in ADM 242 at the PRO, a card index showing the date, place and cause of death for all ranks 1914-20. See also files in ADM 104/144-149, which names all ranks killed or wounded in action between 1854 and 1929. This class of documents enables researchers to find out about wounded seamen; no such index exists for the Army. The Admiralty published monthly alphabetical casualty lists, which included officers and men; however, checking through them is a laborious process unless an approximate date is known.

The RAF Museum at Hendon holds record cards for RFC and RAF First World War casualties. Cards exist for both killed and wounded airmen, outlining the cause of death or injury. However, the records are fragmentary for the earliest part of the war and do not always include casualties from outside the European theatre. Several casualty rolls have been compiled to list air casualties. These include the register of air deaths at the Family Record Centre, Myddleton Place, and another memorial register held at the Imperial War Museum.

The Commonwealth War Graves Commission can supply

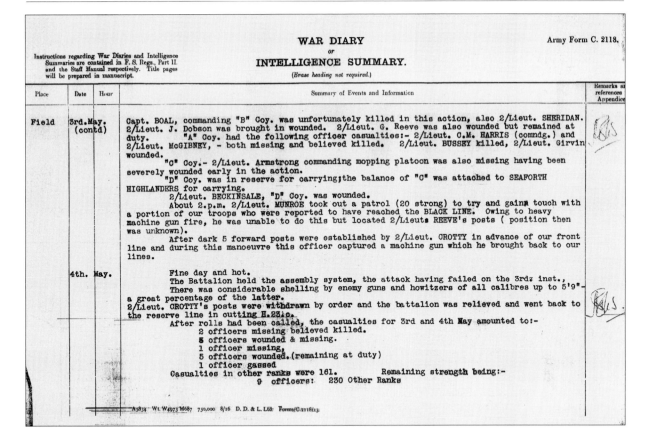

WAR DIARY
or
INTELLIGENCE SUMMARY.
(*Erase heading not required.*)

Army Form C. 2118.

Instructions regarding War Diaries and Intelligence Summaries are contained in F. S. Regs., Part II. and the Staff Manual respectively. Title pages will be prepared in manuscript.

Place	Date	Hour	Summary of Events and Information	Remarks and references to Appendices
Field	3rd.May. (contd)		Capt. BOAL, commanding "B" Coy. was unfortunately killed in this action, also 2/Lieut. SHERIDAN. 2/Lieut. J. Dobson was brought in wounded. 2/Lieut. G. Reeve was also wounded but remained at duty. "A" Coy. had the following officer casualties:- 2/Lieut. C.M. HARRIS (comndg.) and 2/Lieut. McGIBNEY, - both missing and believed killed. 2/Lieut. BUSSEY killed, 2/Lieut. Girvin wounded. "C" Coy.- 2/Lieut. Armstrong commanding mopping platoon was also missing having been severely wounded early in the action. "D" Coy. was in reserve for carrying;the balance of "C" was attached to SEAFORTH HIGHLANDERS for carrying. 2/Lieut. BECKINSALE, "D" Coy. was wounded. About 2.p.m. 2/Lieut. MUNROE took out a patrol (20 strong) to try and gain touch with a portion of our troops who were reported to have reached the BLACK LINE. Owing to heavy machine gun fire, he was unable to do this but located 2/Lieuts REEVE's posts (position then was unknown). After dark 5 forward posts were established by 2/Lieut. CROTTY in advance of our front line and during this manoeuvre this officer captured a machine gun which he brought back to our lines.	
	4th. May.		Fine day and hot. The Battalion held the assembly system, the attack having failed on the 3rd inst., There was considerable shelling by enemy guns and howitzers of all calibres up to 5'9" a great percentage of the latter. 2/Lieut. CROTTY's posts were withdrawn by order and the battalion was relieved and went back to the reserve line in cutting H.23io. After rolls had been called, the casualties for 3rd and 4th May amounted to:- 2 officers missing believed killed. 5 officers wounded & missing. 1 officer missing, 5 officers wounded.(remaining at duty) 1 officer gassed Casualties in other ranks were 161. Remaining strength being:- 9 officers: 230 Other Ranks	

A5834 Wt. W4973 M687 750,000 8/16 D. D. & L. Ltd. Forms/C.2118/13.

details of the last resting place of a casualty or where he is commemorated. The location of the grave gives a strong indication of where the man died; few bodies were moved very far, and many were buried where they fell.

It is a relatively simple matter to find out if a man died during the war; discovering whether or not he was wounded is much more difficult. Even when this has been established, tracking down where and when and in what circumstances is very frustrating. Very occasionally wounds are mentioned on the medal index card; more often the card just gives a reference to the Silver War Badge roll.

Further PRO sources

Once the unit has been confirmed and status as a casualty identified, serious research can start. These two factors decide the sources which can be explored. Having said that, researchers should accept that very frequently this is the end of the road. There may be nothing else left to discover.

For soldiers the next document to consult is the unit war diary. They are in document classes WO 95 and WO 154 at the Public Record Office. War diaries sketch the day-to-day activities of the unit, offering an insight into the life of the man awarded the medals. Other ranks are seldom mentioned by name, although officers frequently rate the odd line or two. It is common to find a nominal roll of officers after a battle, annotating those killed, wounded, missing and the few survivors. These lists may indicate the post each officer occupied, sometimes making it possible to identify patrols and raids he took part in. Arrivals, departures and gallantry awards also feature regularly. Map references often accompany descriptions of where events took place. Many Western Front trench maps referred to can be seen in class WO 297. Those for other theatres of war are in separate classes.

Although few war diaries name other ranks, there are exceptions and many mention senior NCOs. Even when ORs are not referred to individually, significant incidents may be mentioned. If the soldier was killed in action, check the war diary for the day in question. He may have been the only casualty on that occasion and the incident might be mentioned.

The PRO preserves a small number of medical documents, although only a representative sample of the millions created during the conflict. If the medal recipient was a casualty or rendered unfit through sickness, then the files in MH 106 could be checked. Likewise, a few pension documents survive. Some refer to men awarded disability pensions in class PIN 26, others relate to claims pursued by widows and dependants (PIN 82).

The PRO retains a number of documents concerned with wartime courts martial. Records of other ranks tried by district court martial give name, rank, regiment, where tried, what they were charged with and the result of proceedings. The registers are in WO 86/62-85. Records of general courts martial abroad cover proceedings against officers as well as men in WO 90/6-8.

The PRO offers little scope for researching the role played by naval personnel. No ships' logs have been released, and sources outside the PRO provide better opportunities. Records

Portraits of George Reeve found in contemporary reports: as a young ranker in pre-1914 full dress, and as a lieutenant.

for RFC, RNAS and RAF personnel are more extensive. A variety of operational records survive in class AIR 1, detailed within Chapter 9.

Large numbers of British servicemen became prisoners of war, and lists of prisoners were kept by the International Committee of the Red Cross and the **British Red Cross Society**. Enquiries should be sent to:
International Welfare Department
British Red Cross Society
9 Grosvenor Crescent
London SW1X 7EJ.

The **Imperial War Museum** Department of Printed Books holds some useful material to aid research into POWs. Weekly War Office Casualty Lists refer to men taken prisoner, and the IWM holds a run from August 1917 to February 1918. Men taken prisoner before Christmas 1914 were entitled to Princess Mary's Gift Boxes, and some information about them was collated at the time. Details of many are given in the Women's Work Collection.

The PRO has some files relating to POWs, although few are concerned with individuals. Those which do mention names are generally in the form of a list. Men detained in Turkey, Germany and Switzerland in 1916 are listed in AIR 1/892. ADM 1/8420/124 lists prisoners at some German camps in July 1915.

Newspapers

Newspapers are possibly the best source of information about First World War servicemen. Chapter 11 covered newspapers in some detail, but their importance cannot be overemphasised. Each edition of every regional paper was packed with items about local men throughout the war years. The range of war

news published was vast, and there is no better way of sensing the national mood than browsing through local papers printed at the time. By scouring the pages of the weekly paper identified as giving the best coverage of a particular unit, there is a reasonably good chance of finding mention of the man under research, especially if he was an officer, became a casualty, or was decorated for bravery.

Books

Thousands of books have been written about the First World War, many of which assist with medal research. Most can be seen at large reference libraries or military museums. Some of the best-known titles are listed in Chapter 10. The number of books written about the war compensates for the lack of information available about individuals. A wide collection of reference books is a "must" for anyone contemplating regular research into Great War medals. The more research carried out, the greater the need for reference material.

Other sources

Collecting and researching Great War medals awarded to local men is a popular theme. Many different types of memorials can be seen throughout the country, erected to commemorate the fallen in churches, schools, factories and on village greens; Chapter 14 explores this source more fully.

Photographs and postcards have been mentioned previously. Millions of portraits were taken of men in uniform by local studios at home and abroad, and sent proudly home. Theoretically there should be a chance of a photo having been taken of most servicemen; but the huge majority are now divorced from the medals, and reuniting them is extremely difficult. A collection of identifiable First World War photographs, postcards and other ephemera has been compiled by Simon Jervis. The contents have been indexed on computer and searches can be carried out by application to Imperial Soldier Searches, Yew Tree Cottage, Blackford, Shropshire SY8 2ET at a cost of £3.00 with a stamped addressed envelope.

Military museums store a variety of original paperwork from the period. Letters, diaries, journals, memoirs and other ephemera can be superb sources if there is coverage for the unit under research. The Liddle Collection at the Brotherton Library, University of Leeds contains a large selection of records assembled by Peter Liddle, a well-known historian. The archive continues to grow, up-dated by donations of personal memorabilia. Bona fide researchers are given access to the collection by appointment. The telephone number is 0113 233 5566.

County record offices may hold relevant archive material. Paperwork varies from one record office to another, but it is common to find some documentation relating to the recruitment of local men and the activities of units affiliated to the region.

The potential for Great War research is huge, but all too often the only returns for painstaking detective work are photocopies of the medal index card and medal rolls at the PRO. It is intensely frustrating when you read the exploits of the man's battalion, yet cannot glean any information about his individual experiences. Still - he was there, he endured, and he lived or died. Whatever his rank or unit, the medals were hard earned, and were often a paltry reward for years of horror in the trenches, on the seas or over the lines. Those medals which do prove researchable more than make up for those which do not.

Research Notes

David Boyce

The PRO medal index card for David Boyce yielded little information. It did not mention his wound, when he arrived at the Front, or the battalion he served with.

Medal roll WO 329/1687 recorded that David Boyce served with the 9th Battalion, Royal Irish Fusiliers, the County Armagh Battalion. This battalion formed part of Kitchener's "New Army" of volunteers, and served with the 36th Ulster Division through most of the major campaigns after being blooded on the Somme in July 1916.

WO 95/2505, the war diary of the 9th Royal Irish Fusiliers, reported the battalion attack on the first day of the Somme in detail. Fifteen officers and around 600 men took part in the assault; by the end of the day all officers were killed, wounded or missing, along with 518 other ranks. The four assault waves were massacred by German machine guns unharmed by the preceding artillery barrage. Despite huge losses the battalion took their primary objective, Beaucourt Station; as so often, the survivors were later forced to withdraw in the face of heavy counter-attacks when reinforcements were wiped out before they could come up in support. There is no evidence to confirm whether or not my grandfather took part; but family legend insists that he and his two brothers enlisted together, and both of them were wounded in the battle.

The war diary describes numerous actions as the war ebbed and flowed, until 16 August 1917 - the day David Boyce was badly wounded at the battle of Langemarck, part of Third Ypres. The battalion attacked from the area of Pommern Redoubt at 4.45am. The leading companies came under heavy fire as they advanced towards Hill 35, forcing them to merge. The advance was held up for 20 minutes and the supporting barrage passed ahead of the battalion. Once Hill 35 was taken the 9th RIF pressed on, but found enemy wire virtually uncut; they came under heavy fire from "Gallipoli" and other German strongpoints, and suffered many casualties. The attack ground to a halt. The men withdrew, but long range machine gun fire enfiladed the untraversed trench, resulting in more casualties. A further withdrawal was outflanked by the enemy, and the battalion finally retired south of Hill 35 to the starting position.

The war diary reports that No Man's Land was extremely cut up and heavy going - a dry euphemism for a hell of deep mud and shellholes. The artillery support was described as good, but advanced far too fast. The most telling part of the account is the description of the enemy: "The resistance encountered was very stubborn both with MG and rifles, enemy only retired when almost surrounded. Very few allowed themselves to be taken prisoner. They fought practically until every man was killed on Hill 35. Positions were held until our men were right into them."

It is impossible to gain any indication of when David Boyce was hit, or how he got back to British lines; but whatever the exact details, the outlook for a man falling wounded in this dreadful, muddy scene of carnage was fearsome. Total battalion casualties were 36 killed in action, 323 wounded, 12 shell-shocked, 83 missing, and two missing believed killed: a total of 456.

A sketchmap accompanying the war diary referred to a trench map - Frenzenberg Sheet, Edition 2. This map can be seen in class WO 297/1877 and makes it possible to trace the route taken on the day, identifying all the enemy strongpoints. No unit history exists for the 9th Royal Irish Fusiliers, but accounts of their exploits appear in the 36th Division history and several other books; these are covered at the end of Chapter 10.

George Reeve

Research into George Reeve revealed an absolute mass of information from a variety of sources, and space permits only an abbreviated summary of material discovered.

The medal index card for George Reeve was crammed with information. He entered the conflict on 22 August 1914 as Sergeant 7574 Royal Irish Fusiliers. The card confirms his MC and MM, records the date of his commission, and also notes the date of his accidental death. Reeve was also entitled to the 1914 Star, British War Medal and Victory Medal. Reference numbers on the card indicate that they were issued, but notes in the remarks column are indecipherable. Reeve is listed on two medal rolls, one for officers and one for ORs. These make the fate of the missing campaign medals no clearer, and their present whereabouts are unknown.

The Military Medal index confirmed Reeve's entitlement to the MM and gave the *London Gazette* date as 11 November 1916. No citation appears. The MID index revealed that Reeve was mentioned in despatches on 1 January 1916 for gallant and distinguished conduct.

Reeve first appeared in the 1st RIF war diary, WO 95/1482, on 19 April 1915 when he was promoted to acting regimental sergeant major. The following day he was admitted to hospital. He was reconfirmed as acting RSM on 26 June.

On 30 November 1915 the diary records that Lieut.G.Reeve joined for duty after being granted a commission.

A notable incident occurred on 18 January 1916. While visiting outposts Reeve was slightly wounded by enemy snipers, together with a Lt.Kirkby. They were dragged to safety by an orderly, who bandaged them, set off for help, and returned with stretcher bearers. The orderly was under heavy fire the whole time, and was subsequently awarded the DCM - a most coveted decoration - for his bravery.

Reeve took over command of C Company on 9 October 1916. He was listed among wounded officers after the battalion was engaged in fighting around Guillemont and Ginchy during the final stages of the battle of the Somme, 10-14 October 1916.

Reeve next featured on 26 November 1916, when the GOC 4th Division presented Military Medals at Ercourt to members of the battalion for "gallantry and good service up at Ypres in 1915." Reeve was one of 16 men so decorated.

On 22 April 1917 Reeve was posted to B Company. On 3 May the battalion took part in an offensive action near the Roeux Chemical Works, and 2nd Lt.Reeve played a heroic part in the fighting. The war diary tells how, at around 4.25am, A and B Coys. got held up on the near side of the Roeux/Gavrelle road by heavy machine gun fire from the Chemical Works and other strongpoints. The two companies became mixed up with men from other battalions. Reeve, although wounded, gathered his men, re-organized them, and dug in until recalled by order at 10.10pm. He withdrew with few casualties, bringing out his wounded. The OC B Coy was killed in this action; Reeve was wounded but remained on duty - in all nine officers and 161 ORs of the battalion became casualties during that day.

WO/95/2502 is the first battalion war diary for 1917, and Reeve was acting adjutant for part of the time; his duties included the compilation of the diary, so his signature appears quite frequently. On 26 August 1917 the battalion celebrated the third anniversary of the battle of Le Cateau. The survivors, including Reeve, totalled six officers and 84 men; they paraded, and were congratulated by the CO. Lt.Reeve was listed on a nominal roll at Appendix E to the diary.

Witnesses for a field general court martial were ordered to report to 2nd Lt. Reeve MC at 108th Field Ambulance at 10am on 20 September 1917 at Royalcourt. They were required for the trial of 8104 Pte.W. Clarke, A Coy., and 23676 T.Cochrane, D Company. On 5 November 1917 the diary announced that Pte.G.Hanna had been sentenced to death; he was the first member of the battalion sentenced to be shot. The firing party under Lt.Reeve MC were ordered to proceed to Divisional HQ; Pte.Hanna was shot the following morning at 6.40am.

The 1918 war diary, WO 95/2505, was checked. Reeve was acting adjutant and compiled the diary during February 1918. From February he was not mentioned.

The *London Gazette* index for July 1917 is ZJ 1/653. Reeve's Military Cross was listed on page 7242, Volume 111

1917, PRO reference ZJ 1/646. The full citation was given for the action at Rouex Chemical Works:

"For conspicuous gallantry and devotion to duty. He showed great resource and determination in assuming command of his company when all other officers were casualties, in reorganising men of other companies, and in digging in and maintaining his position. He subsequently withdrew with his flanks in the air, and brought all his wounded with him. His skill was most marked."

The Army List details Reeve's career prior to the First World War. The October 1918 issue records Reeve as born on 12 February 1884. He spent 2 years 226 days in the ranks, and transferred to the Reserve on 23 February 1905. After rejoining the following June, Reeve's service in the ranks totalled 8 years 313 days. He was a WO(I) for 185 days, and was commissioned second lieutenant on 10 November 1915. Promotion to lieutenant followed on 24 April 1917.

Army officers' records were released to the PRO in February 1998. George Reeve is listed on microfilm in WO 338, long number reference 119028. This was checked against WO 339 index and referred to class WO 339/49015.

WO 339/49015 is a bulky file about the army career of George Reeve. The file contains a truly superb collection of over 70 papers; to any researcher this sort of resource represents pure gold dust. The file is divided into two sections, one of service papers and the other made up of various reports relating to his death. Most of the service papers dealt with his time in the ranks, which was excellent, as this was unknown territory. The documents made it possible to assemble a complete record of George Reeve's military life.

AFB 217 records George Reeve's original short service attestation, signed on 12 July 1902. He was 18 years 5 months old, born in Spratton near Northampton, a labourer by trade. He enlisted for three years in the 1st Battalion, Royal Irish Fusiliers, with a commitment to nine years in the Reserve. At the time he was 5ft 6½ins tall, 132 lbs, chest 33½ins, 35½ expanded, fresh complexion, brown eyes, red hair, C of E, with no distinguishing marks.

On completion of his service with the Colours Reeve transferred to the Reserve on 23 February 1905. His description at discharge was: aged 21, 5ft 8½ins, chest 38ins, waist 34ins, helmet size 23ins, boot size 9, complexion fresh, eyes brown, hair red, trade labourer. His intended place of residence was 44 King Street, Northampton. Descriptive marks - nil. Total service - 2 years 227 days. His AFB 2077 Parchment discharge certificate assessed his conduct as "very good".

Employment was obviously hard to find in Northampton; and on 10 July 1906 the War Office granted permission for Reeve to rejoin the Colours. He was informed that his recent application to complete nine years service had been successful, provided he remained unmarried. Reeve replied by telegram on 31 October 1906, stating that he no longer desired to rejoin and had found employment. The authority to rejoin was cancelled. Nevertheless, according to Reeve's record of service document, completed on AFB 200, he did in fact rejoin the Colours on 17 June 1906. Somewhere along the line he had a change of heart; perhaps his "good situation" fell through. Reeve's full record of service, taken from several AFB 200s, is as follows:

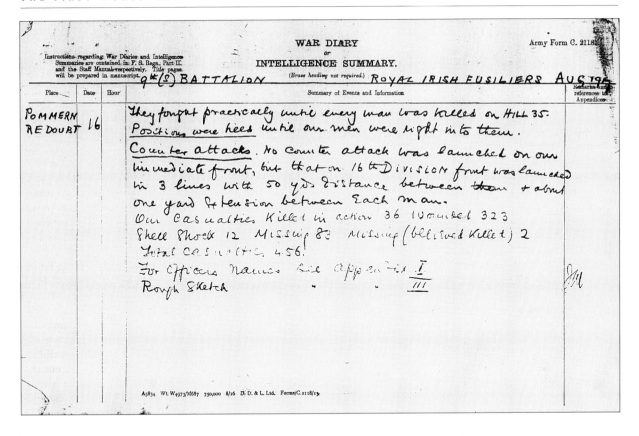

WAR DIARY
or
INTELLIGENCE SUMMARY.

Army Form C. 2118

Instructions regarding War Diaries and Intelligence Summaries are contained in F. S. Regs., Part II. and the Staff Manual respectively. Title pages will be prepared in manuscript.

9th (S) BATTALION (Erase heading not required.) ROYAL IRISH FUSILIERS AUG 191

Place	Date	Hour	Summary of Events and Information	Remarks and references to Appendices
POMMERN REDOUBT	16		They fought practically until every man was killed on HILL 35. Positions were held until our men were right into them. Counter attacks. No counter attack was launched on our immediate front, but that on 16th DIVISION front was launched in 3 lines with 50 yds distance between them + about one yard extension between each man. Our Casualties Killed in action 36 Wounded 323 Shell Shock 12 Missing 83 Missing (believed Killed) 2 Total Casualties 456. For Officers names see appendix I Rough Sketch " " III	

A5834 Wt. W4973/M687 750,000 8/16 D. D. & L. Ltd. Forms/C.2118/13.

12/7/02 ...	Attested Armagh Depot.
24/10/02 ...	Posted
19/10/03 ...	Promoted unpaid LCpl
31/10/03 ...	Paid LCpl.
1/4/04 ...	Granted service pay class I at 6d
12/7/04 ...	Granted 1 Good Conduct Badge
23/2/05 ...	Transferred to reserve on conversion of svce
23/2/06 ...	Reverted.
17/6/06 ...	Private. Rejoined colours to complete 9 yrs under authority WO letter 115/AB/87/279.
17/7/06 ...	Elects service pay class I: Rate 6d.
1/10/06 ...	Paid LCpl
1/3/07 ...	Reduced to Pte
20/7/07 ...	Promoted unpaid LCpl
17/8/07 ...	Paid LCpl
12/7/07 ...	Advanced 1d service pay after 5 yrs svce.
24/3/08 ...	GC Badge restored
4/11/08 ...	Promoted Cpl
7/5/09 ...	Promoted unpaid LSgt
5/3/10 ...	Reduced to Cpl
20/7/10 ...	Promoted paid LSgt
3/7/11 ...	Permitted to extend svce to complete 12 yrs
18/6/11 ...	Promoted Sgt vice Humphries
11/5/14 ...	Permitted to re-engage at Shorncliffe up to 21 years
20/3/15 ...	Promoted CSgt Coy QMS vice Wolsey
9/4/15 ...	Appointed acting CSM
9/5/15 ...	Promoted WOI CSM vice Tynan
10/11/15 ...	Commissioned 2Lt

War diaries were sometimes completed in manuscript, and are not always easily legible. This relatively clear example, found in WO 95/2505, is from the 9th Battalion, Royal Irish Fusiliers. This page includes part of the report on the unit's role in the battle of Langemarck on 16 August 1917, when David Boyce was wounded. Note the comments at the top on the stubborn bravery of the German defenders of Hill 35.

The recommendation form giving Reeve permission to extend his service to 12 years was completed at Bordon on 3 July 1911; he was aged 27 years 5 months and his character was assessed as very good. A medical record sheet accompanied the form; this began on 22 July 1906 at Kilbride Camp, when Reeve was examined and found fit for his original extension of service. He received dental treatment at Aldershot on 26 October 1909, at a cost of 2s.6d. for one filling. Reeve spent a week in Cambridge Military Hospital from 5 November 1909 after the toenails of both big toes were removed.

George Reeve's Regimental Conduct Sheet, AFB 120, made interesting reading. Several misdemeanours were reported: 28/2/07 Dublin Rank LCpl. Offence - (I) Quitting barracks when Company Orderly Corporal. (II) Disregarding Battalion Orders. Reported by Cpl.Schofield and Sgt.Robinson. Deprived of lance stripe 1/3/07 by Maj.P.R.Wood & forfeit one GC badge.

9/3/07 Dublin Rank Pte. Offence - Absent from Reveille till he surrendered himself at Bedford on 22nd inst, dressed in

War Office telegram, which survives in WO 339/49015, informing Mrs.Reeve of George's death - one of three she will have received between 1915 and 1918.

plain clothes. Reported by Cpl.McGerr and LSgt.Schofield. 14 days CB 27/3/07 by Lt.Col.W.Plomer, commenced 27/3/07 to 9/4/07. Forfeit 14 days pay.

13/4/09 Aldershot Rank Cpl. Offence - Making an improper reply to CSgt.Robinson. Reported by Sgt.Schofield and CSgt.Robinson. Severely reprimanded 14/4/09 Lt.Col.Plomer.

4/3/10 Aldershot Rank LSgt. Offence - Absent from Reveille till 1.30am 5/3/10. Reported by Sgt.Schofield and LCpl.Sullivan. Deprived of lance stripe 5/3/10 Col.Plomer.

An Employment Sheet, AFB 2066 dated 29 December 1913, assessed Sgt.Reeve's conduct as very good, with no cases of drunkenness on or off duty. He was employed as assistant regimental instructor of signalling and described as a good telegraphist and an excellent clerk, reliable and trustworthy.

AFW 3040, the next-of-kin card, showed father, George, 44 King Street, Northampton.

A Military History Sheet confirmed George Reeve as entitled to the 1914 Star, BWM, V. It was compiled when he was commissioned and totalled his home service at 12 years 41 days (12/7/02-21/8/14). At the time he had spent 1 year 81 days at the front, from 22/8/14 to 10/11/15. The sheet shows that Reeve passed his 3rd class Certificate of Education on 1 October 1902 and 2nd Class Certificate on 12 May 1904. He was awarded an assistant instructor's certificate of signalling on

22 December 1908. His service to date and next-of- kin details were listed as before, with the addition of mother, Rebecca, and brother, Richard.

Another casualty card up-dated Reeve's medical record; he suffered a gunshot wound to the head on 23 May 1915. A series of telegrams are with the papers, sent to inform his family of wounds received. Two were sent 21/1/16 and 25/1/16, regarding a slight gunshot wound to the leg received on 18 January 1916. He was admitted to 2 Red Cross Hospital, Rouen. Another, dated 16/10/16, states that Reeve was wounded on 12 October; a second sent the next day added that he had been admitted to 20 General Hospital, Etaples, with a gunshot wound to his left leg and slight shell-shock. On 15/5/17 a further telegram informed his mother that he had been wounded on 4 May, but remained at duty.

The final telegram, dated 15/10/18, simply states: "The Army Council express sympathy on learning of the death of Lieut.G.Reeve MC Irish Fusiliers."

A Committee of Adjustment was convened to settle Reeve's accounts on 19 October 1918, whereupon an inventory was made of all his clothing, equipment and personal effects. As a result of their enquiries it was established that his assets stood at £4 7s.5d.; after settling his debts the balance in hand stood at £2 13s.10½d. The balance and property listed were forwarded to his mother. The full inventory of the personal effects and kit of the late Lieutenant Reeve was very detailed. Items listed included:

His cigarette box and cigarettes, a purse containing four

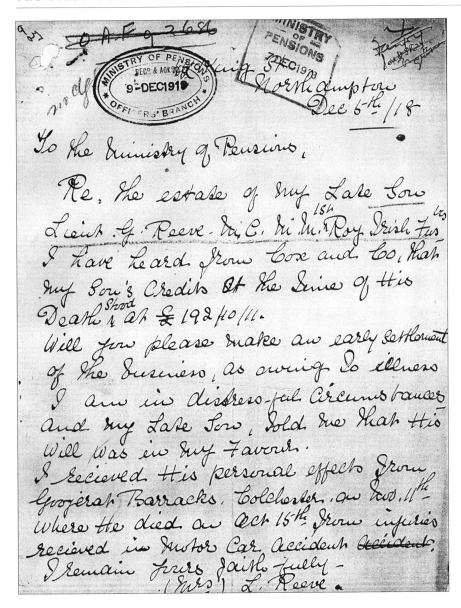

Letter from Mrs Reeve to the War Office requesting an early settlement of George's estate, as she was in "distress-ful circumstances".

coins & 7s.5d. cash, a wallet containing a watch & strap, ring, pencil, photographs, trench coat, puttees, field service pocket-book, bedroom slippers, cased prismatic compass, flask, further wallet containing an advance pay book, letters and photographs, his revolver and holster, ammunition pouch, and all his clothing and other acoutrements.

Two letters from his mother, Lydia Reeve, written during December 1918 to the Ministry of Pensions, are with the papers. She claimed to be in distress, seeking an early settlement of his affairs in her favour. His bankers, Cox and Co., had informed her that George's credits stood at £192 10s.11d.; she claims that George had told her that the will was in her favour (there is no mention of George senior).

The file also contains copies of the inquest depositions from Colchester Military Hospital, dated 17 October 1918. Rosalie March, a single lady, of 31 Hythe Station Road, Colchester, was with Reeve when the accident occurred. His body was identified by Lt.Harold Pike, Adjt. 52KRRC. He last saw Reeve alive at dinner in the officer's mess. Pike stated that Reeve had won the MC and MM and been wounded four times, and that he was an old soldier, promoted for bravery. He said he was perfectly fit except for an injury to the leg. Depositions describing the accident were taken from a number of witnesses; all are with the file.

No will was found for George Reeve. Letters of administration were granted at Northampton District Probate Registry on 3 May 1919 to George Reeve, the natural and lawful father and next-of-kin. Gross value of the estate was £215 13s.9d. The section for Disposal of Medals & Decorations was unfortunately not completed.

The above represents only a brief precis of the papers on George Reeve's file. The benefit of the newly released officers' papers in WO 338 can be clearly seen. Few files are as comprehensive as this one, however, so such excellent results cannot be expected every time.

CHAPTER 16: HELP IS AT HAND

Researching medals is primarily a lone activity. Only the researcher knows where the hunt is leading and what the eventual goals are. Yet there are benefits to be gained from sharing information and passing on new sources. A number of forums exist through which medal researchers can exchange ideas or seek assistance. Medal collectors with shared interests can prosper by collaboration, reducing cost and time spent in archives. Discussion promotes fresh ideas and prevents mistakes. Best of all, teamwork increases the pleasure gained from the hobby, and ensures that you have someone with whom to share success and failure.

No matter how solitary the researcher may sometimes feel when faced by an apparently closed historical door, there is a huge amount of help available. It is rare to find anyone looking at a subject so remote that absolutely no-one else is able to offer useful information. Indeed, it is not unusual to find that several people are simultaneously conducting research into different aspects of the same topic, and all can gain from sharing information. The more experienced researcher in any group may feel short-changed initially if he is doing all the giving without obtaining much in return. However, things may become less one-sided over the passage of time: the budding medal researcher he has nurtured may prove to be a skilled digger who repays his patience many times over.

Before research projects can be shared or assistance sought, the researcher needs to identify where people with common interests might be found. Dozens of societies cater for military enthusiasts and there are usually members with relevant knowledge. Few societies exist purely for medal enthusiasts, but many are dedicated to some form of military research. The membership may have a common attraction to a particular campaign or share interest in units from a particular region. It is a smart move for any medal researcher to join societies whose field of study reflects his own.

There is one society totally dedicated to our subject. The **Orders and Medals Research Society** (OMRS) exists to promote research into all aspects of medals. Members' interests range from the numismatic background through to the more popular aspect of researching the men behind the medals. Altogether there are some 2,500 OMRS members, and their combined knowledge and expertise is unsurpassed. The annual membership fee is £12.00, and this small sum provides each member with a number of benefits.

The society publishes a quarterly journal containing well-researched articles and passing on research information. Members are provided with an opportunity to broadcast their interests, and

a noticeboard allows them to advertise for medals they require. This column regularly includes appeals on behalf of families trying to trace medals awarded to military ancestors. Each new member is introduced through the journal, with a brief list of their interests. This first appearance tends to attract a fair amount of correspondence. As one might expect, medal dealers are keen to offer the new member items which match his advertised interests. Other letters may be more promising. Existing members frequently contact new recruits with corresponding interests; this response can lead to on-going contact and a forged friendship between members from opposite ends of the country.

The OMRS holds an annual convention in London, preceded by a formal dinner for members and guests. The convention provides an opportunity for collectors to meet informally and "talk medals." In recent years the venue has been The Connaught Rooms in Holborn. Numerous stands sell medals, military books, militaria and ephemera. Others exhibit research carried out by OMRS members.

Several regional branches exist under the umbrella of the OMRS. At present there are branches in Manchester, the Cotswolds, Scotland, Sussex and Northumbria, as well as specialised branches for ribbons and miniatures. These are governed by the rules of the parent society.

Anyone interested in medal collecting and/or medal research should give serious consideration to joining the OMRS. Their subsequent involvement depends upon personal preference: some members only wish to receive the journal and visit the convention, while others attend meetings and play a full role. Collectors keen on research can only gain from contact with like-minded enthusiasts.

The **Medal Society of Ireland** pursues similar aims to the OMRS, although on a smaller scale with a membership of around two hundred and fifty. The stated purpose of the society is "to encourage the study of medals and badges in their various collectable forms, with special emphasis on Irish-related material". Annual membership fees are IR£12, although there is a reduced fee of IR£6 for members under the age of sixteen. New members and their interests are introduced via the pages of the quarterly MSI journal, which is full of items on an Irish theme. The magazine carries a small advertising section, priced at IR£5 for insertions in four journals.

Some type of historical or research society has been formed to pursue interest into almost every campaign ever conducted by British forces. The size of membership reflects the popularity of the campaign, but membership will nearly always add to knowledge about "your" war. Most research societies produce a journal or newsletter, which not only contains interesting articles concerning the campaign, but also lists members' interests and introduces less well-known sources of information. Some of the major societies most likely to be of assistance to medal researchers are as follows (see also the list of useful addresses in Appendix VII):

The **Society for Army Historical Research** is centred at the National Army Museum, Royal Hospital Road, London SW3 4HT. Formed in 1921, this is Britain's oldest military research society. The annual membership fee is £18, and members receive an informative quarterly journal. The **Military Historical Society** has over a thousand members interested in various aspects of Britain's military past. The society produces a quarterly bulletin; annual membership costs £10. The **Scottish Military Historical Society** issues a journal and seeks to promote research into all areas of Scotland's military past.

The **Victorian Military Society** seeks to further all research into military matters from the last century until the start of the First World War. A journal is produced four times a year. The **Crimean War Research Society** is concerned with research into all aspects of the war, including medals; a journal called *The War Correspondent* is published four times a year. The **Anglo-Zulu War Research Society** produces three issues of its journal every year; society membership costs £10 annually for UK/BFPO residents and £15 for all others. Researchers interested in Indian awards might benefit from membership of the **Indian Military Historical Society**. This encourages research into all aspects of military life in India, including medals awarded for any of the various Indian campaigns. Four journals appear every year.

The **Naval Historical Collectors' and Research Association** caters for those interested in naval subjects and collectors of naval artefacts. The **Royal Marines Historical Society** exists to further research into the rich and varied history of the Corps.

The societies listed here are but a few of those which exist to further study of different aspects of the nation's military past. They are not there to cater solely for medal collectors and researchers, but medal enthusiasts are well represented in their ranks. Joining a society whose theme corresponds to that under research is inexpensive and can lead to the establishment of useful contacts. The less experienced can benefit from the advice of members well versed in military research. A number of regional societies give the opportunity for members to meet and exchange ideas on a regular basis.

Several magazines provide platforms for seeking help with a research project. Only one publication is devoted specifically to medals, but others offer the possibility to request information through their pages.

Medal News is the only commercially produced magazine aimed at medal collectors. Until recently it was only available on subscription, but now it can be found in major outlets across the country. The publishers are Token Publishing, a specialist publishing house whose postal address is PO Box 14, Honiton, Devon EX14 9YP. Articles in *Medal News* span the whole range of medal- related subjects. Many relate details of research carried out. The magazine focuses attention on current trends in the hobby and reports upon the auction scene.

Feature articles are likely to entertain anyone with even a passing interest in medals, but a couple of regular monthly

Wyke House, Withernsea, the Davis family home.
(Courtesy Jean Nordon)

columns are of particular interest to researchers. The "Medal Tracker" column enables subscribers to advertise for wanted medals free of charge; the same facility is charged at £2.00 per entry to non-subscribers. Classified advertisements at the rear of the magazine are free to subscribers and 50p. per word to non-subscribers. These provide an excellent noticeboard for eliciting help from a dedicated medal-collecting audience. Another small section of the magazine called "On Parade" publishes medal-related enquiries. Typical entries picture medals which cannot be identified, or ask how to develop a line of enquiry. When research comes up against an apparently insurmountable obstacle, this column could provide the key.

Navy News is published by the Royal Naval Association, HMS *Nelson*, Portsmouth, Hants P01 3HH. The magazine contains a section to assist ex-servicemen contact old shipmates. Medal enthusiasts keen to research recent awards may find it a good source for eyewitness accounts and personal reminiscences of an action which interests them. It might even be possible to trace shipmates of the sailor whose medals are under the microscope; their memories of his role in the proceedings would be an excellent addition to research. Some may possess elusive photographs.

The Legion is the Army equivalent of *Navy News*, published by The Royal British Legion. The magazine offers similar services to those mentioned above, and enquiries should be addressed to The Royal British Legion at 49 Pall Mall, London SW1Y 5JY. *Soldier* magazine, the current official Army publication, also includes an enquiry service. *Soldier* is produced fortnightly from Parsons House, Ordnance Road, Aldershot, Hants GU11 2DU.

It must not be forgotten that medal research is not the main purpose of such servicemen's magazine columns, so make your intentions clear from the outset. Many ex-servicemen are reluctant to speak of past experiences; some can be upset by what they perceive as a morbid interest in tragic events which touch them personally, *so be prepared to back off and respect their feelings.* Others are quite happy to narrate events in graphic detail. Try to be tactful, and gauge their feelings before plunging in to ask questions about what could well have been extremely harrowing experiences. It goes without saying that it is also important to meet any costs incurred by anybody responding to an advertisement; and to treat any original material with the greatest care. The personal value to a veteran or relative of a document or photograph far outweighs its notional financial value, so always use registered postal services (and actively encourage correspondents to do the same - elderly people are sometimes too trusting of the efficiency of today's public services).

Medal researchers can profit from other magazines apart from those dedicated to the military. Genealogical publications also provide research opportunities and invite a response from a different cross-section of the public, not specifically interested in military matters but tuned in to the techniques of research.

Family Tree is the most prestigious commercial genealogical publication, packed with authoritative features about family research. While the magazine is primarily concerned with genealogy, a surprisingly large number of items cover military research. *Family Tree* is similar to *Medal News* from a researcher's perspective. Many articles make entertaining reading, but some features are of particular interest. The "Can You Help" page is self-explanatory: readers submit enquiries for publication, requesting assistance from a wide audience. This column could be put to good use by medal researchers seeking information about a unit or establishment. Readers can publish surnames of interest in a "Reader's Interests" column. The minimum charge is £1.24 for a single entry and 32p. for additional entries. The service is designed for genealogists, although there is nothing to prevent any medal researcher taking advantage of it. "Questions and Answers" offers the chance to raise general queries, which are answered by Jean Cole, a well-known genealogist. Many questions put to her request advice into military research, and make informative reading.

The magazine contains a monthly update from the Public Record Office, keeping readers abreast of changes at the PRO and new documentation released. *Family Tree* is full of articles about less well-known research sources and unpublicised indexes that would never be discovered in the normal course of events, and is well worth regular scrutiny by researchers keen to make use of all types of available information.

After looking at the possibilities offered by specialist magazines, consider placing an advertisement or short article in a **regional newspaper** published near where the medal recipient lived. This costs next to nothing and can produce spectacular results. Newspaper advertisements are a good source of anecdotal memories, adding personality to what is known. Correspondents are usually thrilled to find that a friend's or relative's memory survives, and are happy to assist in any way they can - for instance, by taking photographs or copying a memorial inscription.

It is estimated that at any one time in the United Kingdom there are in the region of one million people carrying out some form of family tree research. **Family history societies** exist to further their activities. Most have developed along regional lines to promote genealogical interest in a given locality. They generally publish a journal containing similar articles to those in Family Tree but with a more localised slant. Family tree enthusiasts usually join societies associated with areas where their forebears originated. Medal researchers who specialise in geographically affiliated units might consider joining a family history society in the area of interest. Yearly subscriptions are not extortionate, and several articles of interest are likely to appear within the published journal over the course of a year.

Every such society seems to have its quota of military enthusiasts, and their knowledge can be very thorough. Such people may be primarily genealogists, but they are often acquainted with obscure military research archives in the region. It is not unusual to unearth research carried out into local units by society members who have not the slightest interest in medals. In some cases they have compiled lists and indexes from a host of local sources, and are generally willing to check names against their material.

On joining, new members are normally entitled to publish names they are researching in the society journal and can expect to hear from fellow members who have already conducted research into the names listed. Apart from the specific assistance this may provide, it is also useful to read about the local research facilities detailed in most journals on a regular basis.

It should be stressed that the author does not suggest that all medal researchers should become genealogists: when all is said and done, it is the medals we are interested in. However, some of the facilities open to family tree enthusiasts can be of real value in medal research; it is for the individual to choose how far down the genealogical line to proceed.

Local history societies can benefit anyone researching medals to men from a specific geographic location or units with ties to a particular area. Societies may be associated with counties, towns or any other regional variation. Details can be obtained from the headquarters of the **British Association for Local History** at 24 Lower St., Harnham, Salisbury, Wilts SP2 8EY. Invariably, they have some members with an interest in local military history and good knowledge of local sources. A large number of societies publish a journal.

Paid research services

Some medal collectors are interested in the results of research, but have neither the time nor inclination to do the work themselves. Those with sufficient funds can employ a professional researcher to do the digging for them. Advertisements appear in *Medal News* and *Family Tree* magazines; rates for basic PRO and genealogical investigation are normally specified, although more far-reaching research is considerably more expensive.

The type of service offered and commissioned is a matter for the individuals to decide. Research targets and fees should be agreed in advance to prevent nasty shocks at a later stage. If possible, try to use a recommended researcher; and establish a system whereby the researcher reports regularly on progress made and costs incurred, so that further work can be discussed and agreed in advance.

Many advertisements placed by professional researchers contain the letters AGRA, indicating that the advertiser is a member of the Association of Genealogists and Record Agents. Membership denotes that the researcher is qualified to do the work and bound by the association's code of practice.

Opinions about the use of professional researchers differ. They certainly offer a perfectly adequate service at major archives; but they are less likely to trawl through more obscure sources. For obvious reasons the professional is likely to research your medals along with several others. Each receives equal attention and an accurate, detailed result. However, the collector/researcher doing his own detective work has the incentive of a real personal interest in discovering as much as possible about one medal, group or man. He may not possess the archive familiarity and knowledge of the professional, but this is compensated for by determination and enthusiasm. Certainly the collector can derive more satisfaction from personal research.

Before seeking professional help, weigh up the cost, the time available, the amount of research required and the location of pertinent sources. Consider combining some personal research with that of the professional.

The type of research service offered by some medal dealers is generally sufficient to identify casualties, obtain copies of attestation/discharge papers and medal index card details. Few are willing to delve much deeper. Prices are clearly stated from the outset and results are supplied quite quickly. This can be a useful service for collectors able to purchase a number of medals at one time. It enables them to identify groups worthy of more detailed research, while obtaining basic details of all medals they buy.

Research Notes

Advertisements were placed in appropriate local newspapers, seeking information about all the men being researched apart from Edward Heymer and David Boyce. No place of allegiance could be established for Edward Heymer, and most friends and relatives of David Boyce were already known to the author.

Charles Hoggett

Several replies were received to an article in a Portsmouth newspaper. Most were of a general nature, but one was from Constance Ponsford, Charles Hoggett's great-granddaughter. Her mother told her that old members of the family were buried at Mile End Cemetery, which is now a car park. Her information led to fruitful enquiries in the city archives. Constance never knew Charles Hoggett, but remembers his son (her grandfather) as a very moral man, who died in 1925. Her mother was one of eight children, so Charles obviously had a

Carefree snapshot of "Buster" Davis with a friend while on leave in August 1943. (Courtesy Stephen Escreet)

few grandchildren. Her mother was born at 37 Charles Street. Unfortunately, although very interested, Constance could add nothing more.

Henry Harvey

Several people responded to a request for information in a Guernsey paper. The Harvey name came to prominence again recently, due to a book about the German occupation of the Harvey family home during the Second World War. *The Battle of Newlands* was based on a diary kept by Winifred Harvey, Henry's daughter. Rosemary Booth, from St Peter Port, was involved in the publication of the book and able to give some background to the Harvey family.

Mrs Booth told me about Henry's aunt, Margaret Anne Neve, who lived to 110 years of age. This information led to more discoveries at the Guernsey Archive. She also knew of Harvey papers at the Priaulx Library. Rosemary Booth assisted with contacting the current owners of Newlands, Mr and Mrs Colin Grant; and Mrs Grant kindly sent me photographs of the house and a copy of Winifred Harvey's book.

David Kreckeler, from St Peter Port, sent details of the Harvey family vault and copies of inscriptions from Foulon Cemetery. He also provided photocopies of relevant newspapers and locally published books. One of these was a copy from the Elizabeth College Register of 1931 recording Henry John Harvey (son of Henry James) as an old boy. The extract shows the Harvey military dynasty continuing into the 20th century. It reads: "2970 Harvey, Major Henry John. Born in Guernsey on the 26th May, 1892. Son of Lt.Col.Henry James Harvey, late KOSB, and Beatrice Emmeline Watson. Elizabeth College 1900-10. Shooting VIII, 1909-10. Sandhurst, 1910. 2nd Lieut., KOSB, 1911. Lieut.—— Capt.—— Major——. Went to France in 1914. Was wounded and came home October to May 1915. France again in 1915. Then home service 1915-17. France again in 1917 till November, then home service till November 1918. Volunteered for the Russian Expeditionary Force at Archangel in 1919. War Service: Great War 1914-18.

France. Battles of Mons, Le Cateau,, The Ourcq, Marne, Aisne and La Bassée. Wounded. On rejoining fought in the battles of Passchendaele and Cambrai. North Russia with the Expeditionary Force. Medal, Victory medal and 1914 Star and clasp. Despatches. MC."

The response to this advertisement clearly demonstrates the valuable help it is possible to obtain in this way. Correspondents carried out a great deal of research on my behalf which helped to achieve a well-rounded picture of the Harvey family.

Joseph Full
No response to an article.

George Reeve
No response to an article.

Thomas Davis
Several people responded to an advertisement placed in the *Withernsea Gazette*. A further piece in *The Laurel Tree*, the organ of the IX Squadron Association, brought one reply. Information provided by correspondents painted an illuminating picture of Davis' early life.

Thomas Rhodes Davis was a big, freckled chap with wavy brown hair, known to his friends as "Buster". Apparently he looked like a young Spencer Tracy. All described Buster Davis as full of fun and enormously likeable. Buster was the middle child of three born to Capt. and Mrs Davis, née Violet Rhodes. He had two sisters, Joan and Paddy. There were family connections in the United States, and it seems that they lived in Staten Island for a period.

Buster's mother was a local girl. Her father ran a wholesale fruit business in Humber Street, Hull; Capt.Davis took over the firm when her father became ill, but it eventually folded. He was also associated with the shipping industry, and Buster had intended going into the family business after the war. Buster's father suffered from Parkinson's Disease, and the shock of his son's sudden death had a terrible effect on him. The family moved to London soon afterwards.

The family home still stands. Wyke House is a large four-bedroomed house with extensive gardens. In Buster's time there were oil lamps and no gas supply was installed. Bessie Hodgson, from Hull, wrote about an aunt who worked as a maid at Wyke House. Bessie herself also worked there for a period. Several people remembered happy times at Wyke House before the war, and told of incidents from Buster's childhood.

Jean Nordon, from Withernsea, provided a good deal of assistance. She took photographs of Buster's grave and the war memorial on Withernsea promenade, and of Wyke House. Jean explained that her sister had been very close friends with Buster in childhood. They built "dug-outs" in the paddock and played on the farm where Jean and her sister grew up; the girls taught Buster to ride ponies, and they skated in the winter.

Buster first went to school at Dr Cripps' in Patrington where he was taught by a governess; he later attended Withernsea High School. Buster fed buns cooked by the girls in domestic science class to a donkey tethered in a field. On another occasion he helped concoct an explosive mixture, using chemicals "borrowed" by the GP's daughter. Jean's sister remembered Buster dancing with her when he was home on leave. She described how proud she felt on the arm of a young man in RAF blue.

F.W.Richardson first met him when he was about seven years old; they remained friends throughout Buster's short life, and Mr Richardson provided a letter received from him during his aircrew training in Canada. The letter from 1456334 LAC Davis T.R., No.2 AOS, Edmonton, Alberta, Canada, was dated 7 June. It reads:

"I hear from Mother that you are in the Army and I hope that affairs are progressing favourably. I expect that you have heard that I'm no longer training to be a pilot; I still think that I was given a raw deal and I'm absolutely certain that I should have passed the course in England or Canada, because I had solo'd and all that kind of thing, which is in itself almost a guarantee that you will pass in any country except the USA.

"I'm now training at No.2 Air Observer's School in Edmonton, Alberta. Edmonton is quite a decent town of about 100,000 inhabitants surrounded by prairies and the Rocky Mountains about two hundred miles to the west. The course is much harder than the pilot's course and we have to learn all sorts of stuff that I'd never even heard of before, then for our practical work we charge around in Ansons.

"Before I even came to Edmonton I had three weeks in Trenton, Ontario about 100 miles from Toronto. We hitch-hiked down to Toronto several times and its a pretty good city, we also went down to Niagara Falls which is about 100 miles further. In between leaving Trenton and going to Edmonton we hitch-hiked down to New York but we didn't have that much time there because we had to waste two days waiting for the US Consul in order to get a Visa to visit the States. Although we only had a day there we made the best of our chance, we went up the Empire State Building, had a look at the Normandy, saw the La Guardia Airport - which is supposed to be the most modern in the World - and in the evening we went to a Show on Broadway. Altogether since leaving England I should say I have travelled 14,500 miles of which more than 3,000 has been hitchhiking, so you can see we really get about in this part of the world.

"Please give my best wishes to your Mother and Father, Joyce, Mr and Mrs Shipston, Jean and Lucy. You see I make one letter do a lot of work.

"I'll close now as I want to skip Church Parade. Cheerio! All the very best - Buster".

Buster spent his final leave at Ivy House. Apparently he stole some pastries cooked by "Old Mary", the cook, and she chased him down the yard with a dishcloth. When she heard Buster was dead she was glad he had stolen her jam buns.

Several correspondents expressed delight that Buster Davis was not forgotten and that he was featured in this book. To some it brought back mixed emotions of times both happy and sad, reminding them of how young many of the casualties were and how "they shall not grow old, as we that are left grow old".

CHAPTER 17: FINISHING TOUCHES

Research never really finishes. There is always a niggling question unanswered or a frustrating suspicion that something has been missed along the way. However, there comes a time when most reasonable steps have been taken and it is time to move on. Frequently this point is reached all too quickly; occasionally it takes longer; but always, inevitably, the trail turns cold in the end.

Sometimes attention turned upon a man's civilian career can uncover new twists to his story. Medals denote acts of bravery, achievement and campaign service in military life. Yet every medal recipient began life as a civilian, and most returned to civvy street at the end of their service. In the World Wars, fought by millions of "hostilities only" volunteers and conscripts, their time in uniform only formed a short, if very important period of their life.

Some would disagree, but most believe that research is not complete until the man's origins and subsequent fate are uncovered. To cease research at discharge from the armed forces leaves the job half done. Who knows what befell him afterwards? Nobody would seriously advocate that years be spent following the life of every man awarded medals. Medal collectors can be selective, and look at those offering the best chance of success.

Newspaper obituaries often give an excellent indication of whether further research is worthwhile, drawing attention to notable events and achievements. However, prior to the Great War obituaries were only printed for publicly prominent individuals. Sporting and civil medals found with military groups open up research possibilities outside the forces. For example, a skilled footballer probably continued playing after discharge from the forces, and match reports in newspapers may prove fruitful.

Life-saving awards are a vast subject which really fall outside the scope of this book. The date of the deed is usually engraved on the medal, providing a starting point. A parchment certificate or citation should accompany the medal, describing the act which earned it. Most bodies which award life-saving medals keep archive records which can provide an authoritative account of events. Life-saving makes news, and newspapers around the date shown on the medal are sure to include reports; editors love a hero, and the medal recipient may even be photographed alongside a report which might give some personal background. If the medal was awarded for a particularly spectacular rescue, magazines like the *Illustrated London News* may also have reported the story.

Original papers accompanying medals also give pointers to life outside the armed forces. They may include trade and professional qualification certificates, newspaper cuttings, diaries, letters and a multitude of other documents. Each can be considered on its merits for research potential.

Many ex-servicemen traditionally became policemen, and it is not unusual to find Jubilee, Coronation or police long service medals alongside those earned on military campaigns. Metropolitan Police records are stored at the PRO, but nearly every force maintains an archive. Holdings differ from force to force, but where records survive they can be extremely informative. Police long service awards do not always identify the force of the recipient, but military research normally indicates the region where he is likely to have served. Until relatively recently large towns and cities were policed by their own borough forces; sometimes service records for the old forces were lost or destroyed, but happily a great many survive within the archives of the new amalgamated units.

The fire services also attracted men willing to exchange one uniform for another, and their bravery and long service decorations may well accompany campaign medals. Fire services are arranged regionally and service records sometimes survive, retained by the fire department or local record offices. HM Coastguard has always numbered large numbers of ex-naval men among its recruits, and medals awarded to coastguards are regularly seen with naval awards. Records of service are held at the Public Record Office and offer good opportunities for research.

Chaplains to the forces were eligible for the full range of medals which could be won by their flock. Indeed, many chaplains earned bravery awards as a result of outstanding devotion to duty shown while ministering to their men. After relinquishing their military role they usually returned to the civilian ministry; and their subsequent careers can be followed through the pages of Crockford's Clerical Directory. This lists the names of Church of England clergymen and outlines their appointments. It was first published in 1858 and appears at regular intervals; copies can be seen at major reference libraries. Every church denomination keeps some form of historical archive.

Many records exist for members of the medical profession and these can be explored when researching military medical staff. Medical registers first appeared in 1858 and contain biographical notes on practitioners. The Wellcome Institute for the History of Medicine, 183 Euston Road, London NW1, has a medical history library which can be consulted by appointment; and The Royal College of Surgeons Library,

CENTRAL CHANCERY OF
THE ORDERS OF KNIGHTHOOD,
ST JAMES'S PALACE. S.W.1.

Sir,

I am commanded to forward the Imperial Service Medal which Her Majesty The Queen has been graciously pleased to award to you in recognition of the meritorious services which you have rendered.

I have the honour to be, Sir,

Your obedient servant,

Ivan De la Bere

Brigadier
Registrar of the Imperial Service Order.

David Boyce, Esq.

35-43 Lincoln's Inn Fields, London WC2, can assist with enquiries about individuals. Many universities retain archive material and if the person's medical school can be identified through service papers then these may be able to provide extra information.

With the development of soldier/tradesmen, men frequently followed the trade they had been taught in the forces after discharge. Regional and trade directories can assist researchers to follow their fortunes through the years. Every trade or calling presents opportunities for research. Some are well documented, most are not; it is up to the individual researcher to decide how much effort, if any, to invest. Men who joined a uniformed service or the professions are worth more than a cursory look, but other callings seldom produce results without lengthy research. Once the military exploits, family life and civilian career of the medal recipient have been explored, it is usually time to start afresh and enjoy the whole adventure again with another group of medals. Who knows what might be discovered about the next ones?

* * *

So that's it - all done; no more stones to overturn. Now what do we do with the bundle of paperwork, photos and photocopies assembled along the way?

The answer is, there is no answer; it is entirely a question of personal taste. Every researcher has his own ideas. For some, there is sufficient satisfaction to be gained from basking in the glow of achievement. Documents and medals are put away, out of mind; now and again the paperwork is taken out and reread. Sometimes new ideas spring to mind and research recommences. A chance discovery may hasten steps back towards the Public Record Office.

Others display the results of their labours. Medals can be mounted to make a very attractive wall feature. It is more difficult to exhibit research. Original documentation can be displayed, but photocopied items look fairly unappealing. A photograph mounted next to the medals is probably the most pleasing combination.

Displaying medals poses a problem in the modern age. They may be eyecatching and attractive items, but unfortunately they also draw attention from those with sinister motives. Even an opportunist thief will probably recognize that they have a disposable value, and collections can become the target of burglars. Medals do not even have to be displayed to be stolen - they are likely to be discovered if the house is ransacked. This presents a dilemma. No one wants to turn their home into Fort Knox, but it is sensible to take precautions. Much depends on the value of the medals. A VC may have a thousand times the intrinsic value of a First World War pair, but the sentimental worth of such medals awarded to a relative makes them worth protecting.

Common sense should prevail. If a thief is absolutely determined to steal your property, no amount of barriers will

Letter from St James' Palace to David Boyce accompanying his Imperial Service Medal.

protect it. All that can be done is to make the effort of overcoming protection seem out of proportion to the rewards offered. Most importantly, make sure medals are adequately insured. This means showing the collection as a separate item in a policy; otherwise few insurance companies will pay out the amount required to establish a similar collection. Review values periodically to keep pace with inflation. List all the medals in a collection, and keep the list up to date. Remember policemen are like everyone else: to them one medal looks like any other unless the loser can supply details of the ribbons, shapes and markings, and it is obviously good idea to photograph the collection.

Sadly, valuable awards are sometimes buried away in bank deposit boxes - a very unsatisfactory situation. Surely there is no point in owning something if you cannot see it? A floor or wall safe is a preferable alternative, at least making the collection accessible for your own and your friends' enjoyment. Another solution is a lockable cabinet. Some firms manufacture cabinets fitted with tray drawers to display collections, which can be secured by a vertical bar. This enables medals to be displayed attractively and offers at least a modicum of protection against the thief who is nervous of investing too much time and noise. Each individual must choose the balance of security and expense warranted by his collection.

Research material is a different matter; the researcher is the only person to whom it has any value, so security is not a problem. The simple ring binder is a good way of storing documents, letters, postcards, photos and other paperwork in plastic wallets for visibility; care should be taken to select those made of a material designed to preserve paperwork. Larger items can be displayed to good effect in the various sizes and designs of art portfolio cases. Box files are a less expensive alternative, and medals and paperwork can be stored in the same file. Whatever the system chosen, it is useful to index paperwork, making it possible to retrieve required documents quickly and to identify items which go missing.

Given that research rarely throws up the facts in date order, it is also a good idea to write up the story of the person researched chronologically. This sorts the mass of information into a readable format, enabling the researcher to share his enthusiasm with the uninitiated.

It is important to record where facts were discovered; after a surprisingly short time it becomes difficult to recall particular sources. This is especially important when selling medals. If an exciting piece of information about the recipient has been unearthed, enhancing the value, it may be necessary to prove this by reference to the original source.

So, now comes the time to select the next subjects for research. This does not present a problem for those collectors who specialize in medals awarded to a particular unit or for a particular campaign. For those with wider interests, selecting the next medals to research can present an interesting dilemma. Do they use the knowledge gained while researching the previous group, or do they move on to something different, and fall into similar pitfalls as before?

As years go by, a problem grows: many medals which

come onto the market have already been researched by previous owners, or by dealers keen to enhance the selling price. This poses an interesting choice for collector/researchers. Do they wait until a totally unresearched group within their area of interest comes onto the market? Do they throw away the existing paperwork and pretend that it has not been done, so that they can start tracking it all over again? (If this seems to you to be a sensible choice, then the time may have come for seeking medical help…) Or do they take the completed research and use it as the basis for trying to uncover further material?

Generally the groups already researched tend to be the most interesting ones, and this is an important factor. Nobody wants to pass up a particularly desirable group of medals just because someone else has already looked at their background. By the same token, it would be sad to deliberately buy less interesting material simply because it offered unexplored territory.

Fortunately, millions of medals survive, and new items appear on the market all the time. Families die out and medals are suddenly catapulted to the auction rooms, ready for their story to be brought to the surface. The pleasure gained from unearthing tales about yesterday's soldiers never seems to fade. Finding long-forgotten documents about an individual amongst a pile of moribund paperwork always gives the researcher a thrill; old soldiers and sailors seem to step off the page and come to life as the hunt progresses, developing such a personality that it becomes hard to close the book on them.

Medal research is an absorbing pastime which fascinates a growing number of enthusiasts. It is hoped that this book has demonstrated some of the reasons why medals are so captivating, and that it may have sparked a flame in some readers who had not previously considered collecting them. Perhaps some of those who already collect may also feel that they are missing out on what many of us believe to be the most exciting side of the medal: the man behind it.

Researching medals has certainly taken up a good part of my leisure time since I first contracted the bug. I have no regrets; during the course of research I have started writing for publication, travelled widely, made many friends, and learned a great deal about British military history and life in days gone by. Be warned - researching medals becomes addictive, and you may suddenly find there is no time or money for any other pastimes. Enjoy your research, and I hope the medals you investigate have an exciting story to tell. Who knows? Our paths may cross in the depths of a dusty archive somewhere.

Research Notes: a Summary

Charles Hoggett

Charles Hoggett was the only naval representative among the medals selected. Research was extremely successful. His name leapt from the pages of nearly every class of documents consulted, and a surprising amount of information was brought to the surface. Full career details were found, most family particulars were uncovered, and it was possible to find out the part played by his ship in the action off Syria for which the medal was awarded.

Research yielded no dramatic stories about Charles Hoggett, but a wealth of details about his naval career. The medal itself had given no hint of his long service and his many voyages around the world. His travels in the mid-19th century were brought to life through the pages of ships' musters and captains' log books; and his final selection for the hand-picked crew of the Royal Yacht was interesting in itself.

One or two stones remain unturned; for instance, it was frustrating to find no trace of Hoggett's marriage certificate. However, a full, rounded picture of his life was achieved, and the research was rewarding, enjoyable and rarely frustrating.

Edward Heymer

Edward Heymer led a relatively short but interesting life. All the research targets were met, and a surprisingly large amount of information was uncovered. The fact that Heymer took part in a famous cavalry charge in bloody circumstances gave his story instant colour. Vivid descriptions of the action emerged, and made research exciting.

His origins deserve further exploration. His father had an unusual occupation - an undertaker - a trade he might have been expected to follow. So why did he join the Army? After all, at the time only the fairly desperate or degenerate took the Queen's Shilling. The story of his marriage is also unusual. How did Hester's first husband die? Why did Sergeant Whitfield's widow marry so quickly a lowly private some years younger than herself?

In Heymer's case the story had an unhappy ending when he died a year after discharge, leaving Hester a widow again. Then his will revealed that a son, previously undiscovered, followed him into the regiment. That, and his desire to see his medals pass on to his son, indicate that Sergeant Major Heymer had loved the calling he had chosen to follow. Edward Heymer was a very engaging soldier to research. His story enhances the medal, and there are still areas left to explore. The file remains open.

Henry Harvey

Commissioned officers always offer potential and Harvey was no exception. The discovery of his Guernsey origins posed problems initially, but eventually turned out to be an advantage due to the standing enjoyed by the Harvey family within a relatively small community. His military career was well documented, including the Second Afghan War resulting in the medal. The family life of Henry and the rest of the Harveys was exceptionally well recorded - the best of all the medals researched - owing to the status and wealth they enjoyed (and the remarkable longevity of Aunt Margaret).

The only disappointment was the failure to uncover any portrait of Lieutenant-Colonel Harvey, although there is a good chance that one may be unearthed eventually. Apart from that, research is complete. The personal documentation, such as that found among memorandum papers at the PRO, even helped to

David Boyce (standing sixth from left) with fellow
Post Office workers during the 1950s.

give a feel for Harvey's personality. Nothing further is planned except renewed efforts to find illustrative material.

Joseph Full

Joseph Full's medals proved to have the least research potential of any of those selected. His military service was well documented at the PRO, and his family life was traced through genealogical indexes, but nothing was discovered beyond the bare facts. Full spent many years in the Royal Marines, but never actually fought in a battle, so that avenue of research could not be followed. Still, there was a happy ending: he lived to a ripe old age and apparently died within the bosom of his family. To sum up, research was successful, but slightly disappointing. No further work is planned.

David Boyce

Until researching this book, my branch of the family had no knowledge of the Imperial Service Medal awarded to my grandfather. This is typical of knowledge which can go adrift within a single family. The ISM was frequently awarded to postal staff upon retirement, in recognition of their efforts. The names of recipients were published in the *London Gazette*. David Boyce retired in 1957, and the entry was found on page 303 of the *London Gazette* for Friday 10 January 1958 (W 1/1148); he was simply shown as postman, Southend-on-Sea.

The research into David Boyce has now achieved all the objectives originally set - and has gone beyond them. His battalion was found, and the date and circumstances of his wound were discovered after a lengthy search. The battalion war diary and 36th Divisional History portrayed events very dramatically. Relatives were found to have several previously unknown photographs of him in uniform and, of course, the Imperial Service Medal. Other than that, his family history was already well known. All in all, research was extremely successful and nothing further is planned.

George Reeve

Few medals tell a story like those awarded to George Reeve. They proved exceptionally researchable, and there is virtually nothing left to discover about his life in the forces or outside.

This poignant tale has everything. This was a youngster who lied about his age to enlist; left the Army and then rejoined; suffered several scrapes with authority before clearly deciding to apply himself, and earned promotion to positions of trust. The young NCO came to the fore in wartime: he was mentioned in despatches, wounded four times, decorated twice for bravery, and became RSM of his battalion before being commissioned

Newlands, St Peter Port, Guernsey, once the family home
of the Harveys. (Courtesy Mr & Mrs Colin Grant)

in the field - George Reeve was an authentic hero and leader of fighting men. For a man of such stature to die pointlessly under the wheels of a taxi cab is unbelievably sad, and made doubly so by the timing - a month before the Armistice.

Thomas Rhodes Davis
Davis was the recipient of the sole RAF group among the medals under the microscope. The research carried out was richly rewarded, and a detailed story of his life in and out of

the service was established. All of his bombing missions were researched, in particular the night of the tragic crash returning from Berlin. Several sources were consulted and all added to knowledge of the event.

The article in a local paper led to significant information about his early years, helping to form a memorable picture of "Buster's" personality. The article also led to photographs, adding a face to the story. The results of research surpassed all the original targets, and there seems little more to be done.

APPENDIX I:
RESEARCH CHECKLIST

All medals:
Medal roll(s)/index card
London Gazette
Birth certificate
Baptismal record
Marriage certificate
Death certificate
Will
Family birth/marriage/death certificates
Family wills
Census returns
Ministry of Defence
National military museums
Regimental/service museums
Newspaper obituaries
Newspaper reports on notable events
Campaign histories
Unit histories
India Office Library
Published medal rolls
Published casualty lists
Memorial inscriptions
Commonwealth War Graves Commission
County Record Office
Military research societies
Advertisements:
    Local papers
    Family history societies
    Medal/genealogical magazines

Army Officers:
The Army List
Hart's Army List
London Gazette
Public Record Office:
    Official service records WO 25
    Regimental records WO 76
    Commission papers WO 4, 43
    Memoranda papers WO 31
    Commission books WO 25
    Army Purchase Commission WO 74
    Half-pay records WO 23, PMG 4
    Wound pensions WO 4, WO 23,
      WO 43, PMG 9
    Widows' pensions - various classes

Birth certificates WO 32
Marriage documents WO 25
Birth/marriage/death registers WO 68-9
    Muster rolls WO 10-16
Public school records
Royal Military Academy Sandhurst
Illustrated London News
The Graphic
Who Was Who?
Debrett's Peerage

Army Other Ranks:
Public Record Office:
    Attestation and discharge documents
    WO 97
    Regimental musters WO 10-16
    Regimental description books WO 25
    Depot description books WO 67
    Regimental casualty returns WO 25
    Pensioner discharge documents
      WO 121
    Regimental pension registers
      WO 23, 120
    District pension registers WO 22
    Chelsea admission papers WO 116-7
    Kilmainham admission papers WO 118
    Chelsea in-pensioners WO 23

Royal Navy Officers:
Navy List
Steele's Navy List
London Gazette
Naval Biographical Dictionary (O'Byrne)
Royal Naval Biography (Marshall)
National Maritime Museum
Public Record Office:
    Medal rolls ADM 171
    Honour sheets ADM 171
    Passing certificates ADM 6, 13, 107
    Applications ADM 6
    Promotion candidates ADM 6, 7, 11
    Confidential reports ADM 196
    Examination results ADM 6, 7, 11, 203
    Service certificates ADM 107
    Service registers ADM 196

Surveys ADM 6, 9, 10
Analyses ADM 6, 11
Marriage certificates ADM 13
Half-pay registers ADM 23, 25,
    PMG 15
Bounty payments ADM 106
Widows' pensions PMG 16, 20
Widows' charity payments ADM 23,
    PMG 19
Pensions ADM 22, 23, PMG 15
Wound pensions ADM 22, 23, 181,
    PMG 16
Compassionate Fund ADM 6, 22, 23,
    PMG 18
Muster books ADM 36-39
Casualties ADM 104, 242
Public school records
Royal Naval Colleges
Illustrated London News
The Graphic
Who Was Who?
Debrett's Peerage

Naval Ratings:
Public Record Office:
    Medal rolls ADM 171
    Continuous service records
      ADM 139, 188
    Certificates of service ADM 29, 73
    Muster books ADM 36-39
    Pay books ADM 32-35
    Allotments ADM 27
    Remittances ADM 26
    Greenwich Hospital in-pensioners
      ADM 6, 73
    Greenwich Hospital out-pensioners
      ADM 6, WO 22
    Chatham Chest ADM 22
    Out-pension payment registers
      ADM 22
    Casualty returns ADM 141, 104,
      154, 242
    Naval wills ADM 48, 142
    Greenwich Hospital School records
      ADM 73, 161

APPENDIX II:
P.R.O. MEDAL ROLLS
(WO 100)

Royal Marines Officers:

Army List

Navy List

Hart's Army List

List of Officers of the Marine Forces

Public Record Office: generally as for
RN Officers, with the addition of:

    Half-pay records AO 1, PMG 73

    Obituaries ADM 6, 11

    Greenwich Hospital pensions ADM 201

Public school records

Illustrated London News

The Graphic

Who Was Who?

Debrett's Peerage

Royal Marines Other Ranks:

Public Record Office:

    Attestations index

    Attestations ADM 157, 313

    Description books ADM 158

    Records of service ADM 159

    Effective and subsistence lists ADM 96

    Muster books ADM 36-39

    War diaries ADM 116, 137, 202, DEFE 2

    Births/marriages/deaths ADM 5, 81,
      183-5

    Discharge books ADM 183-5

Royal Air Force Officers:

Air Force List

Army List (RFC)

Navy List (RNAS)

Public Record Office:

    Medal rolls WO 329, ADM 171

    First World War records AIR 1

    Communiqués AIR 1

    Squadron records AIR 1, 27

    Station records AIR 1, 28

    Prisoners of war AIR 14, 20

    Combat reports AIR 50

    K reports AIR 14

Royal Air Force Museum:

    Aero Club Certificates

    Casualty cards

    Aircraft history cards

Public school records

Illustrated London News

The Graphic

Who Was Who?

Debrett's Peerage

Royal Military Academy Sandhurst

Royal Air Force College Cranwell

Royal Air Force Other Ranks:

Main sources for aircrew are largely
the same as those for officers.

Volume		Campaign
1-11	...	Peninsular War
12	...	Egypt
13	...	India Medal 1803-26
14, 15/1, 15/2	...	Waterloo
16	...	Peninsular War Gold Medals/Crosses 1793-1814
17	...	South Africa 1834-53
18	...	New Zealand 1854-66
19	...	Abyssinia, Ashanti, India, New Zealand, Zulu War
20, 21A, 21B	...	India NW Frontier
22-34	...	Crimea
35-39	...	Indian Mutiny
40-41	...	China
46-50	...	South Africa 1877-79
51-54	...	Afghanistan
55-61	...	Egypt
62-68	...	Sudan 1884-89
69-70	...	Burma 1885-87
71-72	...	Sudan 1885-89
80-82	...	Sudan 1896-98
84-89	...	India 1897-98
94-99	...	China 1900
112-301	...	Queen's South Africa Medal
302-367	...	King's South Africa Medal
368	...	Queen's Mediterranean Medal

APPENDIX III:
P.R.O. NAVAL MEDAL
ROLLS (ADM 171)

1 ...	Naval General Service 1794-1815, incl. Camperdown, Trafalgar, Nile; also some records of Algiers, Navarino, Syria, Acre. Syrian campaign nominal roll.	
2 ...	Medal claims for actions in which first lieutenants or commanders were promoted; also some claims for Algiers, Navarino, Acre.	
3 ...	Claims for boat actions 1793-1815 for which the officer commanding was promoted.	
4 ...	Algiers	
5 ...	Navarino	
6 ...	1840-42. List of officers and men serving on HM ships in Syria and China campaigns.	
7 ...	List of claims for Syria and China.	
8 ...	Nominal roll of surviving officers/men entitled to NGS clasps between 1793-1827.	
9 ...	1818-1853. Roll of recipients of Arctic medal.	
10 ...	1818-1855. List of officers/men, RN & RM, employed on Arctic service. Also Burma medal 1824-26.	
11 ...	India GS Medal, clasp Ava	
12, 13 ...	China 1840-42	
14, 15 ...	St Jean d'Acre 1842	
16 ...	New Zealand Medal 1845-66	
17 ...	India GS Medal 1854, clasp Pegu	
18 ...	South Africa/Cape of Good Hope 1850-53	
19 ...	Baltic 1854-55, A-D	
20 ...	ditto	E-J
21 ...	ditto	K-R
22 ...	ditto	S-Z
23 ...	Crimea RM Bde, Sebastopol/Balaclava/Inkerman	
24 ...	Crimea Naval Bde, Sebastopol/Inkerman	

25 ...	Crimea, clasp Azoff	
26 ...	Turkish Crimea, ships A-F	
27 ...	ditto	G-Q
28 ...	ditto	R-Z
29 ...	Indian Mutiny 1857-58	
30 ...	China 1856-60, RM Bde	
31 ...	ditto, ships A-D	
32 ...	ditto	E-J
33 ...	ditto	K-R
34 ...	ditto	S-Z
35 ...	Canada GS Medal 1866-70	
36 ...	Abyssinia 1867-68	
37 ...	Ashanti 1873-74	
38 ...	Arctic 1875-76	
39 ...	India GS, clasp Perak 1875-76	
40 ...	South Africa 1877-79	
41 ...	Egypt 1882	
42 ...	Sudan 1884, clasps Suakin 1884/El Teb/Tamaii	
43 ...	Sudan, Nile/Abu Klea/Kirkeban/Suakin 1885/Tofrek. Khedive's Sudan	
44, 45-48 ...	Burmah 1885-87. Ashanti 1887-1900	
49 ...	Sudan 1888, Gemaizah 1888	
50 ...	Khedive's Egypt Star 1891, Tokar	
51 ...	Khedive's Sudan 1896-1908, Hafir/Soudan 1897/Atbara/Khartoum/Gedarif/Soudan 1899/Bahr el Guazal	
52 ...	Sea Transport Medal 1899-1902	
53-4 ...	Queen's South Africa Medal	
55 ...	China 1900	
56 ...	Africa GS 1902-10	
57 ...	Naval Gunnery Medal	
58 ...	Naval GS 1915	
59 ...	Durbar 1911	
60 ...	Register of medals - indexed	
61 ...	Miscellaneous - indexed	
62 ...	Naval GS 1915, 1915-52	
63 ...	MiD roll 1914-18	
64 ...	Africa GS 1921-52	
65 ...	Royal Humane Society, Albert Medal, RNLI, Naval Prizes King's Gold Medal 1833-1918	

66 ...	King's Gold Medal 1917-48	
67 ...	Foreign orders to naval officers	
68 ...	George V Silver Jubilee	
69 ...	George VI Coronation	
70 ...	Reserve LSGC 1909-12	
71 ...	ditto 1912-37	
72 ...	ditto 1938-49	
73 ...	RN LSGC 1912-19	
74 ...	Decorations to ratings with British Armoured Division in Russia	
75 ...	CGM/DSM index to rolls	
76 ...	Foreign officers recommended for British decorations	
77 ...	1914-18 RNR honours and awards	
78-88 ...	Honour sheets 1914-18	
89-91 ...	Naval War Medals RN/RNVR/RN Aux Service officers	
92 ...	RM/RNR officers	
93 ...	RNR miscellaneous	
94-119 ...	1914-18 RN ratings	
120-129 ...	1914-18 RNR ratings	
130-134 ...	1914-18 Mercantile Marine Reserve ratings	
135-37 ...	OBE 1918-19, names submitted for appointment	
140-45 ...	RN LSGC 1920-47	
146-47 ...	RFR LS Medal	
148 ...	Officer's War Medal issue book	
149-55 ...	RN LSGC application books for medal claims 1925-70	
156-59 ...	RN LSGC register index	
160-61 ...	RFR LSGC medal claims book	
162-3 ...	Index to claims book	
164 ...	1942-45 DSM, BEM, GM, MM, OBE, DSC	
165 ...	1946-72 ditto	
166 ...	Korea Medal and gratuity. List of ships	
167-71 ...	Roll of Naval War Medals 1914-20, RM NCOs and men	
172 ...	List of RN/RM officers holding foreign decorations	

APPENDIX IV: MEDAL ROLLS AT THE INDIA OFFICE LIBRARY

APPENDIX V: P.R.O. SOURCES FOR FOREIGN, IRREGULAR & COLONIAL TROOPS

Medal Rolls are in L/MIL/5/42-141; most can be seen on open shelves:

42-44	...	East India Company GS Medal 1799-1826 (Army of India Medal)
45	...	Indian GS Medal 1854 (General)
46-51	...	Clasps North West Frontier 1849-63/ Umbeyla 1863
52-54	...	Pegu 1852-53
55-56	...	Persia 1856-57
57-60	...	Bhootan 1864-66/ Hazara 1868
61-62	...	Looshai 1871-72
63	...	Jowaki 1877-78
64	...	Naga 1879-80
65	...	Burma 1885-87
66	...	Marine Medals 1801-1860
67	...	China 1842
68	...	Jellalabad 1842 (second issue)
69	...	Scinde 1843
70	...	Sutlej 1845-46
71-72	...	Punjab 1848-49
73-105	...	Indian Mutiny 1857-58
106-07	...	China 1857-60
108-09	...	Abyssinia 1867-68
110-21	...	Afghanistan 1878-80
122-24	...	Kabul to Kandahar 1880
125	...	Egypt 1882
126	...	Delhi Durbar 1903
127	...	Delhi Durbar 1911
128-41	...	Miscellaneous 1845-1911

East India Company:

European Regiment officers
   WO 25/3215-9
Pension registers WO 25/3137
Deserters WO 25/2933

Boer War volunteers:

Attestation/discharge papers WO 126-7
Imperial Yeomanry WO 128
Casualties WO 108, 129

Colonial troops:

Attestation/discharge papers WO 97
Musters WO 12-13
Pension admission books
   WO 23/153-7, 159, 160, WO 22
Casualties WO 25
Description books WO 25

Foreign troops:

British French regiments, Napoleonic
   Wars WO 25
Musters WO 12
Casualties WO 25
King's German Legion officers' records
   WO 25/749-79
KGL birth/marriage/death
   WO 42/52-58
KGL soldiers' papers WO 97
KGL statements of service
   WO 25/1100-14
KGL casualties WO 25/2272-88
KGL musters WO 12
KGL pension documents WO 23

British Foreign Legion:

Statements of officers' services
   WO 25/3236-7
Foreign Veterans Battalion WO 122

War diaries:

Colonial troops, First World War
   WO 95
Colonial troops, Second World War
   WO 169-178
Dominions, Second World War
   WO 179
Southern Rhodesian forces WO 333

APPENDIX VI: REGIMENTAL MAGAZINES

Many regimental journals and magazines are named after the regiment concerned; the following examples are not. Some of the units shown exist today, while others have long since been amalgamated or otherwise ceased to exist. In such cases the run of journals ceased with the disappearance of the regiment or corps, but when amalgamations took place the heritage of the original regiments usually continued to be honoured by the new unit publication.

The Life Guards *The Acorn*
Royal Horse Guards *The Blues*
Royal Scots Dragoon Guards *Eagle and Carbine*
3rd Carabiniers *Feather and Carbine*
5th Dragoon Guards *The Green Horse*
7th Dragoon Guards *Black Horse Gazette*
6th Inniskilling Dragoons *The Inniskilliner*
Queen's Royal Irish Hussars *Cross-Belts*
8th King's Royal Irish Hussars *Cross-Belts*
9th/12th Royal Lancers *The Delhi Spearmen*
9th Queen's Royal Lancers *The Delhi Spearmen*
14th/20th King's Hussars *The Hawk*
16th/5th Queen's Royal Lancers *The Scarlet and Green*
17th/21st Lancers *The White Lancer and the Vedette*
17th Lancers *The White Lancer*
20th Hussars *The Yellow Plume*
21st Lancers *The Vedette*
Royal Tank Regiment *Tank*
Royal Artillery *Gunner*
Royal Engineers *The Sapper*
Royal Corps of Signals *The Wire*
Royal Scots *The Thistle*
The Buffs *The Dragon*
The Royal Sussex Regiment *The Roussillon Gazette*

King's Own Royal Border Regiment *The Lion and the Dragon*
Royal Regiment of Fusiliers *The Fusilier*
Royal Northumberland Fusiliers *St George's Gazette*
Royal Warwickshire Fusiliers *The Antelope*
Lancashire Fusiliers *The Gallipoli Gazette*
King's Regiment *The Kingsman*
Royal Anglian Regiment *The Castle*
Royal Lincolnshire Regiment *The Imps*
Bedfordshire and Hertfordshire Regiment *The Wasp; The Wasp and Eagle*
Essex Regiment *The Eagle*
Royal Leicestershire Regiment *The Green Tiger*
Light Infantry *The Silver Bugle*
Duke of Cornwall's LI *One and All*
King's Own Yorkshire LI *The Bugle*
POW's Own Regiment of Yorkshire *The White Rose*
West Yorkshire Regiment *Ca Ira*
East Yorkshire Regiment *The Snapper*
Cheshire Regiment *The Oak Tree*
Royal Welch Fusiliers *Y Ddraig Goch*
Royal Regiment of Wales *The Men of Harlech*
Royal Irish Rangers *The Blackthorn*
Royal Ulster Rifles *Quis Separabit*
Royal Irish Fusiliers *Faugh a Ballagh*
Gloucestershire Regiment *The Back Badge*
Worcs and Sherwood Foresters *Firm and Forester*
Worcestershire Regiment *Firm*
Sherwood Foresters *The Forester*
Queen's Lancashire Regiment *The Lancashire Lad*
South Lancashire Regiment *Newsletter*
The Loyal Regiment *The Lancashire Lad*
Duke of Wellington's Regiment *The Iron Duke*
Staffordshire Regiment *The Staffordshire Knot*

South Staffs Regiment *The Knot*
North Staffs Regiment *The China Dragon*
The Black Watch *The Red Hackle*
Royal Berkshire Regiment *The China Dragon*
Seaforth Highlanders *Cabar Feidh*
Queen's Own Cameron Highlanders *The 79th News*
Gordon Highlanders *The Tiger and Sphinx*
Argyll and Sutherland Highlanders *The Thin Red Line*
Parachute Regiment *Pegasus*
Special Air Service Regiment *Mars and Minerva*
RCT *The Waggoner*
REME *Craftsmen*
RAVC *Chiron Calling*
RAEC *The Torch*
Intelligence Corps *The Rose and Laurel*
APTC *Mind, Body and Spirit*
ACC *Sustainer*
WRAC *The Lioness*

APPENDIX VII: USEFUL ADDRESSES

Air Historical Branch
Ministry of Defence
Lacon House
Theobalds Road
London WC1X 8RY

Army Medal Office
Government Office Buildings
Droitwich
Worcs WR9 8AU

Army Museums Ogilby Trust
Connaught Barracks
Duke of Connaughts Road
Aldershot
Hants GU11 2LR

Australian War Memorial
GPO Box 345
Canberra
ACT 2601
Australia

Birmingham Medal Society
229 Rednal Road
King's Norton
Birmingham B38 8EA

British Newspaper Library
Colindale Avenue
Colindale
London NW7 5HE

British Red Cross Society
International Welfare Department
9 Grosvenor Crescent
London SW1X 7EJ

Canadian Department of Veteran Affairs
Honours and Awards
284 Wellington Street
Ottawa K1A 0P4

Canada
Commonwealth Forces History Trust
37 Davis Road
London W3 7SE

Commonwealth War Graves Commission
2 Marlow Road
Maidenhead
Berks SL6 7DX

Crimean War Research Society
4 Castle Estate
Ripponden
Sowerby Bridge
West Yorks HX6 4JY

General Register Office (Northern Ireland)
Oxford House
49-55 Chichester Street
Belfast BT1 4HL

General Register Office of Ireland
8-11 Lombard Street
Dublin 2

General Register Office (Scotland)
New Register House
Edinburgh EH1 3YT

General Registry
Finch Road
Douglas
Isle of Man

Guildhall Library
Aldermanbury
London EC2P 2EJ

Historical Research Centre
Central Army Records Office
360 St Kilda Road
Melbourne VIC 3044
Australia

HM Greffier
The Greffe
Royal Court House
St Peter Port
Guernsey
CI

Imperial War Museum
Lambeth Road
London SE1 6HZ

Indian Military Historical Society
37 Wolsey Close
Southall
Middlesex UB2 4NQ

Judicial Greffe
States Building
10 Hill Street
Royal Square
St Helier
Jersey
CI

Life Saving Awards Research Society
Little Saddlers
10 Upper Edgeborough Road
Guildford
Surrey GU1 2BG

Medal News
Token Publishing Ltd
PO Box 14
Honiton
Devon EX14 9YP

Medal Society of Ireland
1 The Hill
Stillorgan
Co Dublin

Military Information Bureau
Archives Section
Private Bag X289
0001 Pretoria
South Africa

Ministry of Defence:
    CS(R)2a (Royal Naval Records)
    CS(R)2b (Army Personnel Records)
    CS(R)2e (Navy Personnel Records)

Bourne Avenue
Hayes
Middlesex UB3 1RS

Natal Archives Depot
Private Bag
X9012
3200 Pietermaritzburg
South Africa

National Archives of South Africa
Private Bag X206
0001 Pretoria
South Africa

National Army Museum
Royal Hospital Road
London SW3 4HT

National Maritime Museum
Romney Road
Greenwich
London SE10 9NF

Naval Historical Collectors and Research
Association
17 Woodhill Avenue
Portishead
Bristol BS20 9EX

Naval Medal Office
HMS Centurion
Grange Road
Gosport
Portsmouth PO13 UA

Orders and Medals Research Society
21 Colonels Lane
Chertsey
Surrey KT16 8RH

OMRS Medal Ribbon Branch
7 Durham Way
Rayleigh
Essex SS6 9RY

OMRS Miniatures Branch
31 Gatcombe

Great Holm
Milton Keynes
Bucks MK8 9EA

Personnel Records Centre
National Archives of Canada
Tunney's Pasture
Ottawa
KIA ON3

Canada
Public Record Office
Ruskin Avenue
Kew
Richmond
Surrey TW9 4DU

Public Record Office of Northern Ireland
66 Balmoral Avenue
Belfast BT9 6NY

(RAF Officers)
Personnel Management Centre
PG 5a(2)
RAF Innsworth
Gloucs GL3 1EZ

(RAF Other Ranks)
Personnel Management Centre
P Man 2b(1)
RAF Innsworth
Gloucs GL3 1EZ

Royal Air Force Association
43 Grove Park Road
London W4 3RV

Royal Air Force Museum
Aerodrome Road
London NW9 5LL

Royal Marines Historical Society
2A Seaview Road
Drayton
Portsmouth PO6 1EN

Royal Marines Museum

Eastney
Southsea
Hants PO4 9PX

Royal Naval Medals OS10
Empress State Building
Lillie Road
London SW6 1TR

Royal Naval Museum
HM Naval Base
Portsmouth
Hants PO1 3LR

Scottish Military Historical Society
4 Hillside Cottages
Glenboig
Lanarkshire ML5 2QY

Scottish Record Office
PO Box 36
HM General Register House
Edinburgh EH1 3YY

Society for Army Historical Research
c/o National Army Museum
Royal Hospital Road
Chelsea SW3 4HT

Society of Genealogists
14 Charterhouse Buildings
Goswell Road
London EC1M 7BA

Victorian Military Society
20 Priory Road
Newbury
Berks RG14 7QN

Western Front Association (1914-18)
PO Box 1914
Reading
Berks RG4 7YP

BIBLIOGRAPHY

General:

British Battles and Medals, Joslin, Litherland & Simpkin (Spink 1988)

British Gallantry Awards, P.E.Abbott & J.M.A.Tamplin (Guinness/Seaby 1971, Nimrod Dix 1981)

British Orders and Awards, A.L.Gordon (1959)

Collecting Medals and Decorations, A.A.Purves (1968)

Spink's Standard Catalogue of British Orders, Decorations and Medals, Litherland & Simpkin (1990)

Ribbons and Medals, H.Taprell-Dorling, ed.A.A.Purves (1983)

The Victoria Cross 1856-1920, Sir O'M.Creagh & H.M.Humphris (1993)

Victoria Cross Locator, D.Pallinger & A.Staunton (1991)

Collector's Guide to Orders, Medals and Decorations, S.B.Vernon (1990)

Tracing Your Ancestors in the Public Record Office, J.Cox & T.Padfield (1992)

Guide to the Records of the India Office Military Department, A.Farrington (1981)

The Medals, Decorations and Orders of World War II, A.A.Purves (1986)

Lloyds War Medal for Bravery at Sea, G.Brown (1992)

Coronation and Royal Commemorative Medals, Cole (1977)

The White Ribbon: a Medallic Record of British Polar Expeditions, N.W.Poulsom (1968)

Never Been Here Before? - PRO Readers' Guide No.17 (1997)

Royal Navy:

VCs of the Royal Navy, J.F.Turner (1956)

Distinguished Service Cross 1901-1938, W.H.Fevyer (1990)

The Distinguished Service Medal 1939-46, W.H.Fevyer (1981)

Naval Medals 1793-1856, K.J.Douglas-Morris (1987)

Naval Medals Vol.II, 1856-1880, K.J.Douglas-Morris

The Naval General Service Medal Roll 1793-1840, K.J.Douglas-Morris (1982)

Alphabetical Naval General Service Medal Roll 1793-1840, C.W.Message (1995)

Naval General Service Medal Roll 1793-1840, A.J.Newnham

The Trafalgar Roll: The Ships and the Officers, R.H.MacKenzie (1989)

Naval Biographical Dictionary, W.O'Byrne (1849)

The Queen's South Africa Medal to the Royal Navy and Royal Marines, W.H.Fevyer & J.W.Wilson (1983)

The China War Medal 1900 to the Royal Navy and Royal Marines, W.H.Fevyer & J.W.Wilson (1985)

The African General Service Medal to the Royal Navy and Royal Marines, W.H.Fevyer & J.W.Wilson

The Naval General Service Medal 1915-1962 to the Royal Navy and Royal Marines for the Bars Persian Gulf 1909-14, Iraq 1919-20, NW Persia 1920, W.H.Fevyer & J.W.Wilson (1995)

Seedie's Roll of Naval Honours and Awards 1939-59, W.W.F.Chatterton-Dickson (1990)

The Naval Long Service Medals, K.J.Douglas-Morris (1991)

The Meritorious Service Medal to Naval Forces, Ian McInnes (1983)

Naval Records for Genealogists, N.A.M.Rodger (1988)

Guide to the Manuscript Collections of the Royal Naval Museum, M.Sheldon (1997)

Records of the Royal Marines - PRO Readers' Guide No.10 (1994)

Record Repositories in Great Britain (PRO 1997)

Army:

VCs of the Army 1939-51, J.F.Turner (1962)

The DSO: A Complete Record of Recipients, Sir O'M.Creagh & H.M.Humphris (1978)

The Distinguished Conduct Medal 1855-909, P.E.Abbott (1987)

For Distinguished Conduct in the Field: The Register of the DCM 1920-22, P.McDermott (1994)

For Bravery in the Field: Recipients of the Military Medal 1919-39, 1939-45, C.Bate & M.Smith (1991)

In Search of Army Ancestry, G.Hamilton-Edwards (1983)

My Ancestor was in the British Army: How Can I Find Out More About Him?, M.J.& C.T.Watts (1992)

Regiments and Corps of the British Army, I.S.Hallows (1991)

Army Records for Family Historians, S.Fowler (1992)

A Bibliography of Regimental Histories of the British Army, A.S.White (1988)

Regimental Journals and Other Serial Publications of the British Army 1660-1980, F.H.Lake

The Military General Service Medal 1793-1814, A.L.T.Mullen

The Three Great Retrospective Medals 1793-1840 Awarded to the Artillerymen, D.D.Vigors & A.M.Macfarlane (1986)

The Army of India Medal Roll 1799-1826, R.W.Gould & K.J.Douglas-Morris (1974)

The Waterloo Roll Call, C.Dalton (1904)

The First Afghan War 1839-42 and Its Medals, A.G.Stone (1967)

The South Africa 1853 Medal Roll, G.R.Everson (1978)

The New Zealand Wars 1845-66, H.G.Longley (1967)

The New Zealand Wars, J.Cowan (1967)

Honour The Light Brigade, W.M.Lummis (1973)

A Casualty Roll for the Crimea 1854-55, F.& A.Cook (1976)

Red with Two Blue Stripes, B.A.H.Parritt (1974)

Casualty Roll for the Indian Mutiny 1857-59, I.T.Tavender

The Medal Roll of the Red River Campaign in 1870 in Canada, G.N.Neale & R.W.Irwin (1982)

The South Africa Campaign of 1879, J.P.Mackinnon & S.H.Shadbolt (rp.1995)

The Silver Wreath: The 24th Regiment at Isandhlwana and Rorke's Drift 1879, N.Holme (1979)

They Fell Like Stones, J.Young (1991)

Casualty Roll for the Zulu and Basuto Wars, South Africa 1877-79, I.T.Tavender (1985)

South African War Medal 1877-8-9: The Medal Roll, D.R.Forsyth

The Roll Call for Isandhlwana and Rorke's Drift, J.Whybra (1980)

The Second Afghan War 1878-80 Casualty Roll, A.Farrington (1986)

Cape of Good Hope General Service Medal: The Medal Roll, D.R.Forsyth

Abu Klea Medal Roll, J.V.Webb

British South Africa Company Medal 1890-97, D.R.Forsyth

The British South Africa Company Medal Rolls 1890-97, Roberts

The India General Service Casualty Roll, A.Farrington (1987)

The Ashanti Campaign, I.McInnes & M.Fraser

British Regiments in South Africa 1899-1902, J.Stirling (rp.1994)

List of Casualties of the South African Frontier Force (Hayward 1972)

South African War Casualty Roll: Natal Field Force (Hayward 1980)

The Last Post: A Roll of All Officers Who Gave Their Lives in the South African War 1899-1902, M.J.Dooner (1980)

Roll of the Bar, Defence of Mafeking, on the Queen's Medal for South Africa 1899-1902, F.K.Mitchell (1963)

Medal Roll of the Cape Copper Company's Medal, D.R.Forsyth

Natal Native Expedition 1906: The Medal Roll, D.R.Forsyth

The Honors, Medals and Awards of the Korean War 1950-53, K.R.Ingraham (1993)

Korea 1950-53: Mentions-in-Despatches, P.Dyke (1989)

Royal Air Force:

VCs of the Air, J.F.Turner (1961)

Register of the Distinguished Flying Cross 1918-95, N.& C.Carter (1995)

In Action with the Enemy: The Holders of the Conspicuous Gallantry Medal (Flying), A.W.Cooper

The Distinguished Flying Medal: A Record of Courage, I.Tavender (1990)

The Battle of Britain - Then and Now, ed.W.Ramsey (1980)

The Meritorious Service Medal to Aerial Forces 1916-28, I.McInnes (1984)

A Contemptible Little Flying Corps, I.McInnes & J.V.Webb (1991)

India General Service Medal 1908-35 to the Royal Air Force (Naval & Military Press 1994)

First World War:

Hart's Army List 1915 (rp.Naval & Military Press)

War Services Supplement of Officers to end December 1917 (rp.Naval & Military Press)

War Services Supplement of Officers to end of December 1922 (rp.Naval & Military Press)

Times Diary and Index of the Great War (rp.Hayward 1985)

Collecting and Researching Medals of the Great War, H.J.Williamson (1990)

Medals, Decorations and Orders of the Great War 1914-18, A.A.Purves (rp.1989)

The World War One Source Book, P.J. Haythornthwaite (1992)

The Naval Who's Who 1917

The Distinguished Service Medal 1914-20, W.H.Fevyer (1982)

The Royal Naval Division, D.Jerrold

The Cross of Sacrifice. Vol.2: Officers of the RN, RNR, RNVR, Royal Marines, RNAS & RAF 1914-19, S.D.& D.B.Jarvis (Roberts Medals 1993)

- *Vol.4: NCOs and Men of the Royal Navy, Royal Flying Corps and Royal Air Force 1914-19* (1996)

- *Vol.5: Officers, Men and Women of the Merchant Navy and Mercantile Fleet Auxiiary 1914-19* (1994)

With Full and Grateful Hearts. A Register of Royal Marine Deaths 1914-19 (RM Hist.Soc.1991)

The 1914 Star to the Royal Navy and Royal Marines, W.H.Fevyer & J.W.Wilson

A Dictionary of Disasters at Sea during the Age of Steam, C.Hocking (1969)

British Regiments 1914-18, E.A.James (rp.1993)

A Record of the Battles and Engagements of the British Armies in France and Flanders 1914-18, E.A.James (1924, rp.1990)

Locations of British Cavalry, Infantry and MGC Units 1914-24, R.W.Gould (1977)

Recipients of Bars to the Military Cross 1916-20. To which is added MCs to Warrant Officers 1915-19, J.V.Webb (1988)

The Meritorious Service Medal. The Immediate Awards 1916-28, I.McInnes (1992)

Old Contemptibles Honours and Awards (1917, rp.1991)

Honours and Awards, Army, Navy, Air Force 1914-20 (rp.1979 from lists in April 1920 Army List; incl.foreign decorations)

White Russian Awards to British and Commonwealth Servicemen, R.Brough (1991)

For Gallantry in the Performance of Military Duty, J.D.Sainsbury (1980)

The Roll of Honour 1916-19, Marquis de Ruvigny

Soldiers Died in the Great War (80 parts, rp.Hayward)

The Bond of Sacrifice, L.A.Clutterbuck

Soldiers Killed on the First Day of the Somme, E.W.Bell (1977)

British Officers Taken Prisoner of War in all Theatres of War August 1914 to November 1918 (1919, rp.1988)

Somme. The Day by Day Account, C. McCarthy (1993)

British Battalions on the Somme, R.Westlake (1994)

The First Day of the Somme, M.Middlebrook (1984)

Tank Corps Honours and Awards 1916-19 (1992)

British Regiments at Gallipolli, R.Westlake (1996)

Our Heroes (1916, rp.London Stamp Exchange)

Orange, Green and Khaki. The Story of the Irish Regiments in the Great War, T.Johnstone (1992)

The Location of British Army Records 1914-18, N. Holding (Fedn.of Family Hist. Socs. 1991)

World War I Army Ancestry, N.Holding (Fedn.of Family Hist.Socs.1991)

More Sources of World War I Army Ancestry, N.Holding (Fedn.of Family Hist.Socs.1991)

Army Service Records of the First World War (PRO 1996)

Territorial Divisions 1914-18, J.Stirling

Air Force List 1918 (rp.)

Royal Flying Corps Communiqués 1915-16, ed.C.Cole

Royal Air Force Communiqués 1918, ed.C.Cole (1990)

The Roll of Honour, Royal Flying Corps and Royal Air Force for the Great War 1914-18, H.J.Williamson (1992)

Airmen Died in the Great War, C.Hobson (1995)

Official History of the War in the Air 1914-18 (6 Vols.), Raleigh & Jones (1922-37, rp.)

The Sky Their Battlefield. Air Fighting, and the Complete List of Allied Air Casualties from Enemy Action n the First World War, T.Henshaw (1995)

Above the Trenches, C.Shores, N.Franks & R.Guest (1990, supplement 1996)

Air Defence of Great Britain 1914-18, C.Cole & C.F.Cheesman

The Royal Flying Corps in France (2 Vols.), R.Barker (1994 & 1995)

Royal Flying Corps: Honours, Awards and Casualties 1914-17, G.L.Campbell (1917)

RAF Records in the PRO - PRO Readers' Guide No.8 (1994)